CHEKHOV

RONALD HINGLEY

CHEKHOV

A BIOGRAPHICAL AND CRITICAL STUDY

LONDON · UNWIN BOOKS

PRINTED IN GREAT BRITAIN
in 9 on 10 pt Plantin type
BY C. TINLING AND CO. LTD
LIVERPOOL, LONDON AND PRESCOT

KS
5/31

INTRODUCTION

ALMOST everyone who writes about Chekhov today has to begin by protesting against a widespread misconception embodied in such phrases as 'a gentle, suffering soul', and 'a wise observer with a wistful smile and an aching heart'. Chekhov, if some of his interpreters are to be believed, was an apathetic pessimist, obsessed to the exclusion of everything else with the futility of life. Among his critics there are even some who, like Lev Shestov, find in philosophic despair a piquant quality which they enjoy so much that they are resolved to detect it in everything Chekhov wrote and said.

This approach, usually known as the 'Chekhov legend', is believed by Soviet Russian critics to be particularly common in England, and though they may be right, it is certainly less common than it was. Nowadays most of us are too busy to contemplate the aimlessness of life for long periods on end, and if we are still interested in Chekhov it is because we find that he has something more valuable to give us than an impression of pervasive dreariness. For some time there have been signs that we have begun to take a more balanced view, and it is as a contribution to this process that the present book is intended.

In making the attempt I am very much indebted to numerous Soviet critics and biographers. This is not to say that I have swallowed their presentation whole. The new Chekhov who is offered for inspection in Soviet Russia is a man of confidence and ringing conviction, whose mission in life was the denunciation of contemporary society. This conception is a great advance on the 'legend', but in the mouths of its more excitable promoters it begins to sound almost equally unreal. Fortunately there is no lack of evidence against which the claims of Chekhov's various interpreters can be tested. His letters alone, numbering several thousand, provide a rich and fascinating fund of material which it is a privilege to explore. I have done my best to exploit these and all other available Russian sources in the hope of showing Chekhov as he was, without forcing him to any preconceived idea of what he ought to have been.

Some confusion about Chekhov the man is inevitable in the

minds of English readers because of the confusion which surrounds Chekhov the writer of short stories. Their bewildering multiplicity and variety has probably done as much as the 'Chekhov legend' to deter many people from sampling what is one of the most satisfying and moving experiences which literature has to offer. Over two hundred of them are available in English, so that their number alone makes the problem of where to begin a difficult one. Constance Garnett did a great service to English readers when she opened up so much of Chekhov's work to them in the early nineteen-twenties, but it is a great pity that she did not insist on her versions being printed in some sort of logical order. In her thirteen volumes of translated stories examples of Chekhov's mature and considered style are sandwiched between early comic sketches, dashed off to pay some outstanding grocery bill. It is as though someone has taken all the stories and shuffled them before handing them over to the printer. Broadly speaking 'the later the better' may be taken as a guiding principle in approaching Chekhov's work.

Where Chekhov's plays are concerned no confusion such as that which surrounds his stories has been allowed to develop, and for a very simple reason—there are so few of them. This is partly why they have attracted more than their rightful share of attention in England.

For every twenty English people who have seen *The Cherry Orchard* there are probably at least fifteen who have never even heard of *Ward No. 6*, and this is to me an example of misplaced emphasis. Nobody who admires Chekhov's plays as much as I do could wish to detract from them in any way, but I believe that the stories occupy a more important position in his achievement. The comparison between these two bodies of work is no doubt meaningless in the last resort, and I only make it because of an impression that Chekhov's stories are not receiving their due in England, at any rate from the non-specialist reader. English writers of short stories have not neglected them, knowing that they could not afford to do so.

In conclusion I must mention certain matters of detail. My policy in handling Russian names has been to attempt clarity before anything else. As foreign readers of Russian fiction know to their cost, every Russian has a great many names. There are often several affectionate diminutives to be taken into account as well as Christian name, patronymic and surname, and all of these may appear in isolation or in various combinations. Chek-

hov would have been called 'Antosha' by his mother when he
was a small boy, 'Anton' by those of his fellow-students who
knew him best, 'Anton Pavlovich' by many of his patients, and
'Mr Chekhov' by hostile reviewers. I have usually called him
'Chekhov', more rarely 'Anton', and once or twice, when anything else would strike the wrong note, 'Anton Pavlovich'. In
rendering Russian names I have used the transliteration system
which is now commonly accepted in English-speaking countries,
but in many instances have presented my characters with their
equivalent English Christian name instead of transliterating the
Russian. Here I have been guided by what I thought sounded
right. 'Nicholas Chekhov' seems quite reasonable, while 'Anthony
Chekhov' would obviously be impossible. Accepted forms, such
as 'Tchaikovsky', have been retained in defiance of transliteration consistency, and the Russian letter 'e' (occurring initially or
medially, preceded by a vowel) is given as 'e' and not as 'ye'.

Though I have kept the titles of standard English translations
in the text, all quotations from Chekhov and other authors are
given in my own version. Where no translation into English
exists I have of course supplied translated titles as well.

All dates are 'old style'; that is to say they accord with the
calendar used in Russia before the Revolution. This calendar was
twelve days behind ours in the nineteenth century, and thirteen
days behind between 1900 and 1917.

Mention must also be made of one matter about which misunderstanding might otherwise arise. On occasion certain thoughts
are represented as going through Chekhov's head, or he is described as having a discussion over 'a glass of beer'. Details of
this kind are, of course, based on the Russian material, and are
in no case the product of my imagination.

I am much indebted to Mr Scharf for some first-hand details
of Taganrog in the late nineteenth century.

Note on Second Edition

The text of the original edition has been left unchanged, except that the opportunity has been taken to correct a few minor inaccuracies thrown up by further research, and occasionally to modify comments which later consideration has shown to be inappropriate. The *Index of References* contained in the original edition is omitted for reasons of space, as is the *Appendix* giving the titles of Chekhov's stories in English translation.

The *Bibliography* has been brought up to date by the inclusion of material from the Select Bibliography in *The Oxford Chekhov*, vol. iii (London, 1964), edited by myself and included here by kind permission of the Oxford University Press.

Frilford, Abingdon
1965

Ronald Hingley.

CONTENTS

CONTENTS

CHAPTER ONE

Taganrog

I

THE FAMILY

ANTON CHEKHOV was born on January 17, 1860, in the South
Russian town of Taganrog. His father kept a small shop, outside
which two signboards were displayed: TEA, SUGAR, COFFEE AND
COLONIAL WARES and DRINKS, TO BE CONSUMED ON OR OFF THE
PREMISES. Many other articles of household use were also on sale,
from hair-oil, penknives and butter to grapes, macaroni,
candles and quack medicines. The clientèle included housewives
from the near-by streets, buying provisions for the week, their
children, in search of a packet of sweets, and their husbands,
who had come to treat the place as an unofficial club. These
were the regulars, but Taganrog, though a sleepy town, did have
a small port, and there were occasional foreign visitors, so that
there was no knowing who might drop in next.

Such customers as bothered to look twice at Anton noticed a
small boy with a large head, who had very little to say for himself, but seemed most interested in their conversation. Even before he started school his father expected him to mind the shop.
At first Anton found it a wonderful game, but before long it had
become a burden, especially when his schooling had begun, and
he discovered that he was still expected to do his share of shop-
keeping in the evening and on holidays. He had to fit in his
homework as best he could, and it was difficult to concentrate on
Greek verbs or algebra in the intervals between weighing cheese
and measuring out paraffin.

If he felt tired and overworked he knew that it was no use
complaining to his father, who believed that hard work was good
for little boys. They might as well learn once and for all that life
was a difficult business—as he had good reason to know himself. He was never likely to forget that he had been born a serf,
or that his own father, Anton's grandfather Egor, had been

energetic and industrious enough to buy the freedom of his family at 700 roubles a head. That had been a long time ago, in 1841, and the family had celebrated the event by expanding its former surname of 'Chekh'. This crude monosyllable had been appropriate to their former station, but something a little more elaborate was required to give them confidence in their assault on the lower ranks of the bourgeoisie. Grandfather Egor had stayed on in the country as manager of a big estate not far from Taganrog, having given his sons as good a start in life as he could contrive. Anton's father, whose name was Paul, became apprentice shop-boy to a wealthy trader in Taganrog. It was a hard life, with plenty of physical ill-treatment and little help from anybody. Paul Chekhov had done well to marry the daughter of a successful cloth-trader, and to set himself up in a small shop of his own. He had six children, of whom Anton was the third. Most of the other branches of the Chekhov family, and most of their friends, belonged to the 'merchant' class, and were in much the same sort of circumstances as Paul. Anton's uncle Mitrofan, for example, kept a small grocery shop at the other end of Taganrog.

The thoughts of Paul Chekhov and his friends were mainly focused on the very serious problem of earning their daily bread. A small shop brought in only a bare subsistence, and they were dimly aware of various economic trends outside their control, which might at any moment lead to bankruptcy and ruin. It is little wonder that they counted their copecks very carefully indeed, or that Chekhov himself, summing up in later life the social milieu in which he was reared, defined it as one in which money 'loomed disproportionately large'.

For the cares of day-to-day existence life offered a variety of consolations, of which the chief were vodka, the society of one's friends, and religion. Of the first two Paul Chekhov partook with moderation. In the third, most people thought, he over-indulged. His full beard and conviction of his infallibility made him a terrifying figure to the children. Anton hated the way his father's face flushed and his voice shook with rage when the dinner was late or the soup over-salted. Paul had a rigid system of living, which he imposed on his family without any thought of consulting them. As a devout Orthodox Christian he strictly observed all the ordinances of the Russian Church. The prescribed fasts were kept. There were ikons—some of his own painting—on the walls of the house, and he made attendance at church compulsory for all members of the family. These devotions were a trial to Anton. The Orthodox Church has a full and complicated ritual; its services are not short, and have an awkward habit of occurring very late at night or early in the morning. If Paul had ever stopped to examine his children, instead of treating them as appendages to his own personality, he would have realized that they were not very pious. Indeed, they were adepts at relieving the monotony of church when they thought they could get away with it. In this they had their mother's sympathy. She knew that it was very wrong when Anton interrupted the droning of the priest with a tremendous sneeze, which surely could not be natural, or, standing in the choir, imitated the opening and shutting of a mouth with the loose sole of his shoe, but somehow she was quite unable to stop herself enjoying the joke.

Paul Chekhov was not content with exacting attendance at service. His great passion in life was religious music, and he had some talent in this sphere, for he could read a score and was a fair performer on the violin. As soon as the boys were old enough they found themselves conscripted into a family choir, which their father was determined to make the finest in Taganrog. Choir-practice was even more of an ordeal than church, for father was never slow to punish a false note or incompletely-stifled yawn with a box on the ears. Sometimes the boys had to tumble out of bed at two or three o'clock in the morning to prepare for matins. Little Anton had very mixed feelings as he stood with his brothers in the cold, dark church, waiting to begin the anthem. There was a certain grandeur and majesty about the ceremony, which made a deep impression on him in spite of his boredom and fatigue, but his chief impressions were unpleasant—a fear that his school-friends might notice the holes in his shoes when he knelt down, and a sense of discomfort at having to remain standing so long. He would shift from foot to foot and yearn for the end of these interminable, mysterious and dreary proceedings. The parents in the congregation looked with satisfaction at small boys so dutiful and regimented, and Paul Chekhov found himself the object of general envy. Other parishioners were less enthusiastic. Paul's anthems were too long for them, and they even appealed to his wife, hoping that she might persuade him to shorten them. They might have saved their breath. Evgeniya Chekhov was already opposed to compulsory church-going on the scale enforced by Paul, and had often pointed out that the children were not getting enough sleep. He used to brush her protests aside. 'Singing strengthens little chests, and going to church develops little souls', he would pronounce—and regard the subject as dismissed.

It is not surprising that Anton grew up with a strong dislike of religious education, in which, he once remarked, 'a certain façade is indispensable. ... Behind this façade torture is inflicted; in front of it people smile and go emotional.' However, his reaction against religion did not go as far as might have been expected. Throughout his life he never entirely abandoned attendance at church and the practice of various religious observances, such as fasts, which formed part of the normal rhythm of Russian life. He was particularly attracted by the Russian Easter services and the sound of church bells. Later in life, when he was living in Moscow, he used to gather his friends together on Easter night for a walk through the city to hear the uninterrupted chiming of the bells in its countless churches. He would spend the whole night in this way, wandering from one church to another.

Church-going and choir-practice were only part of Paul Chekhov's comprehensive educational règime. The process went on remorselessly, and took up most of Anton's time. There were frequent readings in the family circle, at which everyone was expected to keep quiet and listen to father. He usually chose some improving book, occasionally varying it with a local newspaper—which afforded no relief. Even the Lives of the Saints were a little spicier than the Taganrog Town Council Gazette. Sometimes Paul would break off abruptly and ask one or other of the family to repeat what he had just been reading—an unfair habit, which deprived them even of the consolation of daydreaming.

It was only to be expected that Paul's forbidding discipline should be reinforced with frequent applications of the stick. Anton later remembered these beatings as one of the ugliest features of his childhood. At the time they seemed a natural and inevitable part of life, but it was rather a shock when, upon comparing notes, he found that he had one friend at school who was never beaten at home. This particular friend was a lucky exception. Most small boys found that they were regularly thrashed by their fathers, and that any other grown-up person felt he had the right to pull their hair or tweak their ears on occasion, usually under the impression that he was doing good by the process.

In later life Chekhov was not fond of referring to his childhood. When he did mention it he usually spoke bitterly, even describing it—for example in letters to his brother Alexander— as a time of 'torture', and remarking elsewhere 'In childhood I had no childhood.' The rareness of such references is due to his natural reticence, and an unwillingness to parade his grievances in front of others. As often happens the most outspoken expression of his views is to be found in a passage of fiction. The following description, taken from the story *Three Years* is put into the mouth of a fictional character, but there can be little doubt that Chekhov had his own childhood in mind when he wrote it:

'I remember that Father began to teach me, or (to put it more simply) to beat me, before I was even five years old. He used to hit me with a stick, tweak my ears, and clout me on the head. On waking up each morning my first thought was: "Shall I get a beating today?" We weren't allowed to play games. We had to go to matins and early mass, kiss the hands of priests and monks, and read the Psalter at home. . . . I am afraid of religion. Whenever I pass a church, I think of my childhood, and it gives me an unpleasant feeling. When I was eight years old they took me into the shop, and I worked as an ordinary shop-boy. This was bad for my health, because there too I was beaten every day. Later, when I was sent to High School, I used to be at my lessons till dinner time, and from dinner until evening I once more sat in confinement in the same old shop.'

Though he felt that most of his upbringing had been a wasteful and unhappy process, Anton never bore a strong grudge against his father. As a child he regarded Paul with mingled affection and fear. The affection persisted until the end of the old man's life, long after all trace of fear had vanished. Moreover, Anton acknowledged that his father was a man of genuine artistic gifts, for there were not many Taganrog grocers who played the violin and painted ikons. If he had been given the opportunity Paul Chekhov might have been happier as a professional choir-master or member of an orchestra. 'We get our talent from our father,' Anton used to say of himself and his brothers, adding that they derived their soul from their mother. In her they were very fortunate. Evgeniya Chekhov was a very busy woman. With six children to feed and clothe it is not surprising that she had to spend all her time on housework. Family cares gave her no time to cultivate her intelligence, which must be admitted to have been very limited. However, she stopped to do a thing which rarely occurred to Paul—to appreciate her children. They returned her love in full, and were entranced by the exciting stories she had to tell—wonderful fairy-tales, and equally enthralling personal reminiscences of her adventures before marriage, when she had travelled all over Russia. She well remembered the Crimean War, and the British bombardment of Taganrog in 1855, which had forced the family to evacuate, so that her first boy was born in the country.

Like most Russians the Chekhovs were very sociable people, and they lived in an atmosphere where hospitality came as naturally as breathing. They were always ready to put on the samovar or bring out the vodka bottle in honour of any chance visitor, so that, apart from what he saw in the shop, Anton had plenty of opportunities for observing grown-up people at home. What he saw fascinated him, and he would often sit for hours listening to their conversation, heedless of the appeals of his brothers, who wanted him to come and play in the yard. Then there were visits to be returned. The Chekhovs were regular guests at Uncle Mitrofan's house. Anton was very fond of his uncle, a church elder, who was every bit as devout as Paul, but seems to have been a much kindlier man.

The people who understood Anton best during his childhood were undoubtedly his brothers and sisters. This is particularly true of his two elder brothers, whose talent and sensitivity were not far inferior to his own. Alexander was five years older, and naturally exercised the strongest influence. While Anton was still quite small Alexander had begun to smile sardonically at the old-fashioned ways of the family, and it was probably he who made his brothers realize that there was another world outside the lower middle-class section of Taganrog—a world with vastly different standards and exciting possibilities. Alexander was going through a process common among the more gifted sons of poor parents, that of transformation into a member of the 'intelligentsia'. He reacted violently against his upbringing, and, though he never communicated this reaction in its full violence to Anton, his tirades had a stimulating effect. Anton was also very fond of his other elder brother, Nicholas, who lacked Alexander's trenchant independence of mind. Nicholas was a moody and quick-tempered child, with no strength of character,

but he seemed at one time to be the most gifted member of
the family. It was thought that he would make a successful
artist, since everyone praised his drawings, and he had a fair
share of the artistic temperament to match. The other children,
Ivan, Michael, and his sister Mariya, were too young to have
much influence on Anton. It was they who looked up to him,
and they found him a very amusing playmate.

II

THE TOWN

THAT provincial life should be boring and culturally poor was a
self evident fact to any thinking Russian of the nineteenth century. The very fact that Chekhov was born and spent his first
nineteen years in Taganrog possibly gave him a less promising
start as a writer than he would have had in Petersburg or Moscow. Complete lifelessness was the chief impression created by
Taganrog. Apart from the main street it seemed like a dead
town, with interminable straight roads, lined on both sides with
small, shuttered houses. These roads were so wide that, according to a local saying, it was dangerous to go into the middle of
them—you might get lost. There were endless fences, allotments
and waste plots. At night the streets were unlit, or had dim and
depressing gas lamps at rare intervals. Sometimes things seemed
so quiet and dreary that Anton felt he wanted to rush along the
street shouting 'Police!' simply in order to create a diversion.

In letters written later in his life Chekhov often had some
harsh things to say about Taganrog. It was 'completely Asiatic',
a place where people 'do nothing but eat, sleep and multiply,
and have no other interests. Wherever you go you find buns, eggs,
cheap wine, babies at the breast, and nowhere do you see newspapers or books.' Some of these descriptions do the town less
than justice. Taganrog might have been very much worse. It
had a first-class theatre, a moderately good library, and a sprink-
ling of cultured and intelligent people, such as one might have
sought for in vain at Saratov or Tambov. Moreover, Chekhov
was deeply attached to his home town, in spite of the exasperation which it sometimes aroused in him. The small, square,
whitewashed houses, which often had large grounds with ornamental gardens and orchards, the very remoteness of the place
and its soporific atmosphere—all these had a peculiar charm of
their own. Typically enough the railway station was a twenty

B

minutes' cab journey out of town, so that the dreams of Taganrog were never disturbed by shunting locomotives. Its very isolation enabled it to preserve the traditional Russian way of life fairly intact. This could not be said of other places near-by, such as the brisk, commercial city of Rostov-on-Don, thirty miles away, which seemed to have sprung up overnight, and which Russians sometimes described as 'Americanized'. Taganrog was a port, but in spite of this it contrived to look like an inland country town. When Chekhov was a boy the port was losing business rapidly, and had already forfeited its position as one of the main outlets of the Russian grain trade. The harbour was silting up, so that big ships could no longer use it, and though dredging operations were constantly under discussion, nothing effective was ever done. Meanwhile trade went on in a half-hearted way. Small foreign vessels continued to anchor off the roads, and to discharge their cargoes of fruit and wine; the outlandish dress and strange accents of their crews brought a colourful element into the life of the town.

Taganrog did not come within the boundaries of the Ukrainian-speaking part of Russia. As a boy Anton spoke reasonably pure Russian, with a small admixture of provincialisms which sometimes made people smile when he later came out with them in Moscow. In addition to Russians, who formed the majority of the population, Taganrog had a fair number of foreign residents. The most prominent of these foreigners were the Greeks, whose flair for commerce had often enabled them to do very well for themselves. Many of them had arrived as common dock-hands, only to leap with amazing rapidity to the eminence of rouble millionaires. By the time of Chekhov's boyhood names like Mark Valiano and Depaldi had become synonymous among the Russian population with wealth and luxury. The rich Greeks built themselves pretentious palaces, and always occupied the best seats in the theatre. People laughed at them of course. Their appearance and dress were strange. Their names tended to end in '-ides' or '-oulos', whereas every normal name ended in '-ov', '-enko' or '-ovich', but the laughter was generally good-humoured, and often concealed admiration.

III

CHEKHOV'S SCHOOLS

NOT all the Greeks in Taganrog had managed to make a fortune, and among the humbler variety Paul Chekhov numbered several customers. It was they who suggested the choice of Anton's first school—the Taganrog 'Greek School', of which he became a pupil at the age of seven. Calling at Paul Chekhov's shop for a glass of wine, the Greeks had nodded their heads and nudged each other at the competent way little Anton totted up the accounts, and took such an obvious delight in managing the shop. Evidently the boy had a head for business, and, given a proper start, might even make a 'Greek career' for himself. Paul Chekhov was impressed. After all there must be something rather special about this nation, whose ex-pirates and former dock-labourers had cornered most of the town's trade from their slower Slav competitors. Whatever this quality might be, Paul hoped that it would communicate itself in some mysterious way to his son. Any doubts he might have had about the respectability of the school were removed when he remembered that it was attached to the Greek parish church. Anton's mother was less enthusiastic about the idea, being influenced by the wives of school-teachers, whom she sometimes met in the shop. Let Anton go to the *Gymnasium*, the best school in the town, where he would receive a decent Russian education, along with children from the professional classes. However, Paul Chekhov had his way as usual, and it was to the Greek school that Anton was sent, together with his brother Nicholas.

If Paul Chekhov's mind had not been so full of ikons and incense he would probably have realized earlier what a disreputable establishment the Greek School was, instead of allowing his boys to waste a whole year there. Their fellow-pupils, mostly sons of rowdy sea-captains and small tradesmen, were a ragged and unruly crowd, about seventy in number. Some arrived for their lessons with bare feet, and the majority had cuts and scratches to display as the result of constant street-fighting. Their favourite pastime was to raid the harbour for fruit and nuts, a sport which often earned them a sound beating from some heavy-handed dock official. They were of all ages, from small boys of six to hulking adolescents, and the entire school was accommodated in a single room. To each of the five classes was allotted one bench, and pupils were often transferred from one class to another for no better reason than that their particular bench was full. The entire proceedings of the school were in Greek, and the little Chekhovs found their names transliterated on the register into the unfamiliar Greek script. Their complete ignorance of the language was less of a disadvantage than might at first sight appear, for it soon became obvious that no serious instruction was ever likely to be dispensed. The headmaster was a red-headed bully called Vutsinas, whose antecedents were a subject of speculation in Taganrog. It was suspected that he had no qualifications at all for the job of schoolmaster, other than a taste for laying his heavy ruler about his charges. The schoolroom was usually in uproar, and the noise was often reinforced by local urchins, who formed the habit of shrieking choral insults at Vutsinas through the open window, alleging in doggerel verse that he had arrived

'from Cephallonia,
without so much as a pair of pantalonia.'

Vutsinas would rush out and disperse them with blows from his ruler. The most extraordinary stories were told of the punishments inflicted on erring pupils—being lashed to the shutters of the window, or 'running the gauntlet'. This involved the culprit sitting in a chair, while the entire personnel of the school filed past and spat in his face, with a cry of 'You Blackguard!' Such stories are no doubt exaggerated, but it is certain that Anton was unhappy at the school, which he later remembered as having 'spoilt many of my childhood joys'. When Paul Chekhov called to inquire after the boys Vutsinas gave glowing accounts of their progress. He followed the visit by sending them home with written reports, which, when translated, revealed Anton as 'diligent' and Nicholas as 'devout'. Things seemed to be going well until Paul made the mistake of organizing an informal examination in front of his Greek friends to display the boys' knowledge. The result was disastrous, and reflected credit on nobody. Anton and Nicholas seemed to have picked up a smattering of colloquial Greek, of doubtful purity, from their small playmates, but very little else. At last their father realized that the school was a commercial enterprise in the worst Levantine tradition, and that Vutsinas trafficked in spurious education, just as the less scrupulous of his compatriots dealt in rotten oranges and rancid butter.

The school left Anton with a dislike of the Greek language which he never overcame. This was unfortunate, because his next school was the one his mother had preferred—the Classical *Gymnasium* or High School, in which the study of Latin and Ancient Greek occupied about half of his time. It was here that he finished his schooling. At the age of eight he joined a preparatory class, and in the following year embarked on an eight-year course, which took him ten years to complete. This delay was due to a failure to reach the required standard in the third and fifth classes, with the result that he was twice kept down for an extra year.

The *Gymnasium* was a fair specimen of the better type of Russian school. Languages took pride of place in the syllabus. Like most schoolboys Anton had his favourite subjects which were Scripture, Latin and Old Slavonic. Among his dislikes was numbered Mathematics as well as Greek. Apart from these subjects he studied Russian (without showing outstanding ability), German, History and Geography. In attending the *Gymnasium* he received a training comparable, at any rate in the emphasis given to the ancient languages, with the classical education which has played such a prominent part in English schools and universities. Unfortunately his classics were served up in a dry and unpalatable manner, and, though they may have done something for him in the way of mental discipline, they appear to have given him no sort of cultural background. Classical literature did not fire his interest, and it never occurred to him to read a word of it after leaving school. Considering the amount of time he spent on the classics at school, it is remarkable how few traces they have left in his later work and correspondence. Here and there one may find an occasional Latin tag or mythological reference, usually introduced to obtain some sort of comic effect, but there is very little more. In the story *Who Was to Blame?* written in 1886, Chekhov allows one of his characters to speak of the classics with a disrespect which he probably shared himself:

'In my day I had the honour to be taught the Latin language. Nowadays, whenever I chance to see some production of classical antiquity, instead of eagerly exulting, I begin to remember *ut consecutivum*, irregular verbs and the ablative absolute. I grow pale, my hair stands on end, and I dash off in shameful flight like a cat.'

It may be mentioned in passing that Chekhov's mature stories are sometimes considered to be the most 'classical' of Russian works, in their economy, avoidance of overtones, and sense of restraint. There can be little doubt, however, that these qualities were attained independently of his school training.

The faults of the *Gymnasium* were of a very different order
from those of the Greek School. There was none of Vutsinas'
riotous chaos. On the contrary there was a severe and deadly
discipline, which often lay oppressively on the pupils. This was
partly the result of Government policy. Chekhov's school-days coincided with a highly-organized attempt by the imperial Government to stamp out the growing revolutionary movement in
Russia. The Tsar's ministers fully understood the importance of
controlling education. Since much of the trouble arose amongst
university students, it was clearly important to keep a tight
grip on the schools from which those students came. Steps were
taken to reduce the free flow of ideas to a minimum, and to produce docile citizens, rather than men of independent mind. Extreme and repressive measures were instituted in the seventies.
During the next decade they developed into the 'Tsarist Terror'
—a term used, not only by post-revolutionary Soviet critics, but
also by mildly liberal historians writing before the 1917 Revolution. Thus it came about that schools like the Taganrog *Gymnasium* were closely watched by the department of a high
official with the sinister title of 'Minister of Popular Enlightenment'—in other words, of education.

The Minister at this time was a Count D. A. Tolstoy, whose
views on education were such that there is little likelihood of
him ever being confused with his more famous namesake. On the
occasion of a visit to the *Gymnasium*, made two years before
Anton became a pupil, Tolstoy had been horrified to find a portrait of Belinsky on the wall, and, what was worse, copies of his
books in the library. That schoolboys should have free access to
the works of one of Russia's most original thinkers and critics
was clearly inconsistent with the policy of the Minister. The
masters long remembered the embarrassing scene in which he had
rebuked the Head in their presence, and ordered the immediate
removal of the offending objects. From then onwards Enlightenment raged unchecked, with the result that some old pupils
have compared the school with a detention barracks. How serious things became can be judged by the fact that the Minister,
on the occasion of a further visit, expressed his satisfaction at
the 'considerable progress' achieved.

Fortunately governmental machinery was not efficient enough
to organize a really thorough suppression of ideas. However, there
was plenty of uneasiness and unpleasantness. For example, any
master who was unscrupulous enough could hope to gain pro-

motion by his zeal in writing denunciations of his colleagues or pupils for 'political unreliability'. Such was the Latin master, Urban, the most outrageous figure on the staff, who was always denouncing the boys to the masters, the masters to the Headmaster, and the Headmaster to the Ministry. He once informed against the teachers for smoking at a staff meeting 'in the presence of some ikons and the portrait of his Imperial Majesty'. Urban made himself thoroughly disliked by his pupils, and is even said to have driven some of them to suicide. This was a time when Russians of all ages were liable to avenge their wrongs by violence. A home-made bomb, constructed out of a sardine-tin, was actually exploded in Urban's room, but failed to injure him. Luckily there were no other masters quite as bad as this on the staff. They were mainly decent and amiable people, though often odd in their behaviour, and sometimes corrupt. Some of them were not averse to making money on the side by taking in pupils as boarders in their homes—an arrangement of mutual advantage. Everyone knew that the boys' keep was paid for at exorbitant rates, and so nobody was surprised when they passed their examinations with flying colours.

The master for whom Anton had the highest regard was the priest, Father Pokrovsky, a fine upstanding man who looked like a hussar and had a deep bass voice. He was a friend of the Chekhov family, and Anton often met him at the house of his uncle Mitrofan. Pokrovsky was an unusually enlightened and broad-minded Russian priest. His pupils often suspected that he held agnostic views, for he was apparently more interested in literature and politics than religion. He subscribed to the most progressive Russian literary journal, was a keen follower of the satirist Saltykov, and expressed horror if he ever found that his pupils had not read Shakespeare, though he was comparatively indifferent to their knowledge of Scripture. Pokrovsky's classes were general favourites because of his fascinating digressions on all sorts of interesting topics, and it was he who invented the nickname Antosha Chekhonte, which Chekhov later used extensively as a literary pseudonym.

The staff included many other interesting personalities, some of whom reappeared in more or less recognizable form in Chekhov's stories. Among these was the young and sympathetic master Starov, whose matrimonial troubles are reflected in *Ariadne* and *The Teacher of Literature*. Another model was the Inspector, Dyakonov, whose particular brand of unimaginative-

ness was typical of the worst side of the school. He is said to
have suggested some features in the character Belikov, in one
of Chekhov's best-known stories, *The Man in a Case*. This is a
very amusing character-study, in which it has been suggested
that Chekhov has embodied his reaction to the stuffiness of the
Taganrog *Gymnasium* staff as a whole. However, most of the
masters were not so lifeless and unapproachable as Belikov, and
relations between them and the boys were thought to be unusually cordial for a Russian school.

When Anton entered the *Gymnasium* he was a chubby little
boy, with close-cropped hair, dimples and a protruding stomach. He wore the usual school uniform—a peaked cap, a satchel
like an army pack, and a grey tunic with buttons down the
front, one of which, in spite of the Headmaster's strict views on
dress, was usually undone. His abnormally large and round head
was compared by some to the full moon, and soon earned him
the nickname of 'Tadpole'. This alternated with 'The Bomb',
probably derived from his plump figure, and certainly from no
explosive quality of temperament, for he was an easy-going child.
With his fellow-pupils he was a great favourite, though he
made few close friends, being reticent and undemonstrative. In
class he was well-behaved, and usually got full marks for conduct, though there was nothing unpleasantly obsequious about
his attitude to the masters. They too liked him, and he was
often to be seen walking about the corridors of the school, deep
in conversation with the Head. Everyone knew him for a self-
sufficient and good-humoured boy, with plenty of quiet self-
respect, and it was not long before he became known as a first-
class source of entertainment. When any of the masters heard
uproarious laughter and a series of treble guffaws proceeding
from his classroom, they usually knew what was happening. It
was only necessary to fling open the door suddenly, in true
schoolmaster fashion, to surprise young Chekhov reading to a
circle of his friends from an exercise-book. The inevitable con-
fiscation would show that this book contained a number of
amusing stories, which he had either made up himself, or
collected from somewhere. The school gave him ample material
for another of his talents—mimicking the mannerisms and accents
of his elders. It was also noticed that he was usually the first to
label a new master with some grotesque and ludicrously appropriate nickname, which went round the school in a very short
space of time, and often lasted for life.

In spite of Anton's high spirits, his first few years at the *Gymnasium* were a difficult period. Examinations were an ordeal, because low marks led to trouble, both at school and at home, where Paul Chekhov was liable to make them the occasion for a beating. This was extremely unfair, because these failures were really more his fault than Anton's. Anton was not lacking either in aptitude or interest, but he could not help being behindhand with his work so long as his father monopolized his out-of-school hours with duties in church and shop. A proof of Paul Chekhov's hampering effect on his son's progress lies in the immediate improvement which marked Anton's school work after his father left Taganrog in 1876. His last three years at school were fairly successful, though he was never an outstanding pupil. In the passing-out class he was placed eleventh out of twenty-three.

IV
LEISURE ACTIVITIES

DURING holidays at his Grandfather Egor's, Anton first acquired a love of the Russian countryside, which lasted all his life and left many memorable pages in his stories. These visits involved journeys of several days by horse- or ox-cart through forty miles of Ukrainian steppe, and exciting nights of camping on beds of hay under the open sky. Grandfather was a fascinating character, whom Anton remembered for his kindness and his habit of keeping up his trousers by buttoning them to his waistcoat. He was a sturdy and independent old man, who now managed the immense estates of the landowner, Count Platov. The arrival of his grandchildren delighted him, and he thoroughly spoiled them, putting them up in the big house during Platov's absence, just as though they were little counts themselves, taking them for drozhky rides round the estate, and even teaching them to smoke. This easy-going attitude was a novelty to Anton, but there were one or two strict and unexpected rules of behaviour. For instance, it was absolutely forbidden to pick any of the apples in the Count's orchard. One day Anton bet his brother Ivan that he would not only break this rule, but do so quite openly, in his grandfather's presence. The old man was called into the orchard, and came along sucking his pipe, wondering what it was all about. Anton explained that he was going to leap-frog over Ivan, and proceeded to do so, picking the apple in mid-flight. Grandfather was delighted with his impudence, and his laughter rang out through the whole orchard. However, even at Grandfather's life was not all relaxation, and the boys sometimes found that they were given work to do. This too left unforgettable impressions, as Anton later recorded in one of his letters: 'For days on end I had to sit by the milling-machine from dawn to dusk, noting down the weight of the milled grain. The whistles, the shrieks, the noise like a top that issues from the machine under full pressure, the creak of wheels, the lazy tread of oxen, the clouds of dust, the black, sweaty faces of fifty-odd people—all this engraved itself on my memory like the Lord's Prayer.'

Taganrog also provided a number of out-of-door pleasures, which must have done a lot to repair the inroads on Anton's health made by overwork. He loved bathing and fishing, and for a time was attracted by the favourite sport of his schoolfellows —the snaring of wild birds. He could sometimes raise the price of a theatre ticket by selling them in the bazaar for a few copecks. In lazier moods, when the weather was warm, he was quite happy sitting with his brothers on the step of the shop, listening to the distant strains of the band which played on the bandstand in the park. On the whole, though he was a normal boy, and occasionally enjoyed street games with his friends, he kept very much to himself, and often preferred reading on his own. Most of all he enjoyed the fascinating pastime of observing his elders, those grave and peculiar creatures, whose actions often seemed so difficult to explain. It was only rarely that he took part in the more daring escapades of his friends, as on one occasion when they removed a policeman's sentry-box to the front door of the Chief of Police, rang the bell and ran away.

So far as Chekhov's future is concerned, the most important of his leisure activities as a boy were those which centred round the theatre. The possession of a theatre with a very high standard of acting was one of Taganrog's main cultural assets, and he availed himself of it to the full. He first attended at the age of thirteen, and found it so exciting that he soon became a regular member of the audience. A visit to the theatre was quite a difficult undertaking; though seats were cheap, money was scarce, and it was necessary to start queuing early, so as to make sure of a good place in the gallery. Moreover, there was an element of risk as theatre-going was against school rules, and the school Inspector used to scrutinize the audience carefully in the hope of detecting *Gymnasium* pupils. Anton and his friends took counter-measures, which were bizarre but effective, depending chiefly on a liberal use of false beards and dark spectacles. Everything about the theatre delighted Anton. The repertoire was varied, and ranged from popular operetta and a dramatized version of *Uncle Tom's Cabin* to more serious items, such as the plays of Shakespeare and the Russian stage classics of Griboedov, Gogol and Ostrovsky. Anton was enthralled, especially when he was taken back-stage, and had an opportunity to meet the actors. Here was an exhilarating new world of bright lights and gaiety, which made every-day life seem sordid and unromantic by comparison. It was not long before he had infected his family and friends with his enthusiasm, and had become the moving spirit in a number of private theatrical performances produced before small audiences in private houses. Anton was a very clever mimic, particularly of pompous elderly people, and it is easy to understand that he was a great success in such parts as the Mayor in Gogol's *Inspector-General*.

So obsessed was Anton with the joys of acting that he was constantly improvising some escapade or other with a theatrical slant. His skill in make-up and impersonation must have been uncanny, if one story about his childhood is to be believed. It is said that he dressed up as an old beggar, and succeeded not only in deceiving his uncle Mitrofan with a long recital of his woes, but also in extracting a donation intended for his starving children. At home his burlesques and impromptu scenes were an almost daily occurrence, and often required the co-operation of his brothers. Stretching his neck and making the veins stand out like an old man's, Anton would entirely change the expression of his face. In an old and quavering voice he would answer the questions of the 'Bishop' (one of his elder brothers), in an oral 'examination for the rank of Deacon' in the Russian Church. Another favourite scene began with Anton, in the role of dentist, laying out his instruments on the consulting-room table. A cry of pain would resound from outside, followed by the appearance through the door of a wild figure—Alexander Chekhov, with a look of agony on his face as he clutched his swollen cheek. A series of comic contortions followed, culminating in the moment when Anton, thrusting the fire-tongs into his patient's mouth, executed a sequence of painful wrenches, and triumphantly withdrew a huge and evil-looking 'tooth', which was soon seen to be an old cork.

Play-acting of this sort was necessary to Anton for many reasons. It provided an outlet for his high spirits, and enabled him to indulge the instinct for entertaining which had early shown itself as one of the most striking features of his character. People noticed that he did not laugh very much himself, but that he was never tired of amusing others. After enduring the obtuseness of older people during the day, it was a wonderful relief to take one's revenge in the evening by ridiculing their absurdities. Inevitably Anton's imitations began to acquire a keen satirical edge. He suffered from his schoolmasters in class, and got his own back outside by guying their mannerisms. He capitalized his visits to church by learning to reproduce the ponderous address and lumbering syntax of the clergy. Anton and Alexander continued to find this style very amusing long after their schooldays were over, and often parodied it in their adult correspondence. In origin Anton's imitations were purely oral. Later on he found that he had only to write some of them down to find a market for them in one of the Russian comic magazines. The first article published by him is said to be a word for word transcript of one of his early oral parodies. There could be no clearer illustration of the close link between his boyhood love of mimicry and his first steps as a writer.

v

A DOMESTIC CRISIS

DURING Anton's first six years at the *Gymnasium* there were no major changes in the outward pattern of his life. At about the age of fourteen, however, he began to notice that his father's face was growing longer and his temper worse. Things were going badly in the shop. Small tradesmen were among the first to feel the pinch of Taganrog's rapid commercial decline, and Paul Chekhov was steadily losing business to larger concerns. By 1874 his turnover had dwindled to the trifling sum of about three roubles a day. He cast this way and that in an attempt to improve matters, for example by moving his shop to a site nearer the station, where he hoped to attract the custom of travellers. This was not a success, and another of his enterprises—the building of a house—proved completely calamitous. Hitherto the Chekhovs had always lived in rented premises, and Paul calculated that the ownership of his own house would lead to certain economies—saving the rent, and enabling the family to take in boarders. Unfortunately he fell a victim to unscrupulous builders, who had arranged to be paid by the brick, and were determined to make the most of the opportunity. The new house turned out a squat and miserable structure with unnecessarily thick walls, a permanent monument to Paul's lack of practical acumen.

In order to build the house he had borrowed a large sum of money. By 1876 this had not yet been repaid, and business was worse than ever. Paul was forced to declare himself bankrupt, and was in danger of being locked up in the debtors' prison. He therefore decided to leave Taganrog for Moscow, calculating that the arm of the law (which was harsh, but not particularly efficient) would not reach this immense distance. The circumstances of his leave-taking were humiliating. It was not safe to leave the town openly, so he did the first stage of the journey at the bottom of a cart. Only when he was well out of town did he dare to show his face, and boarded the Moscow train at the next station up the line. In Moscow he hoped to restore his fortunes, after which he could expect to make a triumphant return to Taganrog—a plan which never came near realization.

The two elder sons were already in Moscow. Alexander was now a student of mathematics at the University, and Nicholas a pupil of the Institute of Painting, Sculpture and Architecture. The rest of the family remained in the south for the time being. The three youngest children were dispatched to their grandfather's, and for a short time only Anton was left behind in Taganrog with his mother. Evgeniya Chekhov was driven to distraction by the family disaster, which she was very far from understanding. She soon discovered that Anton, for all his apparent light-heartedness, had a better grasp of practical affairs than she. He found that she relied on him to negotiate with money-lenders and sell the furniture, and she was constantly asking his advice. Paul Chekhov's letters from Moscow were not very encouraging, and he seemed to be having little success with his project of setting up another small shop. In return Evgeniya sent him pathetic, semi-literate letters, in which the refrain 'Just try and not worry about that!' occurs again and again. She was still afraid that he might be discovered by the authorities and arrested as a debtor, and one of her suggested devices for outwitting the law charmingly illustrates her simplicity: 'Write us a post card saying you are going to Tambov. Write and say I'm just off to Tambov (or anywhere else you like).'

Besides Anton, Evgeniya Chekhov had another adviser—the

lodger, Selivanov. He had always been on excellent terms with the Chekhovs and used to say that he considered himself a member of the family. Selivanov was a low-grade clerk in some government office, but it soon became known that successful all-night gambling for high stakes at the Taganrog Commercial Club had made him a man of property who might easily become an asset to the Chekhovs. Soon after Paul Chekhov's disappearance his creditors began pressing for the compulsory sale of the house, and it was in this crisis that Evgeniya turned to Selivanov. He was extremely helpful. He questioned her very closely about the exact state of affairs, told her not to worry, and promised to arrange the whole matter for her. Soon he was explaining apologetically that he had bought the house himself, and even Anton's mother, for all her vagueness about practical affairs, realized that she had been the victim of a mean trick. Selivanov had used his knowledge of her situation to acquire the house at a low price. To make matters worse some of Paul's creditors managed to make good a claim to most of the furniture. Evgeniya, who now had no other course open to her, decided to collect the three youngest children from their grandfather's and join her husband in Moscow. What was Anton to do? It seemed a pity to interrupt his schooling now that he had only three years to go, and was doing fairly well at the *Gymnasium*. Selivanov, who may have been feeling rather ashamed of himself, solved the problem by offering Anton a home. In return he was expected to give lessons to a nephew of Selivanov's.

The loss of the house and furniture, coming on top of Paul's bankruptcy and flight, was, of course, an absolute catastrophe for the Chekhovs. Anton, now an intelligent and sensitive boy of sixteen, could not fail to be deeply upset. Twenty-seven years later, when he wrote *The Cherry Orchard,* he had not forgotten what it felt like to lose one's home. However, distressing as things were, so far as Anton's development was concerned, the disappearance of his family was perhaps a blessing in disguise. The life on which he now embarked was not an easy one, but at least it had the advantage that he was more or less his own master. The chief problem was bound to be money. Still, he had a roof over his head, and he soon found that he could provide at any rate the bare necessities of life by coaching junior *Gymnasium* boys. It was often a heart-breaking task, which meant trudging long distances through Taganrog, sometimes in icy mud and cold, with a threadbare overcoat and shoes out at heel. While he was going through the mechanical process of helping his pupils with their homework he could not help listening to the sounds in the house, trying to detect whether the samovar was being put on—which would at least mean a warming cup of tea before he began the long walk home.

Just before the Christmas of 1876 Alexander managed to scrape together enough money to pay Anton's train fare to Moscow, so that he was able to spend the holidays with his family. Thus it came about that he made the first long journey of his life. It was young Michael Chekhov who took upon himself the role of guide to the Kremlin and the churches, and who later testified in his memoirs to the 'shattering impression' which the city had produced on Anton. The return journey had to be delayed until Easter, because there was no money to pay for the ticket, and Anton had to elicit a 'medical certificate' from a friendly doctor to account for his long absence from the *Gymnasium*. His visit was an expensive luxury which the Chekhovs could not afford again, and they saw no more of him until he left Taganrog for Moscow in 1879.

VI

ALONE IN TAGANROG

DURING Anton's last years in Taganrog his thoughts were often with the family, and the news was rarely good. Alexander's letters were always welcome, because they were written with delicious irony, and were full of all sorts of private jokes which only Anton could understand. They were also saddening for what they revealed of the family's poverty and sufferings. A letter from Moscow usually meant errands for Anton. Alexander would ask for a pound of tobacco, which cost only half as much in Taganrog as in Moscow, and his mother would often want him to sell some article from among the pitiful remnants of furniture left by the creditors. Her letters were unrelievedly gloomy, and they were given an extra flavour of pathos by her entire ignorance of punctuation. Hoping to cheer her up Anton used to write back as amusingly as he could, but she was too upset to laugh. 'We've had two letters from you full of jokes,' she complained, 'but we only had four copecks at the time for bread and lighting and we were expecting you to send us money, we're very miserable Mariya hasn't got a winter coat.' Nobody could have helped liking Anton's mother, who was so good-hearted and hopelessly naïve in her distress. It was many years before she could bring herself to believe that return to Taganrog was impossible, and she still did not give up hope of recovering the house from Selivanov. She wrote asking Anton to have a long talk with him, pointing out that 'human life is very short and if he does us a good turn he will live a long time but if he won't even live as long as a year I've entrusted the whole matter to St John the Theologian.' However, Selivanov was not a man to yield to pressure from this quarter.

Though outward circumstances conspired to depress him, Anton's three years of isolation in Taganrog were not a period of dejection. His intense zest for life and consciousness of his own developing personality were enough to maintain his spirits. Now that he was at last free from his father's interference and able to give due attention to his school work, he found that he enjoyed it more. His enjoyment was still marred by examinations—a nerve-racking prospect, for he could certainly not afford to be kept down again for an extra year. Meanwhile new pursuits were beginning to appear, replacing some of the old ones. He began to take an interest in the opposite sex, and was flattered to find that some of the pretty High School girls were not slow to return the compliment. He was able to extend his experience of life in other directions by the hospitality of Selivanov's nephew, the supervision of whose studies now earned him his board. This nephew was a Cossack boy from the wilds of the Don steppe, where Anton sometimes joined him for the holidays. Hard riding and straight shooting were the rule in this rough cowboy community, and the Cossack way of life made even Taganrog seem sophisticated. The hunting instinct was so strongly developed in these parts that most people's time seemed to be entirely devoted to the unremitting and systematic massacre of wild life—even the domestic animals were allowed to run wild so that one might have the pleasure of hunting them for the table. Anton was often woken early in the morning by the sound of shots—it was the neighbours, slaughtering the day's dinner.

It is not surprising that the passage of time, together with all these new influences, combined to bring about big changes in his personality and outward appearance. Those who had known him as a plump little boy often failed to recognize this slim and strikingly handsome youth with light-coloured hair and hazel eyes. His height, when fully grown, was just under six feet. The breadth of his features gave an unmistakably Slav imprint to his face. His childhood friend Sergeenko remarked that you could find at least one peasant in every Russian village who looked just like Chekhov, 'with Chekhov's facial expression and Chekhov's smile.' His character had also developed enormously. Thrown upon his own resources as he was, he was learning to make his own decisions and to stick to them. He was still slow to communicate his feelings to other people, for he retained much of the reticence which characterized him as a small boy, the origin of which may have lain in the snubs and rebuffs so often inflicted in his infancy. As his school friends often found, it was difficult to draw him out. For instance, in spite of the Ministry of Popular Enlightenment, there was no lack of discussion about politics among the senior *Gymnasium* pupils. They were keenly interested in public affairs, secretly read their Pisarev, Bakunin and Herzen, mirroring in their arguments the ideological wrangles of their elders at the universities. They ranged into partisans of left and right. Anton was one of the few who refused to take sides. 'I want to get married,' he would say with an enigmatic smile and a shrug of the shoulders, when people challenged him for his opinion.

He displayed a similar evasiveness when questioned about what he intended to do after leaving school. 'I'm going to be a priest,' he would say with a grin, realizing that this remark could not possibly be taken seriously by anyone who knew him. With regard to his career, however, he had made a decision, and one which was of immense importance in conditioning his subsequent development. It is not known what precise factors persuaded him to take up medicine. His contact with a kindly German doctor on the occasion of an illness during his seventeenth year—a chill contracted while bathing—probably had something to do with it. So far as the choice of university went, Moscow was clearly indicated because it had a good medical faculty, and the family home provided him with a convenient base of operations.

His interest in the theatre showed no signs of flagging, and he had much extended another early interest—reading. Taganrog Public Library was one of the important places of his childhood. Even when he was quite small he was fond of going there, often with a gang of his school-friends. Their chuckles and whispers as they huddled together over the comic papers

C

sometimes aroused an angry 'Shush!' from an adult reader. Now Anton's reading was beginning to take in more serious works, though it was mostly done for pleasure, without any vestige of a plan. One of his earliest surviving letters written in 1876, and addressed to his brother Michael, is devoted partly to this theme. It has some of the patronizing touch of the sixteen-year-old giving advice to a junior, but is interesting in showing the kind of book which was attracting his attention. He advises Michael to read Goncharov's *Frigate Pallas* and Cervantes' *Don Quixote*. He speaks with favour of Turgenev's essay *Hamlet and Don Quixote,* though he adds, 'You won't understand it, old chap'. (Michael was eleven at the time.) He is severe on Michael's enthusiasm for *Uncle Tom's Cabin,* saying that he himself had recently re-read it 'for research purposes', and that it had made him feel as though he had eaten too many currants and raisins. This preoccupation with long and serious works—which, of course, included many others besides those mentioned in the letter—had not made him any less interested in the comic papers. A large number of humorous weeklies were being published at this time in Russia, with names like *The Dragonfly, Alarm-Clock* and *Fragments.* There was something about these publications which appealed to Anton, and before long he was producing a manuscript magazine of his own, *The Stammerer,* which he used to send to his brothers in Moscow. Alexander was very interested. As a university student without private means he had been forced to find some way of earning money, and had already become a contributor to the comic papers. His sense of humour was not unlike Anton's, and he thought that he could place some of Anton's short sketches along with his own. 'Your anecdotes will catch on,' he wrote to Anton in 1877. 'Today I am sending two of your witticisms by post to *Alarm-Clock,* to wit: *Which sex adorns itself to best advantage?* and *God has granted.* The rest are weak. Make them as short and snappy as you can.'

Dramatic writing played the biggest part in Anton's literary activity at school. He wrote several short farces, but put his most serious work into a long play, called *Fatherless.* Alexander, whose criticism he valued highly, had strong words to say about this play. Though he said it showed some talent, he condemned it as utterly false. *Fatherless* occupies a very obscure place in Chekhov's work. The play has not survived It was identified by the Russian editors of Chekhov's *Collected*

Works (1933) with the extant play sometimes known in English as *Platonov* (published posthumously in 1923 without a title). But there is no serious evidence to bear out this identification. Though neither *Fatherless* nor Chekhov's other schoolboy experiments in writing have survived, their loss is almost certainly not to be regretted from a literary point of view.

It was in August 1879 that Chekhov at last left Taganrog, bearing with him his school leaving-certificate and an official identity-card, which was required for travel within Russia. As he settled down in the train for the long journey to Moscow he realized very clearly that one epoch of his life had just ended, and that another was just about to begin. There was nothing about him at this time to suggest unusual ability, even to those who knew him best. All that seemed to have happened during the past few years was that a high-spirited and ordinary boy had changed into a high-spirited and ordinary young man. Nobody, least of all Chekhov himself, had the remotest suspicion of what lay ahead.

CHAPTER TWO

Early Years in Moscow

—————————— • ——————————

I

CHEKHOV'S ARRIVAL

In Moscow the family were looking forward to Anton's arrival with intense excitement. They had thought and talked about it all the summer, and, as usually happens in such situations, he turned up at the moment when he was least expected. Michael was sitting idly on the door-step, when he suddenly found himself addressed with mock formality as 'Mikhail Pavlovich'—just as though he had been a grown-up—by a tall young man with a deep voice, who had just arrived in a cab. Suddenly realizing who it was, he tore off to tell his mother. For a moment everything was forgotten in the exchange of kisses, embraces and excited exclamations. When things settled down, and Evgeniya began to take stock of her son, she felt proud to see him so tall and attractive-looking, with such a modest air of self-possession. Everyone said how much he had changed. For his part, Anton, when he had time to look around, could not help being horrified by what he saw of the family's living conditions. Things were even worse than he had been led to expect from their letters. Their present quarters consisted of an evil basement, so damp that it filled with steam whenever the stove was lit, and situated in the brothel area of Moscow. It was dark and over-crowded. Through the windows, which looked out on the street, only the feet of passers-by could be seen.

Anton arrived rather later than had been expected. After the school final examinations and passing-out ceremonies were over he had stayed behind in Taganrog to apply for a scholarship of three hundred roubles a year, awarded by the Town Council. This he eventually obtained, and when he arrived in Moscow he had four months' instalment—a whole hundred roubles—in his pocket. The sum was promptly swallowed up by the family's debts, but it did mean that Anton's arrival brought an immediate minor alleviation which must have been very welcome. In addition to the money, he had arranged to introduce two paying guests—Taganrog school-friends who were also about to enter the University. These two were speedily joined by a third, who was unknown to the Chekhovs, but whose parents had somehow heard that they were a thoroughly respectable family, and had accordingly sent him along. Evgeniya Chekhov did not charge very much for board, and she saw to it that her lodgers were really well fed, but their arrival did make a big difference to the family finances. It began to look as though matters were already on the mend, with Anton as the person chiefly responsible.

The arrival of four young men doubled the size of the household, and it was obvious that the Chekhovs would have to make yet another move—the twelfth since they had first appeared in Moscow. A five-room flat in the same street was the best they could manage, and it still left them rather cramped. Michael, who almost worshipped Anton, was overjoyed at being put in the same room as his hero. It was he who again acted as guide to Moscow, and one of their first visits was made to the University, where Anton enrolled as a medical student.

It was thrilling to begin this completely new life and programme of work, but Chekhov had many things to think of besides the excitement of joining Moscow University. The condition of the family did not altogether surprise him, for letters from Alexander and his mother had not left him under any illusions about their mode of life. However, it gave him a considerable jolt to convince himself by the evidence of his own eyes that they were fast degenerating into slum-dwellers, the normal background of whose lives consisted of overcrowding, damp, vermin, the all-pervading smell of cooking and stale food, and the quarrels of neighbours. It was heart-breaking to think of the younger children facing the cruel cold of the Moscow winter in thin coats and dilapidated boots. Obviously Anton must somehow make it his business to improve things—it was clear that nobody else could be depended upon to do so. His father's star was very much in decline. For many years he had been unable to obtain work, and had begun to feel that he must be almost unemployable. Recently he had been taken on as a clerk by a big firm of Moscow wholesalers at a salary of thirty roubles a month, which was not nearly enough to support a family. The arrangement did have its advantages because Paul Chekhov had to live near his work, and could only visit the family on holidays —it is easy to see what a relief this must have been to his younger children, and, one cannot help feeling, to his wife. Anton felt sorry for his father. The menacing figure who had dominated his boyhood was beginning to look like a pathetic elderly man, and very soon Anton found himself regarded as the head of the family.

He did not seek this position, but neither of his elder brothers was capable of filling it. Alexander and Nicholas were still going through a rather unwholesome, though very natural, phase of mutiny against the lower-middle-class traditions in which they had been brought up, and, in particular, against anything which smacked of what they called Taganrogism. They plunged, as deep as their scanty resources would permit, into the Muscovite night life of the late 'seventies and early 'eighties, with its tawdry cabarets and cheap liquor. It was no uncommon thing to find either of them asleep in bed at twelve o'clock in the morning, stertorously breathing stale vodka fumes. Alexander did make some contributions to the family exchequer. He refused to live with them—protesting with some truth that he would be unable to work properly in such a disordered ménage—and supported himself as a student in various ways, chiefly by contributing articles to humorous magazines. When he had anything to spare he sent it to his mother. Nicholas was a much worse case, and was more of a liability than an asset. An extremely gifted painter, he soon had commissions on his hands, but a combination of laziness and ill-health made him neglect his really great opportunities.

Things would have been difficult enough for Anton even if he had had only himself to think of. He had just started a strenuous five-year course at the University, and knew that it would be a long time before he was earning any money as a doctor. How he was going to rehabilitate the family in the immediate future he simply could not see. In the meantime Alexander had shown him a way of making a few extra roubles, and before long the family began to notice that medicine did not occupy the whole of Anton's time. He was often to be seen sitting at the bottom of the garden, where he would scribble away in an old exercise-book, but nobody knew quite what he was doing. He refused to allow anyone to look inside the old trunk which he kept in his room, and which was full of papers. His mother must have had some idea of what was going on because she once playfully threatened to burn the trunk, which would 'teach him to make fun of people'. However, making fun of people was quite a serious thing for her son that winter. One afternoon each week he used to rush out of lectures in order to buy *The Dragonfly*, a Petersburg humorous magazine. Too impatient to wait until he got home he would fumble with the pages in the street, careless of frost-bitten fingers in his eagerness to turn up the 'Pillar-Box'. This was a section of the magazine in which the editor used to inform contributors of his views on their work, and of his decision about publishing it.

II

THE COMIC PAPERS

IN *The Dragonfly* dated January 13, 1880, Chekhov at last found a notice addressed to himself: 'To Mr A. Che---v, Moscow. Not bad at all. We will publish your contribution. Our blessing on any future exploits.'

Almost as exciting as this was the arrival, a week later, of a letter from the editor, telling Chekhov that he was to be paid at the rate of five copecks a line for two humorous sketches which duly appeared in one of the March issues. This only brought in a few roubles—not much perhaps, but it was thrilling to see his work in print, and he decided to persevere. During the rest of the year he continued to contribute to *The Dragonfly*, which accepted ten of his articles. Things seemed to be going well, but before very long he received a number of rebuffs from an editor who evidently did not think that politeness paid dividends. He was never quite so rude to Chekhov as he had been to one contributor, whom he advised to 'take a good dose of castor-oil', but his comment on one article was: 'Very long and colourless. Rather like a long paper ribbon drawn out of the mouth of a Chinese.' Worse still, towards the end of the year he pronounced: 'You are withering without having bloomed. A great pity.'

This epitaph on his writing career had an air of finality which made it very discouraging to Chekhov. Was it to mean the end of his literary earnings, which, trifling as they were, had already become a genuine factor in the family budget? This could not be allowed to happen, so he decided to abandon *The Dragonfly* and try his luck elsewhere. During the year 1881 he published thirteen items, most of which found their way into a Moscow magazine, *The Onlooker*. This was much more interesting than writing for *The Dragonfly* because the editorial office was just around the corner, and Chekhov was able to drop in for a chat with the editor, compositors and other contributors. The atmosphere was homely but hectic. The editor was eccentric; his weakness for grandiose projects went together with a poor business head. His extravagant talk about how he was going to increase the circulation, and crowd the other comic papers off the market, contrasted vividly with his actual achievements. His staff was small and inefficient, and the paper did not survive long. Subscribers were irritated by its irregular and unpredictable appearance—usually well after the promised date—and withdrew their support. While *Onlooker* lasted, the Chekhov family supplied the bulk of the contributions, Anton and Alexander producing the reading matter, while Nicholas made himself responsible for the illustrations.

When *Onlooker* failed, Chekhov had no difficulty in finding other markets for his work. His publications in 1882 totalled thirty-one—some of them of considerable length—and he placed them in a variety of magazines, such as *Alarm-Clock, Travelling Companion, Moscow, Light and Shade, Diversion* and *Worldly Chatter*. None of these contributions was signed in his own name. Pseudonyms, usually with an exotic or whimsical flavour, were very much in the style of the comic press. One contributor signed himself *Pup* (which means navel), and Alexander Chekhov, with a taste for the polysyllabic, used *Agafopod Edinitsyn*. Anton's staple pen-name was *Antosha Chekhonte*, though he used a wide variety of others, such as *My Brother's Brother, The Man without a Spleen, Prose Poet, Screw Number 6* and so on.

By the end of 1882 Chekhov had completed three years as a writer of inconsiderable comic trifles. During this time he had done little more than establish himself as an average contributor to one of the least reputable sections of the Russian press. There was nothing in his work which could have enabled the most keen-sighted literary prophet to predict the brilliant future which lay ahead of him Nor was he under any illusion himself about the quality of what he sometimes used to call 'my literary excrement'. If he had ambitions in the direction of serious writing, he realized that they could never be achieved by comic journalism. Writing was simply a convenient spare-time occupation, which happened to be the easiest way of earning the money so desperately needed by his family. He still hated having to pay

so much attention to money, and loathed hearing it discussed
by his father's business friends, who seemed to think of little
else. It was only in later life, however, that he fully assessed
the extent to which poverty had handicapped him, contrasting his
early struggles with the easy lives of writers from wealthy families—such as Turgenev and Tolstoy—who 'receive from nature
as a gift what we lower-class writers buy at the cost of our
youth'. Chekhov's early correspondence shows quite clearly that
it was not a desire to create literary masterpieces which first
impelled him to write, but the need to pay his family's bills.
Their position forced him to be continually worrying about
money—a habit which pursued him into the 'nineties, when there
was much less occasion for it.

During his early years in Moscow money worries were aggra-
vated by the dishonesty and rudeness of his editors. Chekhov
said that he knew most of them 'only from behind', because they
were not even polite enough to turn around when he came into
the office, but would merely snarl 'Don't let him in!' When he
did get in they would often refuse to read his work: 'What!
You call that a contribution? Why, it's shorter than a sparrow's
nose. We've no use for that sort of stuff.' The rates of pay
were miserable, and usually came out at five to seven copecks
a line. It was hard work extracting even this from the average
Moscow editor, and Chekhov often had to go as often as ten
times to the offices of *Alarm-Clock* to pick up the paltry sum of
three roubles. Sometimes an editor would flatly refuse to part
with money, and would suggest payment in kind: 'Wouldn't
you like a theatre ticket?' or 'How about some trousers? Go
along to my tailors and order yourself a pair.' These visits to
editorial offices were a great waste of time and shoe-leather.
Luckily Michael Chekhov, who was always ready to do anything
for Anton, agreed to take over the collecting. He used to do his
rounds equipped with an 'official document', bearing Anton's
signature, and certifying 'that the bearer has occupied the position of my brother since the year 1865'. It was a job that demanded much patience and ingenuity. Often the only way to
get money was to waylay street vendors as they returned to the
office, and take the sum off them in small change under the
nose of the editor.

Before Michael took over, Anton must often have felt that
it was more trouble to collect his earnings than to write. He
wrote easily and quickly, and soon found that it was not always

necessary to work in the privacy of his room. At meal-times
or in the circle round the samovar the family would sometimes
notice that he had lost the thread of the conversation, and that
he was staring straight ahead, obviously thinking of something
else. At such times they knew that he had an idea for a story.
He wrote his stories straight off, without a pause, in a very short
space of time. When he left them half-finished he found that it
was no use taking them up again. He had to start afresh with
something else.

He was learning to insulate himself against noise and inter-
ruptions, though they irritated him at times. Paul Chekhov was
usually away, but on holidays one could hear the insistent ca-
dences of his voice, as he read aloud for hours on end from
tracts which he bought in the street for a copeck each. He continued the habit long after anyone except his wife had ceased
even to pretend to listen to him. Sometimes Nicholas would be
drawing, using Michael as a model, and grumbling 'When *will*
you learn to sit still?' Someone would wind up the musical box,
and Anton would hear a cracked rendering of tunes from
Offenbach's operetta *La Belle Hélène*, which brought with
it memories of the Taganrog theatre. There was a constant
stream of guests, most of whom had no hesitation in interrupt-
ing him with a discussion of literature or a request for medical
advice. He soon found it was no use trying to get any privacy,
and taught himself to ignore the hubbub. On the rare occasions
when there was no noise going on he began to have an uncomfortable feeling, and he sometimes used to ask Michael or Nicholas to strum away on the piano to help him concentrate.

Increased poverty had not cured the Chekhovs of their inveterate hospitality, and they were constantly entertaining.
Their attitude was that it was better to pawn the hearth-rug
than to be left without vodka or tea to offer their guests. These
guests included people of all ages and descriptions, from
Michael's and Mariya's small playmates to Paul Chekhov's
friends from his place of work. Some of them were from other
branches of the Chekhov family, most of whom were in commerce. These were good-hearted, vulgar Moscow burghers, without any shred of intellectual interests, who knew that they
could find a hearty welcome and the kind of evening's entertainment that they liked. There would be plenty to drink and
much coarse laughter; as soon as they got warmed up they
would start singing their favourite drinking songs, accompanied

by Nicholas at the piano. Half tipsy, Paul Chekhov would sometimes hold up an authoritiatve hand, and insist on the company
rendering an anthem. Anton was reminded of choir-practice of a
very different type which his father had conducted in the old
days at Taganrog. Anton and Alexander were ready enough to
join in these orgies, but they found that they had very little in
common with the cruder elements of the family, who, for some
reason, used to call themselves the 'Chokhovs'.

Their own friends were rather different, though they often
shared the Chokhovs' love of a rowdy evening. They consisted
of fellow-students and fellow-journalists. Many were hangers-
on of the comic press, who could not lay claim to any particular
success in life, but were colourful figures in their ill-fitting,
worn-out clothes. They were always anxious to exchange the
latest piece of scandal with Chekhov before returning to
their impossible garrets and blowsy mistresses. Chekhov visited
them in turn, drank beer and wine with them, gave them free
medical advice, vetted their manuscripts, and even passed
their work off as his own when they had difficulty in finding a
publisher. They enjoyed the company of this young student, who
shared many of their interests, and was always willing to help
them. His conversation was lively and sophisticated, with an
attractive tang of malice when he retailed the newest and
spiciest piece of newspaper gossip. Above all he was valued as a
sympathetic confidant, before whom his friends could pour out
their troubles. He was always more of a listener than a talker.

III

CHEKHOV'S EARLY WRITINGS

THE character of Chekhov's first literary efforts was determined by the standards of the Russian comic papers. These
papers were numerous, but did not vary very much from each
other in general style, nor did their humour differ greatly from
what was fashionable at the same time in other countries. Certain themes were established as funny, and these themes are
readily recognizable to any one who has ever picked up a
humorous magazine. Popular humour has perhaps not altered
very much since the time when Chekhov was writing, except
that it has certainly been speeded up. Few modern readers
would have the patience to read through jokes like this early
contribution of Chekhov's:

'A fine frosty noon. The sun glitters on every particle of snow. There are no clouds or wind. A couple is sitting on a boulevard bench.

"I love you," he whispers.

Pink dimples play on her cheeks.

"I love you," he continues, "The first time I saw you I realized what it is I live for. I learned the purpose of my life! Either life with you—or total non-existence! My darling! Mariya Ivanovna! ... I love ... Answer, or I shall die. Yes or no."

She lifts her large eyes to him. She wants to say "Yes". She opens her mouth.

"Oh!" she screams.

On his snow-white collar two huge beetles are chasing each other. Oh, horrors ! ! !'

It must be admitted that Chekhov's jokes were not all quite so cumbrous as this one and that he showed great resource in putting them together. Many were in the form of captions to funny pictures supplied by his brother Nicholas or other artists of his acquaintance. Though he was full of ideas himself Chekhov let it be known that he would pay ten copecks to anyone who supplied him with a new subject, and his publications did credit to the ingenuity of everybody concerned. They include these *Problems of a Mad Mathematician:*

'I am chased by thirty dogs, of which seven are white, eight grey, and the remainder black. Which of my legs do the dogs bite, the right or the left?' 'My mother-in-law is 75 years old, and my wife is 42. What time is it?'

Comic advertisements were something which could always be relied upon when other ideas failed:

'Coffins of every type in store. Discount for those dying whole-sale. Gentlemen in process of expiring are warned to beware of imitations.' 'Dr Chertolobov treats the poor free of charge on: February 30, April 31 and June 31, and at greatly reduced terms on February 29.'

Many of these 'advertisements' concerned books with ridiculous titles:

'IN LEUKHIN'S BOOK-SHOP there are on sale the following fright-ful books: *Passionate Love, Self-Taught,* or *Oh, you beast!* by Idiotov. Price 1 rouble 80 copecks. *Collected Letters* by Doctor Merzavtsev. Price 4 roubles. *The Memoirs of a Woman's Stocking,* or *So much for Innocence!* Price 1 rouble 50 copecks.'

In the sort of article Chekhov was contributing there was an unwritten law that all the characters should be given funny names. To an English ear, of course, many quite ordinary Russian names sound funny. However, a reference to the dictionary will show the non-Russian speaker that inventions such as Shchelkolobov, Krivomordenko, Merzavtsev and Ivan Tarakan-ovich are in fact constructions of the 'Captain Reilly-ffoull' type. Others, such as Idiotov, Krokodilov and Lieutenant Zyumzum-bunchikov are patently absurd without any such reference, and it is not surprising to find among Chekhov's foreign characters a Monsieur Pas-de-Quoi and a Herr Wanze.

Not all Chekhov's early publications were brief and frag-mentary. However, the same glib facetiousness runs through almost everything he wrote, and he attempted a wide variety of genres. An example of the kind of burlesque which derived directly from his boyhood love of mimicry is his first contribu-tion to *Dragonfly*—*The Letter of a Don Landowner to his Learned Neighbour.* This 'letter' followed closely the text of some of his early imitations in the family circle. It purports to be written by a semi-literate and dogmatizing old fool, and takes the form of a defence of science. Both the style and thought-processes of the landowner are ridiculed. His 'scientific' deductions include:

The day is short in winter because it shrinks from the cold.
No one can live on the moon, because rain is necessary for life, and that falls down, not up.

The text is packed with comic periphrases, mis-spellings and malapropisms. During this period Chekhov repeatedly reverted to such mockery of the uneducated, in burlesques of school-girls' essays and reproductions of speeches by servants who use long words which they do not understand. There are also many examples of literary parody, including alleged 'Translations from the Spanish', or 'from the Portuguese'—imitations of a type of magazine-story popular at the time. Some of Chekhov's early jokes were worked up into episodes and might almost be dignified with the name short stories. An example is *A Nasty Story*. This concerns the attempts of a young lady to induce her artist friend to propose to her. The artist is very timid, but he obviously has something on his mind. Finally, long after his manoeuvres have thoroughly exasperated both the reader and the heroine, he tells her that he has an important question to ask:

' "You are just the woman I need. To the devil with the rest! Elena Timofeevna! Be my—" She submissively rested her head on his shoulder.

'Tears of happiness shone in her eyes.

' "My dear! Be my ... model!" '

A Nasty Story is an early and crude specimen of the literary genre known as the Little Story which Chekhov developed with great skill in the years 1883-85. Like other early examples it is not very successful.

Not all Chekhov's early work was comic. *The Unnecessary Victory* is a piece of literary imitation unusual because of its length and comparatively serious treatment. It was written after an argument between Chekhov and the editor of *Alarm-Clock*, as a result of which Chekhov undertook to produce a full-length novel with a foreign setting, as good as the translated novels which were appearing in Russia at the time. His chief model was the Hungarian novelist Jokai Mor, and the imitation was near enough to convince some readers that it was actually Jokai's work. It describes the adventures of the daughter of a gypsy violinist. Chekhov makes a brave show at treating subjects of which neither he nor most of his readers had any first-hand knowledge—the Hungarian nobility and the night life of Paris. The flavouring of the novel is exotic and romantic in true magazine-story manner. Like all Chekhov's early work it abounds in extravagances: 'The Baron laughed contemptuously and spat to one side. His spit flew a distance of twelve feet.' The editor of *Alarm-Clock* soon found that he had got more than he bargained for, and began to complain that the story was too long. It has no literary merit and is not well-known in Russia, although it appears that several early films were based on it.

The Unnecessary Victory can hardly be called a serious work, but at any rate it is free from the cruder forms of clowning imposed upon Chekhov by the comic press. Other and more serious stories afford proof of his desire to experiment with literary form, and incidentally contain by far the most promising examples of his early work. The story *Because of the Apples* was an attempt at a form of writing which had once been very popular in Russia, but which was now becoming obsolete. This is the 'philanthropic story', of which the prototype was Gogol's *Overcoat*, and of which Turgenev's *Sportsman's Sketches* contain some of the best-known examples. Chekhov's story concerns a brutal landowner (a stock figure in 'philanthropic' literature) who catches a peasant couple stealing apples in his orchard. 'I hope I am not disturbing you,' he says in a dangerous and silky voice, and proceeds to humiliate them by forcing them to beat each other. *The Mistress* is another story with a strong 'philanthropic' element. It concerns the tragic disorganization of a peasant family created when a rich and spoilt woman decides to take a handsome villager as her lover. Here both upper and lower classes come in for equally severe treatment from Chekhov, and this is one of the first stories in which he shows the squalor of Russian village life.

The most remarkable and interesting of these early *Chekhonte* stories is undoubtedly *Belated Blossom*. It is a study of the Russian nobility in decline, and its subject-matter has an affinity with that of *The Cherry Orchard*. On the one hand Chekhov shows the Priklonsky family, impoverished aristocrats, consisting of an old widowed mother, a drunken son and a good-hearted but feeble daughter. They are all failures, and in describing their wasted, unhappy lives Chekhov seems to touch for the first time that distinctive but elusive note for which some of his later work is famous. The vigorous doctor Toporkov, who has risen to wealth and success after starting life as a servant's son, is set in contrast to the Priklonskys—an anticipation of the relations between Lopakhin and the aristocratic owners of the cherry orchard. In *Belated Blossom* the treatment is crude, and the story dissolves in a welter of sentimentality, highly untypical of Chekhov; however, it is certainly the most successful of his early attempts at serious writing.

With a few exceptions, such as *Belated Blossom*, the style of Chekhov's early work is uniformly frivolous. It is chiefly remarkable for a number of irritating tricks, such as one sometimes finds in a schoolboy's letters. Chekhov was obviously uneasy about the quality of his material, and sought to redeem it by the use of various extravagant devices. Among these are the grotesque names of the characters, malapropisms and puns. The reader is exasperated by the recurrence of certain favourite metaphors, such as 'cats were scratching his heart' to convey mental anguish. Various stock methods of expressing hyperbole also weary by repetition. Chekhov obviously delighted in the incorrect Russian of the uneducated, and went to great pains to give a phonetical transcription of their speech. However, his own Russian was far from impeccable at this period, and contained a number of glaring provincialisms. His prose is often strained and hysterical. Exclamation marks cover his pages like a rash, together with shrieks of joy or dismay such as are found in boys' magazines. ('Yaroo!' 'Owch!', to give them their English equivalents). Wearisome also is his fondness for pseudo-classical periphrases, whereby a lawyer becomes 'the acolyte of Themis' and an after-dinner nap 'the embrace of post-prandial Morpheus'.

IV

CHEKHOV'S OUTLOOK AS A STUDENT

CHEKHOV'S effervescent humour was not exhausted by his efforts for the comic papers. Just as in the Taganrog days, his sallies and improvisations could usually be relied upon to keep the family and their guests amused. Some of his friends, particularly those who did not know him intimately, must often have wondered whether a serious thought ever entered his head, since they heard little from him but a torrent of high-spirited nonsense. As in his boyhood he continued to conceal his deeper thoughts and feelings from others, but they did emerge on occasion. He was already tiring of the Russian comic press. He had no illusions about its worth, and gave expression to his contempt at an occasional irritated outburst:

'The word "newspaper-writer" means at very least a scoundrel. I'm one of them; I work with them; I shake hands with them; I'm even told that I've begun to look like one from a distance ... But it's only temporary. I shan't die as one ... All I get out of my writing is a nervous twitch.'

It was a long time before literature presented itself to him in the light of a whole-time career. For the moment his policy was clear—he was going to be a doctor, and he took his studies very seriously. The medical course was exacting, and it would have been beyond the power of most students to combine it with intensive literary work. However, Chekhov took it fairly well in his stride. His attendance at clinic and lecture-room was regular. Like many other students he was worried by the prospect of failing his examinations. They were the one unpleasant feature in a programme of which he otherwise approved. He hated the mechanical process of 'cramming' a lot of facts which were immediately forgotten afterwards, and which took him away from the more interesting and valuable side of his studies. 'These examinations very much handicap senior students,' he wrote, 'just as saluting hinders policemen in the execution of their duty.'

His attitude to medicine varied according to the mood of the moment. Sometimes it 'tormented' him, sometimes it seemed to be the 'only salvation' from his trials and difficulties. However his views vacillated, medicine was becoming more and more necessary to him, and he was soon calling it his 'legal wife' in contrast with literature, his 'mistress'. In spite of their relationship the two lived in very friendly rivalry as complementary activities, each providing a welcome refuge and relaxation when the other became irksome.

As a man and a writer Chekhov owed an immense amount to medicine. The most casual glance at his fiction shows to what extent he was indebted to his profession for subject-matter. However, the chief importance of medicine to him was perhaps the way in which it conditioned and reinforced his general outlook on life. At the age of twenty-two he had no firm philosophical view, but was already giving evidence of one of his most characteristic mental qualities—an ability to reserve judgment on complicated questions. He was never much impressed by abstract theorizing, particularly when it was religious or metaphysical, and the only kind of generalizations which attracted him were those which could be tested against evidence. This approach was natural to him, but there can be no doubt that his scientific training helped to strengthen it.

As during his school-days, he carried his scepticism into the realm of politics, and in this respect differed from many of his fellow-students. The average young intellectual was politically conscious, and felt that everyone else ought to be so too. It was a period of intense political dissatisfaction which found various forms of outlet, from impassioned private debate to public violence, and which led to the popular association in the West European mind of the Russian and the bomb. Since

Chekhov's boyhood the internal situation had deteriorated. Revolutionary activity had culminated in the assassination of Alexander II in 1881, followed by an intensification of repressive measures under his successor. Some of Chekhov's fellow-students suffered exile in Siberia for their activities. Though Chekhov took no part in politics, he disliked official interference just as much as did his more politically-minded contemporaries.

The 'eighties were notorious in Russia for a general lowering of social morale and for a 'stifling' atmosphere. Chekhov was touched by the general depression, and there were many ways in which he was directly affected. His stories were at the mercy of an obtuse and apparently arbitrary censorship, which was liable to ban them entirely, or to strike out whole passages, often on no discernible principle. Like every other Russian he had to be careful what he said in public. In the summer of 1881 he was attending the All-Russian Exhibition in Moscow, when he heard the news of a very serious railway accident which became the talk of the newspapers for months afterwards. Chekhov was horrified, and remarked to his companion that such catastrophes were only possible in 'our brutish Russia'. A general, wearing a dark blue forage cap and white epaulettes, rushed up to him and said: 'What did you say, young man? Repeat your words! "In our brutish Russia", I believe. What is your name? Who are you?' Having taken particulars the General withdrew with a cry of 'You'll answer for this!' It was no laughing matter. Chekhov was seriously worried, for he knew that if his remark was reported to the police it might lead to serious consequences. Fortunately, however, the General must have decided not to pursue the matter farther.

Though politically neutral, Chekhov was not, even in these early days, indifferent to the social condition of Russia, but the comic magazines did not seem a very appropriate place in which to register a protest. They were themselves a typical by-product of social depression, their flippancy and facetiousness being symptomatic of a desire to avoid genuine issues.

CHAPTER THREE

'Fragments'

I

LEYKIN AND THE LITTLE STORIES

ONE day in the early winter of 1882 Chekhov was walking through the streets of Moscow when he heard a shout, and a sledge drew up beside him. The occupant, a prosperous-looking gentleman who was smoking a cigar, introduced himself as Nicholas Leykin, the proprietor and editor of the Petersburg magazine *Fragments*. Leykin at once took Chekhov into the nearest tavern for a glass of beer, saying that it was too cold to discuss business in the street. He explained that he had had his eye on Chekhov for some time, and that he wanted him to write for *Fragments*, suggesting eight copecks a line as remuneration. This was more than he had so far been receiving, and the proposition looked all the more attractive because Leykin was known to be prompt in settling up. Chekhov, whose first work appeared in *Fragments* in November 1882, before long became a mainstay of the paper, and from this point onwards his writing provided him with a dependable small income.

Chekhov had heard of Leykin long before this meeting, and knew him to be a wealthy man who had founded his fortune on a flair for the commercial possibilities of humour. Leykin was himself a prolific writer of humorous stories, which Chekhov had admired ever since he had first read them as a boy in Taganrog Public Library. Authorship had given the proprietor of *Fragments* more insight into the problems of his contributors than was to be expected from other editors of comic papers. At the same time no one was ever likely to mistake Leykin for an aesthete, and it was Chekhov himself who described him as a 'bourgeois to the marrow', interested only in the market value of his publications. His editorial policy was clear-cut. 'Keep it short and funny.'

Chekhov was delighted with his new employer. '*Fragments* is now the most popular magazine,' he wrote to Alexander. 'It's read everywhere, which is not surprising. Working for it is like having a diploma. Now I have the right to look down on *Alarm-Clock*.' Chekhov and Leykin corresponded frequently, and they understood each other well enough to have no hesitation in airing their differences. Leykin jealously watched his protégé, and became annoyed whenever he saw the signature *Antosha Chekhonte* in someone else's paper. However, Chekhov soon made it clear that he did not intend to abandon the other papers entirely. 'If I sent you the whole of what I sometimes manage to write in a single good winter evening's work,' he wrote to Leykin, 'you'd have enough material for a month. But it so happens that I do more than one evening's writing, and produce a whole quantity of stuff. Where, then, am I to send this quantity?' Chekhov pointed out that he had to earn between 150 and 180 roubles a month, 'otherwise I'm bankrupt', and that it was impossible to earn this sum in *Fragments* alone. Leykin, who was a sensible man, accepted the situation, particularly when he realized that Chekhov tended to use other publications as a dumping ground for his inferior work.

Chekhov's chief complaint against *Fragments* was directed against the rigidity of Leykin's 'programme'. It was irritating having to keep a story within the statutory length of 100 lines, particularly when your pen ran on and on, and when you at last felt that you were writing something worth while. 'What's happened to my *Tragic Actor*?' he asked. 'It might have turned out quite a decent story if it hadn't been for your frameworks. As it was I had to cut down the very heart and kernel of it.' However, in spite of all 'frameworks' Chekhov's work for *Fragments* did coincide with a great improvement in the quality of his writing. It was in *Fragments* that he first made extensive use of the Little Story, a literary form which grew directly out of Leykin's programme. Although he chafed under Leykin's restrictions, he certainly derived some benefit from them. For example, they checked a tendency to verbosity which was a feature of his earlier style. Some of his first approximations to the form of the Little Story such as *Papa* and *A Nasty Story* suffer from a long-windedness which was not possible in *Fragments*. They are clumsy in comparison with the pithy, neatly-turned work which he now began to produce. It was now that he first began to develop the extreme economy of expression which eventually became an outstanding quality of his style. Concrete evidence of this is provided by the texts of some of the earlier stories as altered by him in 1883 for inclusion in a volume of collected stories which in fact was never published. A comparison with the versions as originally printed a year or two before shows that Chekhov's revision was devoted principally to toning things down. Fanciful proper names are replaced by a more sober variety, exclamation marks disappear, and faulty Russian, put into the mouths of doorkeepers and coachmen to raise an easy laugh, is frequently corrected.

Besides an improvement in technique, Chekhov's work for *Fragments* brought an enormous increase in output. In 1883, the first full year of his association with Leykin, the number of his publications rose to 112—more than three times that of the previous year. During the following three years also the number of publications was in each case over a hundred, which meant that Chekhov was now turning out stories and articles at the rate of two or three a week. Not all of them were Little Stories, for he continued to produce various specimens of more undignified comedy, such as the comic advertisements and short jokes of which examples have already been given. Many of these were acceptable to Leykin as well as to the other papers, and Chekhov often published them in *Fragments* alongside his Little Stories. It is interesting to notice that he usually graded his pseudonym according to the quality of his work. *Antosha Chekhonte* was regularly used for his best contributions, while a number of others, such as *The Man without a Spleen*, were reserved for the feeblest.

Chekhov was already in his fourth year as a student when he began working for *Fragments*, so that this intense productivity coincided with the most arduous stage of his medical studies. It was only possible because of the ease with which he wrote. He would dash off a story in a few minutes, at a single sitting, and settle down to another one before the ink was yet dry. An examination of the Little Stories does something to explain this facility. They are constructed more or less on a formula. Anyone who has read more than a dozen of them will quickly begin to realize that they consist of a series of ingenious variations on a limited number of themes and settings. The characters are not drawn with depth or subtlety, though this does not stop them from being extremely funny. They consist mostly of such favourite comic types as mothers-in-law, corrupt officials, pompous dignitaries, obsequious underlings, jealous husbands, unfaithful wives, dentists, insects, drunks, ignoramuses, foreigners and those in love. The background of the stories was often dictated by topical considerations. Towards Christmas and the New Year, for example, Chekhov was expected to exploit the comic potentialities of seasonal drunkenness, and his stories had to be particularly attractive because this was the time of year at which Leykin hoped to gain new subscribers. In the summer 'bungalow stories' were the rule. It was then that many town-dwellers would rent a *dacha* or bungalow, usually in the country near their place of residence. Husbands very often had to travel to work during the 'bungalow season', while their wives amused themselves in the country, so that the 'bungalow husband' provided Chekhov with a useful variant of the Unfaithful Wife joke. The 'bungalow season' was also recognized as the peak period for proposals of marriage, and many of Chekhov's stories are devoted to the wiles of young women and their mammas in what he called 'the hunt for suitors'.

Among other favourite settings were the offices of civil servants, weddings, funerals, railway-trains, doctors' consulting rooms, drinking-parties and the theatrical world. Thus Chekhov's Little Stories were constructed to a simple recipe: take a stock setting; mix in two or three stock characters, with funny names to taste; simmer gently through a hundred lines of print, and bring suddenly to the boil.

II

SATIRE

PERHAPS the most interesting new feature in the Little Stories is an element of social criticism and satire, which had been almost completely absent in Chekhov's earliest work. It is true that he had attacked the selfishness, brutality and incompetence of the Russian upper classes in such early works as *The Mistress*, *Belated Blossom* and *Because of the Apples*, but the social criticism of these has a derivative ring. It seems to spring rather from a reading of Turgenev and Gogol than from firsthand observation of Russian life. The satire of the *Fragments* period is entirely different, being fresh, direct and hard-hitting. *Fragments* was a particularly suitable magazine in which to publish this sort of material, since the Petersburg censorship was laxer than the Muscovite, and Leykin used to sail as near the wind as he conveniently could.

As anyone familiar with Russian conditions might have predicted, it was the official class which became the chief target for
Chekhov's satire. The Russian civil service certainly asked to be
made fun of, with its hierarchy of fourteen ranks, each of
which had a pretentious and polysyllabic title. They ranged
from the eminence of an 'Actual Privy Councillor', who rated
as a General, and was addressed as 'Your Supreme Excellency',
down to the smaller fry, such as 'Collegiate Assessors' and the
like, who had to be content with a mere 'Your Honour' from
their underlings.

To judge by the productions of Russian satirists, who had
long made it one of their chief butts, the Russian civil service
had all the worst faults traditionally associated with a bureaucracy. It was inefficient, corrupt, and was riddled with place-
seeking, bribery and hypocrisy. These qualities had been held
up to ridicule in a whole series of works, of which the best-
known is probably Gogol's play *The Inspector General*. The
bureaucracy was of course the instrument of Tsarist administration, and the writer who attacked it was liable to get into
trouble. Even Gogol had confined his onslaughts to unimportant provincial officials, and it was only through the personal
intervention of the Tsar that he was able to have his *Inspector
General* produced on the stage. Chekhov and his editors had to
exercise discretion, but they managed to deal a number of very
shrewd blows. Chekhov's exposé of officialdom is, broadly speaking, in the Gogol tradition, and much of it is devoted to the
same faults—the taking of bribes, corruption and inefficiency.
He pays particular attention to the mentality induced by the
bureaucracy, making fun of excessive preoccupation with rank,
of the extreme arrogance of higher officials towards their juniors
and a corresponding degree of cringing obsequiousness in the
opposite direction.

Alexander III's Russia had many of the unpleasant features
associated with the 'police state', and though Chekhov wished
to protest against them he had to tread more carefully here
than in his attacks on officials. Policemen have always struck
the popular imagination as funny, but in the Russia of the
'eighties it was not advisable to laugh at them too openly. However, two stories in which Chekhov makes fun of policemen
became particularly famous: *A Chameleon* and *Corporal Prishibeev*. In *A Chameleon* a man has been bitten by a dog, and a
police official arrives on the scene to investigate. 'Hold the

dog!' he shouts. 'Biting is against the law these days! I'll teach people to let dogs loose.' When he hears that the dog belongs to some local General he immediately changes his tune. 'It can't have bitten you,' he says, 'it's too small.' Then it appears that the dog does not after all belong to the General, and the policeman changes colour again, only to reverse once more when it turns out that the dog in fact belongs to the General's brother.

Corporal Prishibeev is perhaps the best known of all Chekhov's early comic stories, so much so that the word *Prishibeev* is said to have passed into the Russian language. The Corporal, a retired NCO, whose passion in life is for prohibiting things, is seen in the dock at the local court, charged with disturbing the peace. His fellow-villagers have a lot of complaints to make about his behaviour. He keeps interfering with the village activities, pulls the children's ears, and has made himself a sort of unofficial one-man 'Watch Committee'. 'A day or two ago he went around the huts, and gave orders not to sing songs or put on the light,' runs part of the accusation. 'He says there isn't any law that songs should be sung.' Prishibeev, speaking in his own defence, confirms what the villagers say, but claims that he is performing a public service. After all, there must be someone to stop people doing what they like. 'Where is it written in the law that the people should be given freedom?' After the hearing Prishibeev is condemned to imprisonment for causing a public nuisance, but is still completely unable to understand that he has done anything wrong. As he leaves the dock he bellows menacingly at the crowd, from sheer force of habit: 'Move along there!'

Leykin, to whom *Corporal Prishibeev* was sent, had to tell Chekhov that its publication was forbidden by the censor. He said that he could not understand how the censor could find anything 'liberal' (that is to say anti-Government) in it, and wrote that he could only throw up his hands in bewilderment if asked in what way it could possibly appear dangerous. The censorship archives, which have since been examined by Russian editors of Chekhov, show the reason for the ban—'an exaggeration of the harm caused by an intensification of police activity'. Both Leykin and Chekhov were surprised at the censor's ruling, and this certainly suggests that Chekhov did not consciously intend his story as an attack on the mentality of Russia's rulers. However, many contemporary readers did regard it in this way, an interpretation which it can very easily bear, and which is usually adopted by Soviet critics of Chekhov. It is interesting to note that Chekhov, who had learned to accept the censor's rulings in a spirit of slightly exasperated fatalism, eluded the ban in this instance by sending his story to another paper.

Another target of Chekhov's satire during this period comes under the general heading of the Russian word *poshlost*. This word is notoriously hard to translate, and 'vulgarity' is only an approximate equivalent. It implies a mean, self-satisfied and limited attitude to life, and finds one characteristic expression in an excessive addiction to food, such as Chekhov describes in *The Siren*. This consists entirely of an excited discussion of the respective merits of various dishes by a gathering of gluttons. 'The most succulent smell of all,' claims one of them in a typical access of *poshlost*, 'is that of spring onion, when it's just beginning to brown, and hisses through the whole house, the little rascal.' An over-emphasis on food is only one of the component elements in *poshlost*, a concept which has been well described by Professor W. H. Bruford, who says that it implies 'everything that is reprehensible morally, socially or aesthetically, the ignoble, caddish, shabby in every form'. It seems to imply most of all a mediocre and restricted sense of values, of which a typical exposé is to be found in Chekhov's story *Joy*. The hero, a stupid youth called Mitya, rushes home one day in great excitement. 'I'm known to all Russia,' he shouts. After the suspense has been built up in the usual way it turns out that the reason for all this fuss is that Mitya has 'got his name in the paper' for being run over by a carriage while drunk.

Poshlost persisted as a target for Chekhov's criticism long after *Antosha Chekhonte* had become a thing of the past, and Chekhov's savage onslaught on this quality appealed to many of his readers (including Gorky) as one of the most important features of his work. The theme is to be found in such mature tories as *Betrothed* and *The Teacher of Literature*. In these stories the close connection between *poshlost* and food is fully maintained. It is amusing to notice in passing that any mention of 'roast turkey' in Chekhov's writing is usually a prelude to the evocation of *poshlost*.

The satirical element in Chekhov's early stories has been particularly stressed by many recent Soviet critics, and there can be no doubt that they are right in claiming an important place for *Antosha Chekhonte* among Russian satirists. It is unlikely, however, that Chekhov took himself very seriously in this role, or often thought of himself as flaying the vices of his generation. Many of his *Antosha Chekhonte* stories are free from any satirical element, and consist of amusing anecdotes, intended purely for entertainment. Moreover, one must beware of reading a satirical intention into many stories where it is completely absent. When, for example, Chekhov retails the absurd harangues of some uneducated cook or door-keeper, he is often concerned only to raise a laugh, and is not necessarily indicting the educational system of imperial Russia.

III
CHEKHOV AS A COLUMNIST

CHEKHOV'S interest in the contemporary Russian scene was increased by an excursion into journalism which he undertook at Leykin's request. Between July 1883 and October 1885 he was responsible for a fortnightly column of comments on Moscow life. Although *Fragments* was published in Petersburg, it had a great number of subscribers in Moscow, whom Chekhov undertook to supply with tit-bits of topical, and preferably scandalous, interest. This was not his first attempt at journalism. He had already published a few commentaries on the news and the theatre in other comic papers, but it was in *Fragments* that he first brought out a regular series of such articles. The column, which was called *Fragments of Moscow Life,* had already been in existence for some time, but Leykin had so far failed to find anyone who could handle it to his liking. He suggested the assignment in a letter of June 10, 1883, in which he defined with his usual clarity the programme to which Chekhov should adhere. The articles were to be between 100 and 120 lines in length, and were to be paid for at the same rate as the stories. They were to be devoted to all outstanding Moscow events of a scandalous character, and were to be as humorous as possible. Chekhov's task was to 'mock and scourge', and on no account to praise anything. In replying to this letter Chekhov said that he was not confident of being able to satisfy Leykin, but Leykin was pleased with what he sent, and said that he could not have wished for anything better.

The character of Chekhov's journalism, as emerges from the programme, was completely in accordance with the traditions of the Russian comic press. The column was to be written with a mixture of a sneer and a snigger. Chekhov did his best to avoid the extremes of triviality into which some previous columnists had fallen. He promised not to denounce café proprietors for the dirtiness of their napkins, or bakers for baking beetles in their buns, but the very nature of Leykin's stipulations made a certain amount of pettiness inevitable. It was a type of pettiness very much to the taste of Moscow subscribers to *Fragments*, who knew that they could turn to the column for entertaining and highly malicious gossip. Chekhov's success was partly due to the extravagance of his abuse. He did not hesitate to give the name of his victims—indeed, Leykin required him to do so whenever possible. The following is a typically outrageous broadside directed at the novelist Boleslav Markevich. 'Here is a piece of news as pleasant as yesterday's vinegar stew or a chronic cold in the head. Boleslav Markevich is dramatizing his long, fat, tedious ink-blot, his *Abyss*. As if this daub hadn't already taken up enough newspaper space he's decided to put it on the stage. Spare us, Boleslav Markevich! Do us that favour!'

Chekhov touched on a wide range of subjects in his column. Many of them were scandals drawn from the law-courts. He had not lost his interest in the theatrical world, and theatre gossip naturally occupied a large place in his articles. Although he was always saying how hard it was to obtain suitable material, he seemed to manage fairly well. He ransacked the Moscow press, picked the brains of his journalist friends, and began to acquire the reporter's news-instinct. Nobody in Moscow knew that he was the author of the column, and he thought it prudent to keep his authorship secret. He used the pseudonym *Ruver*, and got Leykin to change it to *Ulysses* when he feared that some of his Moscow acquaintances were on the scent. He often had to sit by while his friends discussed who this provocative columnist could possibly be. One of them once told Chekhov that he had found out. 'He lives in Petersburg. Gets his material sent over from here. A talented swine!'

In style and general approach Chekhov's column was much of a piece with his *Antosha Chekhonte* fiction. It was natural that he should begin to tire of it in 1885, the year in which he first began to show definite signs of outgrowing the *Antosha Chekhonte* phase. His contributions of *Fragments of Moscow Life* grew rarer, and petered out in October of that year.

IV

EXPERIMENT AND DISSATISFACTION

CHEKHOV continued to experiment in a wide variety of literary
forms, as he had previously done during the period 1880-82.
Most of these experiments were devoid of serious literary intention, though they were often highly entertaining. One of them,
The Shooting Party, is of particular interest, being the only
novel which Chekhov ever produced. Equally interesting (and
perhaps surprising to many English readers of Chekhov) is the
fact that this is a detective story. It employs the usual technique of concealing the murderer's identity until the last moment,
suspicion being meanwhile switched from one character to another. *The Shooting Party* makes excellent light reading. It
would be contrary to detective story ethics to spoil the ending
by revealing the plot, but it can be said that Chekhov makes
use of an extremely ingenious and surprising device which was
applied with great success many years later in one of Agatha
Christie's best-known Poirot stories. *The Shooting Party* is not a
completely homogeneous work, and in parts it reads rather like
a parody. All the same, Chekhov's first biographer Izmaylov
found evidence—particularly in passages of nature-description—
that Chekhov took more pains with his novel than with many
of his other productions during the same period, and used it to
try his hand at serious writing.

Most of the literary forms attempted by Chekhov at this time
could not, in the nature of things, lead to anything serious.
They are a proof of his versatility, and, to a certain extent, of
his restiveness. He continued to be dissatisfied with his status as
a humorous writer, and found his constant clowning increasingly
irksome.

'Quite honestly,' he told Leykin as early as March 1883, 'it is
difficult to chase after humour. Sometimes you turn out stuff
that you even find nauseating yourself. You can't help crossing
over into the sphere of the serious.'

As time went on, Chekhov found himself more and more 'in
the sphere of the serious'. During the years 1885-87 he can
be observed gradually disengaging himself from the comic maga-

zines. When the transformation was over a new writer was seen to have emerged—Anton Chekhov, who seemed to have surprisingly little in common with *Antosha Chekhonte*.

Though Chekhov's use of his favourite pseudonym, and the style of writing associated with it, persisted after 1885, *Antosha Chekhonte* was obviously on the way out in 1886, and by the end of the following year he was practically extinct. Accordingly Chekhov's biographers usually anticipate *Chekhonte's* decease by including an 'obituary' of him at this stage. The main theme of such obituaries is often a discussion of whether Chekhov's concentration on farce during his early years had a good or bad effect on his later development. This is not a question which is easy to decide. The *Antosha Chekhonte* manner flourished for over seven years, and filled something like a million words of print. It has been seen that this huge output resulted in some shoddy work, and the view has been put forward that Chekhov injured his health by writing so intensively at a time when he had many other calls on his energies. However, though he sometimes grumbled about having to do it, he certainly enjoyed himself turning out funny stories, and it is arguable that they did not seriously harm either his health or his literary development. In Russia the view seems to be gaining ground that the *Antosha Chekhonte* phase represents a by no means negligible literary achievement in itself, overshadowed though it is by Chekhov's later work. It has been claimed that, if Chekhov had never written anything serious, the best Little Stories would still entitle him to a place in the literary history of his period. They would certainly not have been forgotten by the ordinary Russian reader. They give a vivid impression of Russian life of the early 'eighties in an amazing variety of aspects, almost all classes of society being represented. Chekhov's powers of observation were sharpened by his treatment of such a wide range of subjects, and the humour which he cultivated as *Antosha Chekhonte* continued to serve him, though in rather a different way, after he changed his style.

V

VOSKRESENSK AND BABKINO

IN a celebrated passage of his correspondence, written at the age of twenty-eight, Chekhov describes his personal history in the following terms:

'A young man, the son of a serf, who had been a shop-hand, a choir-boy, a *Gymnasium* pupil and a student; who was brought up to defer to rank, to kiss the hands of priests and to submit to other people's ideas; who gave thanks for every bite of food, was often beaten, used to walk about the streets without goloshes, who fought, tormented animals, liked to have dinner with his rich relations; who played the hypocrite before God and man without any necessity, purely through consciousness of his own insignificance—this young man squeezed the slave out of himself, drop by drop, and woke up one fine morning to realize that it was not the blood of a slave, but real human blood, that ran in his veins.'

Although the more outstanding examples of 'slavishness' quoted here belonged to Chekhov's childhood, it was a long time before he had completely purged his personality of all undesirable traces left by his environment. It is fortunate that he managed to dodge a number of pitfalls which lay in his path. He had never been in any real danger of being swallowed up in the Taganrog tradesman milieu of his father. It would have been very easy for him, however, to remain a successful writer of funny stories. Much worse, he might have become discouraged and lapsed into the position of the 'unsuccessful man'—a typical figure in the history of the Russian intelligentsia. Of this half-comic, half-pathetic character-type he had two examples before his eyes in his elder brothers.

Alexander was already well established in the role by the year 1885. Whereas it had once been he who had given literary advice to Anton, the position was very quickly reversed, and it was soon Anton who was trying to persuade editors to accept Alexander's work. Anton was continually trying to help Alexander with his writing, but he also had to advise him on general, everyday problems, for his brother had a talent for mismanaging his personal, as well as his literary, affairs. Nicholas Chekhov remained even more shiftless than Alexander. Everyone was always grumbling about him. Why did he get up so late? Why did he drink so much? Why did he never answer letters, or remember to forward the illustrations he had promised to the editors of comic papers? It was often Anton who had to make his excuses for him. He did what he could for both his brothers, but their weaknesses were more than his advice or example could overcome.

Unsatisfactory though these brothers may have been, Chekhov would have been hard put to it to find people of superior calibre among his Moscow acquaintances, and it was an extremely lucky accident which began, about the year 1883, to extend his social contacts into a new sphere. His younger brother Ivan had already held for some years the post of school-teacher in a small town not far from Moscow, called Voskresensk. Ivan was provided with a large and comfortable flat, and so his mother was able to bring Michael and Mariya over for the summer holidays, which made a wonderful break from Moscow. It was not until 1883 that Chekhov himself took advantage of this opportunity to give himself a change of scene. During his first three years in Moscow he had hardly left the city, except on an occasional excursion to some nearby *dacha* resort, made partly in search of copy. Perhaps he found himself too busy to take a holiday, or perhaps he found all the relaxation he needed in Moscow itself. In any case it was time he gave himself a change of air, for he was working too hard and too long, and there were already signs that his health was never likely to be very good.

Voskresensk immediately gave him a taste of Russian provincialism which put him in mind of Taganrog, though it was a much smaller place, with none of Taganrog's more exotic qualities—the port, the foreign population and the theatre. However, Chekhov found it fascinating. The bustle of city life had half driven from his mind his love of the countryside. It was delightful to be able to bathe and fish again, and to take country walks in search of mushrooms—a favourite occupation of all the Chekhovs, big and small. In Voskresensk Chekhov found that his family already had a large circle of friends, many of whom he had already met in Moscow. The Chekhovs and their friends would go for long country walks in the evenings, during which the children ran ahead, while their elders followed sedately behind, deep in conversation.

Chekhov, in his broad-brimmed hat and hooded cloak, soon became a well-known figure in Voskresensk. He was a regular visitor to the inn, to the magistrate's court and to the local government offices. He used to have long conversations with the postmaster, who gave him the theme for *The Civil Service Examination*. He made friends with an old man who shared his passion for fishing, and this gave him subject-matter for more stories. A particularly rich fund of material was provided by his new contacts in the medical world. Chekhov was in his last year as a medical student when he first made the acquaintance of Doctor Arkhangelsky, a distinguished and charming man, who was in charge of the Voskresensk hospital. During consulting hours Chekhov used to attend the hospital, and would sit on a stool observing the patients as they told their stories. He was interested in what they had to say both as a doctor and as a writer. Sometimes he helped to give treatment, and was thus able to earn an occasional rouble to pay his bill in the local inn. Almost every patient provided him with material for a new story, but this material did not always harmonize with the programme of the comic press, being often too tragic or sordid to lend itself to facetious treatment. For the time being Chekhov stored up the more serious themes in his mind, but made free use of the comic ones.

1884 was marked by an event to which Chekhov had been eagerly looking forward during the whole of the past five years. In the summer he graduated from Moscow University, and was at last in a position to take up his chosen profession—a profession which was especially important in Russia, where good doctors were scarce. He was given an opportunity to practise medicine sooner that he had expected. Returning to Voskresensk that summer, he learnt that the doctor in charge of a small near-by hospital was going away for a few weeks, and he accepted an invitation to act as substitute. The work was arduous and not altogether pleasant. He had an incompetent assistant, and it became necessary to co-opt his brother Michael (now a law student at the University) to supervise the dispensing. It was not long before Chekhov was faced with his first operation. The patient was a small boy who screamed and kicked, while the peasant woman who had brought him set up a howl. Chekhov, who was further embarrassed by the undisguised interest of his two assistants, seems to have lost his nerve. He decided not to go through with the operation, and sent an urgent message to a doctor in the local town, who performed it for him.

Michael Chekhov records another experience which purports to confirm an early reaction against medicine on Anton's part. Among his first patients in Moscow were some friends of Nicholas Chekhov, the Yanov family. Anton treated the mother and three daughters for typhus. Finally the mother and one of the daughters died on the same day. The daughter died in agony, fiercely clutching his hand as she expired. He seemed to feel the cold grasp of the dead girl for a long time afterwards, as Michael Chekhov rather melodramatically puts it, adding that this experience caused Anton to give up medicine and devote himself to literature.

Anton would certainly not have thanked his brother for writing about his medical work in this way. He did not, as Michael suggests, give up his profession after one or two set-backs; on the contrary, he seems to have made a very capable doctor, though he certainly exaggerated his prowess on the numerous occasions when he claimed to be a better doctor than writer.

Proud though he was of his profession, Chekhov could see that his position had already changed considerably since the days when he had looked forward to supporting the family on a doctor's salary. He was now earning enough as a writer to choose between the two careers, but he did not allow the dilemma to worry him unduly; he made no deliberate and clear-cut choice in 1884, but allowed the problem to settle itself during the years which followed The result was that his medical work became increasingly subordinated to his writing, but was never entirely abandoned. However hard he might be working on a story he always found it impossible to refuse help to the sick people who were constantly appealing to him. Moreover, he maintained throughout his life a keen interest in medical theory, and projected several pieces of research, including a history of medicine, a portion of which remains in manuscript. He always retained a curious feeling that he had a 'debt to medicine' and his research projects were important to him as a means of repaying that debt.

Returning to Voskresensk as a qualified doctor, Chekhov continued to meet interesting people in the neighbourhood.

Many of his new friends belonged to the professional classes. Academic learning was represented by the Slavophil historian Golokhvastov. Colonel Maevsky, an artillery officer, who commanded a unit in the neighbourhood, brought Chekhov into touch with military society, and gave him the background for stories such as *The Kiss* and for the play *Three Sisters*. It was at a ball at brigade headquarters that Ivan Chekhov first fell in with a certain Kiselev, the owner of a large house at Babkino, near Voskresensk. This meeting led to a further extension of social contacts with consequences which were of some importance in Chekhov's development.

Kiselev took a great liking to the Chekhovs, and they rented

E

a *dacha* on his estate for three summers in succession, beginning in 1885. Babkino was a delightful place. The Kiselevs
owned a large house, with grounds consisting of an 'English
park' with woods, fields and a river. At one end of the park
stood the low wooden *dacha* which the Chekhovs occupied.
They arrived at one o'clock on a May morning, stumbled
around in the darkness until they managed to light the lamps,
then marvelled at the huge rooms and furniture. Anton quickly
installed himself and cleared away his trunks, had a bite of
food and a drink of vodka. It gave him a pleasant feeling to
look through the window at the dark shades of trees and the
river. He heard the nightingale sing, and could not believe his
ears. He had forgotten he was not in Moscow.

The Chekhovs soon settled down to a pleasant country routine.
Early rising was the rule, and Anton was usually at work by
seven o'clock each morning, writing away on an old table which
had once been part of a sewing-machine. The main meal of
the day was at one o'clock. In the evenings they all went over to
the big house for a social evening with their hosts. The Kiselevs
rated higher in the social scale than the Chekhovs, but quickly
made it clear that their attitude was very friendly. Madame
Kiselev won Evgeniya Chekhov's heart with the present of a
pot of jam, and the two families became much attached to
each other. There were usually guests from the surrounding
countryside as well, and Chekhov found himself meeting people
who were among the most educated and cultured in Russia.
Madame Kiselev's father, for instance, had been Director of
the Imperial theatres in Moscow. He took great plesure in
Chekhov's company and gave him the subjects for some new
stories. It was at Babkino also that Chekhov met Boleslav Markevich, and he must have been glad that he had sheltered behind
a pseudonym in attacking this elderly novelist so viciously in his
Fragments of Moscow Life. Chekhov found him pompous and
stuffy, an exception to the general run of Bakino society, which
was very congenial to him.

The company in which Chekhov moved at Babkino seemed to
live almost entirely for the arts. There were frequent musical
recitals, and there was much talk of the composer Tchaikovsky,
who was an ex-suitor of Madame Kiselev. Chekhov now began
to acquire a love of music which he had so far had little
opportunity to develop. Among his other Babkino friends was
the painter Levitan, a highly coloured figure with a long record

of amorous successes to his credit. He and Chekhov shared a love of practical jokes and theatrical horseplay. Sometimes they would dress up as Bedouins, and enact improvised scenes in the garden. All of this was highly diverting to the Kiselevs' two children, who were devoted to Chekhov and for whom he wrote a nonsense story which he illustrated by pasting in newspaper-cuttings.

CHAPTER FOUR

'New Time'

I

CHEKHOV AND PETERSBURG

BY the year 1885 it was becoming obvious that Chekhov's literary reputation would be decided in Petersburg rather than Moscow. Though Petersburg was actually the seat of government, Russians tended to give Moscow an equivalent status by speaking of their 'two capitals'. The difference in intellectual atmosphere between them was something which nobody could miss. Moscow had the reputation of being stolid, comfortable and old-fashioned, whereas Petersburg looked towards the West, and felt comparatively modern and sophisticated. In some ways Petersburg occupied a position of cultural leadership, so that, however strong their local patriotism, Moscow writers were usually flattered when they found themselves accepted in the other capital. This was certainly true of Chekhov. Though he had spent the first years of his writing career in Moscow, and must have begun to feel himself a Muscovite by adoption, it was in the Petersburg press that the bulk of his early work had been published. He had usually found his Petersburg publishing contacts helpful and businesslike, whereas their Moscow counterparts were often the reverse.

It was therefore quite natural that Chekhov, having made a reputation for himself in *Fragments*, should begin to contribute to another Petersburg publication, *The Petersburg Gazette*. His association with this paper, more serious in character than those for which he had so far been writing, marks the next landmark in his progress. *The Petersburg Gazette* differed from *Fragments* in imposing less severe limitations, for it would accept longer contributions, and they did not necessarily have to be funny. All the same the first few stories sent in by Chekhov had nothing very unusual about them; *The Last of the Mohicans*, with which he made his début on May 5, 1885, is a typical study of a hen-pecked husband in *Antosha Chekhonte* style. It was not long, however, before Chekhov began to take a holiday from light-hearted comedy, and some of his early stories in *The Petersburg Gazette* show him plunging into quite the opposite extreme. This is particularly true of *Sorrow* and *Misery*, both of which certainly live up to their names, and also of *The Huntsman* which might appropriately have had a similar title. These are all studies of intense unhappiness, and must indeed have seemed a remarkable achievement for a writer who was known only by his comic works. Stories like these were beginning to attract attention in Petersburg among people of serious literary tastes who would have been ashamed to be seen with a copy of *Fragments* in their hands. Consequently by the time Chekhov paid his first visit to the city in December 1885, this visit was in many ways overdue.

He arrived to find himself the talk of the editorial offices. Immediately he went to the offices of *Fragments*, where the garrulous lady-cashier welcomed him as 'our best contributor' and was soon giving him her opinion of Leykin—'a difficult man'. He next met Bilibin, Leykin's right-hand man on *Fragments*, and then called on *The Petersburg Gazette,* where he said he was received like the Shah of Persia. All this was very pleasant, but not of great consequence. His next visit turned out to be the most important of his stay. It was made to Alexey Suvorin, the proprietor of *New Time*, a daily paper with a pro-Government policy and a very big circulation. Chekhov must have felt very thrilled as he knocked on Suvorin's door. Leykin had seemed important enough in the not so distant past, but he was a minor figure compared with Suvorin, and writing for *New Time* brought more prestige than either *Fragments* or *The Petersburg Gazette* could bestow.

The interview was short and formal, but performed the useful function of giving Chekhov an advance in money against his future work for *New Time*. He wrote home describing Suvorin in absurd terms. 'Young man,' he reports him as saying, 'I am satisfied with you, but you must go to church more often, and don't drink vodka. Let me smell your breath.' Assured of his guest's temperate habits, Suvorin ordered tea and gave him further advice before dismissing him: 'You must save money. Tighten your belt.' Whether or not it really was conducted in such an eccentric fashion, this meeting turned out an important event in the lives of both Chekhov and Suvorin, for their

association later developed into a close friendship. Meanwhile
New Time provided an excellent vehicle for Chekhov in the
next stage of his career.

The visit to Petersburg had the effect of a sudden whirlpool
in the pleasant and uneventful flow of Chekhov's life. His first
reaction was excitement at finding himself recognized by a person of Suvorin's standing. He was delighted too by the prospect
of earning more money, since he was to be paid at the rate of
twelve copecks a line for his work in *New Time*—half as much
again as he had been getting from Leykin. 'I'm devilish rich
now,' he wrote to a friend on his return. 'Can you believe it,
I'm working for Suvorin.' As soon as he had time to calm down
he began to think really seriously about his position as a writer,
as many references in his letters show. 'All Petersburg has its
eye on the Chekhov brothers,' he told Alexander, generously including him in his triumph. 'Invitations and hymns of praise
from everyone ... It made me feel ashamed at having written
carelessly in my shirt sleeves. If I'd known I was being read like
this, I wouldn't have written to order as I did.'

His first story for *New Time* was soon finished and dispatched.
It was *The Requiem*, which was published on February 15, 1886,
and began a period of two years during which nearly all his
best work appeared in Suvorin's paper.

Chekhov had hardly time to recover his equilibrium after his
intoxicating experiences in Petersburg, when a new and even
headier draught of encouragement arrived in the shape of a letter
from Grigorovich. This letter was entirely unexpected, and
threw Chekhov into a state of wild excitement. Grigorovich,
whose work is little known outside Russia, was a figure of real
eminence in the literary world. He was now a man of sixty-five,
and, though he had published nothing of importance for many
years, was remembered for his work as a pioneer of the
'natural school' in the late 1840s. Together with Dostoevsky,
Turgenev and other writers, he had written stories of a 'philanthropic' type, and thus was one of the founders of a movement
which contributed to the development of the Russian realist
novel. Chekhov could hardly believe his eyes when he saw
Grigorovich's signature at the end of the letter, and wondered
what he had done to deserve such a flattering piece of attention.

The letter reached Chekhov in March 1886. It was about a
year previously, Grigorovich wrote, that he had first noticed one

of Chekhov's stories in *The Petersburg Gazette*, and since then he had read everything which appeared above the signature *Chekhonte*. There was no doubt that Chekhov had 'talent'—it soon became obvious that this was Grigorovich's favourite word. While expressing his high opinion of Chekhov's talent, which he said was outstanding in the present generation of writers, Grigorovich made it clear that his admiration was directed rather at what his protégé might write in the future than at his actual achievements. He had some direct practical advice to give: 'What you need is respect for your own talent—a rare gift. Give up writing to a time-limit. I don't know what your resources are. If they are limited, then go hungry, as we went hungry in our day, and preserve your impressions for work which is thought out, polished, and not written at a sitting, but during happy moments of inward harmony.'

Chekhov was not slow to reply, and he tried to strike what he thought Grigorovich would consider the right note: 'Your letter, my kind and warmly loved benefactor, struck me like lightning. I almost burst into tears, was overcome by emotion, and I now feel that it has left a deep trace in my soul.' After a preamble in this style, Chekhov went on to confirm that 'if I have gifts which ought to be respected, I swear by the purity of your heart that I haven't respected them hitherto.' None of his friends in Moscow had ever suggested that he had it in him to become a great writer; Moscow highbrows and aesthetes would laugh at the idea. As for his friends and relations, they had always taken a patronizing attitude to his literary work, and had never stopped urging him not to abandon his proper business (medicine) for scrawling on paper. Chekhov offered this, together with the fact that he was up to his ears in medicine, as some measure of justification for the 'grievous sin' of not respecting his own talent.

'Up to now,' Chekhov admitted, 'my attitude to literary work has been extremely frivolous, careless and haphazard. I don't remember a single story on which I worked for more than twenty-four hours, and I wrote *The Huntsman*, which you liked, in a bathhouse! I have been writing my short stories in the way reporters write their accounts of a fire—mechanically, semi-consciously, without bothering at all either about the reader or myself ... I have been trying as hard as I could, while writing, not to waste on my stories images and pictures dear to me, and which, God knows why, I preserved and carefully concealed.'

With regard to work with a time-limit Chekhov wrote that he would abandon it, but not in the near future.

'There's no possibility of getting out of the groove into which I've fallen. I don't mind going hungry—I already have done so—but it isn't a matter of me alone.' He promised to tackle something serious in the summer, when he had more leisure. Meanwhile, 'My hope is all in the future. I'm only twenty-six. Perhaps I shall be able to achieve something, though time passes quickly.'

Chekhov asked for Grigorovich's portrait, which he received, together with a further long letter approving his intention to do some serious work in the summer. Chekhov's gratitude was no less real for being expressed in a rather florid (and quite untypical) style. He wrote more naturally to Bilibin, who was about his own age: 'The old man wants me to write something big and throw up working to a time-limit. He argues that I've got real talent (the words are underlined in his letter) and in proof of my artistic qualities makes extracts from my stories. He writes warmly and sincerely. I'm pleased, of course, though I feel that G. has gone a bit too far.'

II

1886 ACTIVITIES

DESPITE the successes of 1886, which were enough to turn the head of any less balanced young man, Chekhov had sufficient reason for being unable to face the future with complete optimism. Several years earlier he had begun to develop a persistent cough, which troubled him particularly in damp and cold weather. It was in 1884, twenty years before tuberculosis so tragically put an end to his life, that he first suffered a discharge of blood from his lungs, and thereafter the attacks became more frequent and more serious. These were symptoms ominous enough to alarm the most ignorant layman, yet Chekhov so clear and level-headed in everything else, refused to read the danger signals where his own health was concerned. When his family or friends noticed on his handkerchief the bloodstains which he did his best to conceal, he always hastened to assure them that it was nothing serious. 'It's not tuberculosis,' he kept saying, as though he could alter the facts by denying them. However, even in the mid-'eighties there were moments when he realized that the matter was not to be so lightly dismissed. 'I ought to go south, but I can't afford it' he told Leykin, adding that he feared to submit himself to examination by his medical colleagues. For more than ten years Chekhov tried to ignore his disease, until in 1897, at a time when it must have become much less susceptible to treatment, it would allow itself to be ignored no longer.

Chekhov always had too many other things to think about when he should have been paying attention to his health. Much of his time in 1886 was devoted to editing a collection of his short stories for publication in book form under the title of *Motley Stories*. He had already made two such collections. The first was planned in 1883, when he was not yet well enough established to obtain the solid support of a publisher. He revised the stories, got Nicholas to do some illustrations and even had the type set up, when the project fell through for lack of money. This collection was to have been called *At Leisure*. The next year had seen the publication of a collection of stories devoted to the theatrical world, also chosen from work which had already appeared in the press, and called *The Fairy Tales of Melpomene*. *Motley Stories* promised to be a big improvement on this, and Chekhov had gone to considerable trouble editing its contents, weeding out the more grotesquely farcical elements. He personally supervised the placing of advertisements in the Moscow press, and got one of his friends to produce a design for the cover. The cover designs on Russian books of this period were usually hideous, and *Motley Stories* was no exception. However, Chekhov was pleased enough and the design went through, though it was bad enough to cause some objections at the Petersburg end.

By the time the book appeared Chekhov had lost a lot of his enthusiasm. 'It's a mixed salad,' he told Grigorovich, 'a promiscuous hash of undergraduate sketches, plucked by the censor and the editors of humorous publications. I'm sure that many people will be disillusioned when they read it. If I'd known that I was being read, and that *you* were following my progress, I wouldn't have had such a book printed.'

In spite of Chekhov's strictures *Motley Stories* created quite a stir, and was even reviewed in the literary monthlies or 'fat journals'. It was in these publications that most of Russian literature (for example, the novels of Turgenev, Tolstoy and Dostoevsky) first saw the light of day, and Chekhov was very surprised to find them deigning to notice his work. True, his reception was not uniformly favourable. Though *Russian Thought* praised the book, *Virgin Soil* described it as 'the ravings of a madman'. The *Northern Herald* published a long article by the well-known critic Skabichevsky, which was more of a sustained diatribe against the Russian comic press than a serious criticism of Chekhov's book. Chekhov found that he was extremely sensitive to public comment on his work. Reviews, both favourable and unfavourable, irritated him. He was amazed and not altogether pleased to find himself rated in some quarters as a better writer than Korolenko, a contemporary for whom he had the highest admiration. On the other hand, the grating and polemical tone of the adverse reviews aroused in him an exasperation against critics which lasted for most of his life.

Whether he liked it or not Chekhov was already becoming a well-known figure. His stories were given public readings; wherever he appeared fingers were pointed in his direction and he was overwhelmed with new acquaintances. He was pleased, of course, but more than a little puzzled. Whether or not he could write well by his own standards he simply did not know so far. He certainly intended to make the attempt, but regarded his present achievements as unworthy of attention. It was confusing to find that they were making him a celebrity and he drew the conclusion that public taste was frivolous and undiscerning. 'I feel embarrassed for the public's sake,' he said. 'The only reason it trots after literary lap-dogs is that it hasn't the power of discerning literary elephants, and I am deeply convinced that not a soul will know me when I do start to write seriously.'

Chekhov's new literary friends in Petersburg disliked the name *Antosha Chekhonte*. Grigorovich told Chekhov that he could not help being angry with a man who thought so little of himself as to hide behind a pseudonym. Suvorin agreed, and when Chekhov sent in his first story to *New Time* over the usual signature, he quickly received a telegram from Petersburg asking permission to use his real name. Rather against his will he agreed. He was used to signing himself *Chekhonte*. Moreover he wanted to keep his own name in reserve against the day when he fulfilled his ambition of publishing serious articles in medical journals—an attitude which shows how far he still was from regarding writing as his chief business in life. Meanwhile he continued to use the pseudonym for his work in *Fragments* and *The Petersburg Gazette* throughout 1886 and 1887, allowing it to lapse in the following year.

III

1887 ACTIVITIES

JANUARY 1887 brought the usual round of parties. Chekhov complained that, what with guests, long conversations, medical conferences and so on, he never had a free day, and that throughout the festive season his study was continually being 'taken by storm'. When the seasonal festivities were over there was his own birthday and name-day on the seventeenth to be celebrated. The Chekhovs were now renting a small house of red stone which looked like a tiny castle, and was much better suited to their needs than any apartment they had occupied before. Chekhov was able to instal himself in a proper study on the ground floor. The walls were covered with piles of books, for he now had a library of about a thousand volumes, most of them picked up secondhand in the Moscow markets. He could not afford complete editions of authors, so the books were isolated volumes of all shapes and sizes. They lay jumbled together with old numbers of various 'fat journals' and copies of humorous magazines, some of which he hung on to for old times' sake.

The house was usually full of young people, including a number of 'interesting young ladies', to quote Michael Chekhov's description of such attractive visitors as Lika Mizinova and Varya Eberle. There were guests almost every evening, and everyone was particularly surprised and happy on one occasion when a distinguished-looking old gentleman, with an expensive and carelessly-knotted tie, unexpectedly arrived, and soon became the life and soul of the party with his outrageous compliments to the girls. It was Grigorovich, who stayed until late at night and insisted on escorting Dolly Musin-Pushkin home. When he got back to Petersburg he was full of his experiences at the Chekhovs'. 'Anna Ivanovna, my dear,' he said breathlessly to Suvorin's wife. 'If only you knew what went on at the Chekhovs'!' And raising both his arms to the heavens he exclaimed, 'A Bacchanalia, my dear, an absolute Bacchanalia!'

In early 1887 Chekhov was full of his plans to make a long journey such as he had not undertaken since he had first arrived in Moscow. Babkino was a charming place to spend the summer, but this year he found himself yearning for something a little less urbane, and he wanted to go to the south of Russia. Although he had never been passionately attached to Taganrog, he felt a desire to revisit it, and to renew contact with the family of his Uncle Mitrofan, of whom he had always been very fond. Then he wanted to travel in the wild country of the Don, which he felt would give him a new lease of literary and psychological energy, since it formed such a striking contrast with anything he had seen since his boyhood.

He took the train for Taganrog at the beginning of April, and was soon absorbed by new sensations and sights. As he drew farther south, and the climate became noticeably warmer, he was intrigued by scenery which had all the charm of something well known, but half-forgotten. The steppe, the typically shaped steppe-hillocks, the watering stations and the buildings —all these seemed like old friends as he watched them through the window of his carriage. He was alive and thirsting for sensations; all of them, good, bad or indifferent, made a lively imprint on his mind. He was met at Taganrog station by his younger cousin George, though he did not recognize his old playmate of eight years ago in this dapper young man, dolled out in what passed as the height of fashion in Taganrog. At Uncle Mitrofan's Chekhov received a rousing welcome, and he found the old man in the thick of his duties as a church elder, supervising the Easter celebrations. Chekhov attended the cathedral services, and met a number of old friends among the congregation. It was exciting to walk round Taganrog again, and to renew acquaintance with familiar sights. He had forgotten its dreariness, its streets thick in half-congealed mud and the dismal impression produced by the closed shutters. One of his walks, as might have been expected, took him past the house in which he had spent his last three years in Taganrog—the house which had been acquired from his father by Selivanov. Selivanov was there no longer, and the place was deserted. It was strange to remember the fuss and upset of ten or eleven years ago, when the loss of the house had seemed the end of the world to the Chekhovs. As he looked at it again he decided that he would not agree to own it for all the money in the world.

Taganrog was merely the jumping-off point for his journey

into the Don steppe. Chekhov had agreed to officiate as 'best man' at a wedding in Novocherkassk. He wrote home to say that he executed his functions successfully, in spite of his borrowed dinner-jacket, absurdly wide trousers, and a missing stud, for which they would have had him thrown out in Moscow. There was a wonderful selection of rich and eligible young women at the reception, but he was so drunk that he took the bottles for women, and the women for bottles. The local girls thought he was very witty and amusing in his cups, and the boldest of them, anxious to show that she was no stranger to polite manners, kept tapping him on the arm with her fan, and saying: 'Oh, you are awful.' Before he left, the local habit of kissing 'like a pump' had given him 'A feeling in his mouth like over-sweet raisins, and a spasm in his left calf.'

Towards the end of April Chekhov was in the heart of the Don steppe at Ragozina Ravine, as the guest of a Cossack family. It would be hard to imagine any greater contrast with the life he was used to in Moscow. The walls of the house were covered with guns, sabres, whips and hunting tackle. If Chekhov wanted to cross the yard in the middle of the night he had to wake up the old servant to protect him from a horde of ferocious dogs. The diet was a never-failing source of surprise. There was no vodka or pepper. The staple food was goose and turkey, and a form of soup that reminded him of 'the kind of slops that are left when a lot of fat market-women have had a bath.' It was amusing to observe the type of 'rational agriculture' carried out on the farm, which consisted of: 'an uninterrupted round of slaughter, which does not stop for a single minute during the whole of the day. They kill sparrows, swallows, hornets, ants, magpies, crows—so that they shan't eat the bees; so that the bees shan't spoil the blossom on the fruit trees they kill the bees, and to prevent these trees exhausting the soil, they cut down the trees. In this way they are left with a cycle, which, though original, is based on the most recent scientific data.'

In May, when the time came to return to Moscow, he did not want to go. 'If only I had an extra two or three hundred roubles,' he wrote to Leykin, 'I'd travel over the whole world.' He returned sunburnt and with a 'host of impressions' in his head. After a few weeks he retired to Babkino for an unusually long stay of about three months. He had not meant to stay as long as this, especially when he began to find that Babkino was losing some of its charm, partly owing to the coldness of this particular summer and the absence of heating in the *dacha*. A visit to Petersburg had been planned, and he hoped to join friends in a *dacha* on Lake Ladoga, but gave up the idea because of ill-health.

Before Chekhov went south Suvorin had suggested that he might be allowed to publish a number of his *New Time* stories in book form much as Leykin had published *Motley Stories* the previous year. The terms he proposed were generous, and Chekhov hastened to make a selection of sixteen stories, which eventually appeared in August under the title *In the Twilight*. The literary standard of the new book was, of course, immeasurably higher than that of *Motley Stories*, and it made a big contribution to the already rapid growth of Chekhov's reputation. Without consulting Chekhov himself, his brother Alexander and Suvorin entered *In the Twilight* for the 'Pushkin Prize for Literature', awarded by the Academy of Sciences. Chekhov said there was no possible chance of his being given this prize and he was rather annoyed that the entry had been made. However, he admitted that he was pleased and flattered in October 1888 when he heard from Grigorovich that the application had been successful. The adjudicators considered that he did not deserve the full award (a thousand roubles), and assigned him half of this amount. All the same it was a great honour, and incidentally a welcome addition to his income. Chekhov wrote back to Grigorovich, saying that he didn't want to show false modesty and claim that he was unworthy of the prize, but that he knew he owed his good fortune chiefly to Grigorovich himself for championing him in the Academy. The award was a very exciting event for Chekhov, but he still could not help being amused by the status of 'great writer' which it appeared to confer, and tried to show his friends that it had not gone to his head by signing some of his letters 'Schiller Shakespeareovich Goethe.'

IV

A NEW APPROACH

THOUGH Chekhov realized so clearly early in 1886 that he must somehow manage to write less if he was to do himself full justice, this year in fact became the most prolific in his life and saw the publication of about a hundred-and-twenty separate items, totalling over 200,000 words. In 1887 there was only a very slight decrease in quantity, and not until the year after that did a steep fall at last occur.

The writings of 1886 and 1887 present a complicated picture. There was comedy in the style associated with *Antosha Chekhonte*, which continued to appear in *Fragments* and elsewhere, but which was gradually petering out during these two years. At the opposite pole were the *New Time* stories, which Chekhov produced as and when he could (the average rate was about one a month) and which contain his best work of the period. The *Petersburg Gazette* stories occupy an intermediate place between these two styles, veering now towards the gay frivolity of the first, now towards the conscientious artistry of the second. Although they were usually signed *Chekhonte*, many of them were serious in character, and one or two— notably *Typhus* and *Volodya*—were quite up to *New Time* level.

The most surprising thing about Chekhov's work at this crucial period in his development was the way in which he immediately showed himself to be possessed of a high degree of skill in handling genuine human feelings. *Fragments* and the other comic papers had given him little enough exercise in this difficult craft, yet he at once began to practise it with distinction, if not with the complete subtlety and precision which he was later to attain. The humiliation of a weak and dependent person which had formed the basis of a comic anecdote like *A Daughter of Albion* reappeared with vastly different effect in *An Upheaval*. In *The Schoolmaster* Chekhov could continue to use the machinery of the Little Story to squeeze the last drop of comic juice out of an absurd situation, and yet leave the reader near to tears before he had finished with him. A number of delightful sketches, such as *Grisha* and *An Incident*, opened up a new vein—studies of children—which was not to last for many years, but which contributed some minor masterpieces. No doubt many of these stories now seem better than they in fact were because of the careful revision which Chekhov gave them later in his life, but it is clear that he was already very far from being a novice when he began the serious treatment of human emotions.

This is nowhere more evident than in stories which present the love of men and women, a theme which was to appear in some of his most moving pages written later in life. Grigorovich, never slow to record his enthusiasm at the exciting qualities

which he found in Chekhov's fiction, singled out stories like
Verochka for special mention, telling Chekhov that they proved
'what I have already known for a long time—that your horizon
completely embraces the motif of love in all its most subtle and
intimate manifestations'.

Though they are not important compared with his later work,
Chekhov's best stories of 1886 and 1887 were already showing
definite signs of originality. One of the first original features that
people noticed was the way in which he insisted on atmosphere rather than incident. To put it differently, he was apparently more concerned with the moods of his characters than
with their adventures, and *nastroenie,* the Russian word for
'mood', began to be used increasingly in discussion of his work.
Russians say that he wrote the 'literature of *nastroenie'*—indeed, they usually claim that he invented this way of writing.
The point was not only that Chekhov was particularly skilful
at conveying a mood, but also that there was a distinctive
quality about the kind of mood he preferred to deal in. This
quality usually eluded those who tried to define it. Adjectives
like 'haunting', 'wistful', 'poetic' and 'melancholy' obviously came
near the mark, but were somehow unsatisfactory all the same,
and they were the sort of words which Chekhov himself did not
like hearing applied to what he had written. Perhaps the best
way of introducing the 'Chekhov *nastroenie*' is to quote a very
well-known paragraph from his story *The Beauties.* This appears in a description of a young Armenian girl of extraordinary
beauty, called Masha:

'It was not desires, delight or pleasure that Masha aroused in
me, but a deep, though pleasant, sorrow. This sorrow was as
indefinite and vague as sleep. For some reason I felt sorry for
myself and for my grandfather' (who was also present) 'and for
the Armenian' (Masha's father) 'and for Masha herself. I had a
feeling as though all four of us had lost something important
and vital which we should never find again. Grandfather also
grew sad. He stopped talking about grazing and sheep. He grew
silent, and looked pensively at Masha.'

This passage, which has always been recognized as especially
typical of Chekhov, happens to be a good description of the
effect which his best stories of 1886 and 1887 were already
producing on their readers. The feeling of 'deep, though pleasant,

sadness', of having 'lost something important', is expressed with
particular power in one really outstanding story of 1887, *The
Kiss*.

The hero of *The Kiss* is an artillery officer called Ryabovich,
a small, round-shouldered man, with spectacles and side-whiskers
like a lynx. The story tells of an occasion one May when his unit
happened to be quartered in a village for the night, and the
officers were invited over to the house of a local retired
general. They did not much want to go, but could not very
well refuse. The General was only fulfilling what he too considered to be a social duty, and his family and friends were not
very interested in the officers either. However, they were too
well-bred to show it, and immediately started up an animated
conversation. Ryabovich felt rather out of it. His face, lynx-
like side-whiskers and spectacles seemed to be saying: 'I am
the most timid, modest and colourless officer in the whole
brigade.' Wandering about the large house while his comrades
danced, played billiards or talked to the young ladies, he somehow got lost and ended up in a dark room. As he stood there,
a sudden rustle of a dress was heard, and a woman's voice
whispered breathlessly 'At Last!' Two soft, fragrant and unmistakably feminine arms were thrown round Ryabovich's neck.
A warm cheek was pressed against his, and he was tenderly
kissed. The woman who had kissed him at once gave a little
cry, and jumped away from him with apparent disgust. He too
almost cried aloud and rushed out of the room.

He felt embarrassed when he got back to the party, because
he could not help thinking that everyone must know what had
just happened. After a bit he grew more confident, and began
to forget that he was so drab and round-shouldered, and that
he had lynx-like side-whiskers and a 'nondescript appearance'
—an expression he had once accidentally overheard applied to
him by a woman. He went up to his hostess, and, adjusting
his spectacles, told her how much he liked her house. At supper
he ate mechanically, and thought about his adventure. It was
mysterious and romantic, but not difficult to explain. One of the
girls at the party must have had a rendezvous in the dark room,
and had mistaken him for her young man. He found himself
wondering which girl it could be, and decided that none of those
present was a suitable candidate.

When the party was over the officers walked back to their
billets through the garden, and for a moment all were silent,

F

wondering if they would ever have a large house, family and garden of their own, like the General. Then they all started talking and laughing. Their path lay along a river. The far bank was lost in darkness, and in places stars were reflected by the dark water. They quivered and dissolved—the only sign that the river was flowing swiftly.

Thoughts of the kiss filled Ryabovich's mind for a long time afterwards, as he pursued the dull routine duties of an artillery officer which contrasted so strongly with his adventure. One evening he decided to tell his friends about the kiss, and found to his amazement that the whole story could be recounted in a single minute. It seemed to him that it would be possible to go on talking about it all night.

Some time later the brigade again passed through the same village. Ryabovich went once more to look at the river which ran near the General's house, and realized that his mind had been full of unspecified longings and hopes ever since he had been kissed. He at last saw all these fancies for what they were—idle day-dreams:

'The water flowed he knew not where or why. It had flowed just like this in May. In May it had poured from the stream into a big river, from the river into the sea, then it had evaporated and turned into rain. Perhaps it was this same water which now flowed again before Ryabovich's eyes. With what purpose? Why?

'The whole of life appeared to Ryabovich as an incomprehensible, pointless joke. ... Lifting his eyes from the water and looking at the sky he again remembered how fate had caressed him in the person of the unknown woman, remembered his dreams and fancies of the summer, and his life seemed to him extraordinarily bare, impoverished and colourless.'

The Kiss stands right in the middle of Chekhov's line of development as a short story writer. A summary cannot of course begin to convey anything of its real quality, but it does throw into relief some of the more obvious methods of procedure which were to become a permanent part of his technique. Chekhov's manner of handling his hero is quite characteristic. Although Ryabovich is presented with absolute seriousness, there is nevertheless a flavour of humour in the treatment of this comic little man, which reveals him as a very distant relative of hundreds of other comic little men in the Little Stories. The power to make a character amusing and pathetic at the same time was already a distinctive feature of Chekhov's approach.

In having one central character, through whose eyes the whole of the action is seen, *The Kiss* follows what was becoming the normal pattern for a Chekhov story. It is also typical in showing how much could be made of what was, on the surface, a very unimportant and trifling incident. Ryabovich himself knew that the incident was not unimportant or trifling, but it began to seem so as soon as he tried to put it into words and found that he could tell the whole story to his comrades in a single minute. What Ryabovich failed to do on this occasion Chekhov was able to accomplish through his skill in creating *nastroenie*, and it is wholly characteristic that the production of *nastroenie* should be closely linked with descriptions of nature and evocations of the past and future.

As *The Kiss* and many other stories show, the technique of *nastroenie* was well within Chekhov's grasp in 1887, and it continued during all his subsequent writing to contribute one of the most moving and powerful effects at his disposal. However, Soviet critics are beginning to suggest that a little too much has been made of Chekhov's *nastroenie*, although they admit its great importance. As they point out, an admiration for the Chekhov atmosphere has sometimes blinded his interpreters to other equally important features in his work. Chekhov had many achievements of a different kind ahead of him after writing *The Kiss*.

CHAPTER FIVE

Successes and Doubts

I

THE STEPPE

EIGHTEEN-EIGHTY-EIGHT was an especially important point in Chekhov's literary career because it was in this year that he at last managed to concentrate properly on his work, reducing the number of his stories to ten. It was also important for the biggest of all his literary promotions, an invitation to contribute to one of the literary monthlies or 'fat journals', in which Russian readers were accustomed to read their best fiction-writers. This was *The Northern Herald,* a Petersburg publication, for which Chekhov settled down to write *The Steppe* in January. He took up his pen with a new feeling of responsibility, though he spoke of this story as a trifle. 'The thought that I am writing for a "fat journal",' he wrote, 'and that people will take my trifle more seriously than it deserves, jogs my elbow as the devil jogs a monk's.'

The Steppe was turning out much longer than anything he had produced since first trying his hand at serious work, and the care which he expended on it gave him the new experience of 'writing without hurry, as a gourmet eats snipe'. As the story progressed he expressed doubts of its merit in a number of letters to Petersburg, for he was anxious that his friends should not expect too much. 'Small-scale writing has spoiled me,' he said. 'It turns out that I am not yet able to do anything big.'

One of his fuller advance accounts, which was sent to Grigorovich, still makes a valuable commentary on *The Steppe*: 'I describe the plain, the lilac-coloured distance, sheep-drovers, Jews, priests, thunderstorms at night, inns, trains of wagons, steppe birds and so on. Each chapter consists of a separate story, and all the chapters are linked in close relationship like the five figures in a quadrille. I am trying to give them a

common flavour and a common tone, which is all the easier
for me because a single figure runs through all the chapters. I
feel that I have achieved much, and that there are passages
which have the smell of hay, but the general result is something strange and not excessively original. Through being un-
accustomed to write at length, and through a constant, familiar
dread of writing something superfluous, I fall into excess. Every
page turns out compact, as though it had been put through a
press; impressions jostle, pile up, and crowd each other out.
The pictures are tightly wedged together, following in an uninterrupted chain, and are therefore tiring. The general result is
not a picture, but a dry, detailed catalogue of impressions,
rather like a synopsis. Instead of an artistically integrated picture
of the steppe I give the reader a Steppe Encyclopedia. My
first pancake has turned out a dumpling.'

It was no novelty to Chekhov's friends to find him over-severe
in judging himself, but in fact *The Steppe* does not hang together so well as his later long stories, and some of its readers
may very well agree that it suffers from being a collection of
episodes.

This fault is only a minor blemish in what did prove, as
Chekhov intended it should, a literary achievement of greater
magnitude than anything he had written previously. All the
same, *The Steppe* exhibits no abrupt change of writing technique. In making the chief character a small boy, and in
presenting everything as it would appear to him, Chekhov was
repeating a process which had led to some of his most delightful
earlier sketches. The pictures of the Russian countryside contained in the story are composed in a manner peculiar to him,
but one which had already been used by him in previous nature
descriptions. It was recognized, however, that he had carried
his descriptive method to a new level of excellence in *The
Steppe*, and though he feared to bore his public with so many
'prose poems', they turned out to be one of the chief attrac-
tions.

Chekhov's individual manner of describing nature had not
usually emerged in his comic work, where nature played a very
minor role, and served chiefly as an amusing accessory. It was
in some stories published in the *Petersburg Gazette* that he
first showed what he could do in the way of serious landscape-
description—a feature of *The Fish* and *The Huntsman* which
especially appealed to Grigorovich. Chekhov wrote these stories

at a time when his interest in nature had been aroused by visits to Babkino, where the landscape was characteristic of central Russia. It was quiet, flat and unassuming, but delightful to those who knew it, and Chekhov often found that it agreed very well with the mood of his stories. His visits to south Russia in 1887 revived childhood memories of a very different type of scenery, and it was this part of the world which figured in *The Steppe* and several other stories of the same period. His descriptions enjoyed great success among readers who knew and loved the Russian countryside and Chekhov even found himself referred to as 'the greatest Russian landscape painter.'

Chekhov is often claimed to have evolved a new technique of describing nature in prose, particularly because of an unusual concentration on brevity and vividness. The aim he set himself, was to summon up a picture in his reader's mind 'when he closes his eyes', and he found that this could be done without long descriptive passages. The method was to seize some characteristic detail, carefully selected for its aptness in suggesting the whole. He applied this method quite consciously, and had an illustration of it to offer from one of his own stories. This was *The Wolf*, which contains the sentence:

'On the dam, which was covered with moonlight, there was not a trace of shadow; on the middle of it the neck of a broken bottle glittered like a star.'

Chekhov underlined the point in a letter to his brother Alexander, in which he said: 'You'll get the effect of a moonlit night if you write that a piece of glass from a broken bottle flashed like a bright star on a mill-dam.'

The practice of evoking a scene by quoting a piece of minor but vivid detail is frequently claimed as an invention of Chekhov's. It is often contrasted with the technique of earlier writers, such as Turgenev, whose descriptions are usually fuller and have an abundance of detail which a modern reader cannot always bother to assimilate.

The second point about Chekhov's nature-descriptions is the way in which they are linked with the moods of his characters. Nature is an important ingredient in the distillation of *nastroenie,* as stories like *The Kiss* show. Chekhov was rapidly learning to subordinate nature-descriptions, along with all other elements in his writing, to his most important aim—the evocation of a mood. For this reason *The Steppe* was not an altogether typical story, being more saturated with nature than anything else he wrote. However, the technique was quite characteristic. Flashes of vivid detail gave vigour and pungency to his prose, startling into attention readers accustomed to the more leisurely manner of earlier writers. The prose style of *The Steppe* had other features which were already beginning to be recognized as unmistakably Chekhovian. For instance, homely comparisons were lavishly used to illustrate majestic natural phenomena. 'It was as though someone had struck a match across the sky,' he wrote when he wanted to convey the impression made by lightning and thunder on his small hero. 'A pale, phosphorescent streak flashed and died down. There was the sound of someone far away walking over an iron roof. They were probably walking in bare feet because the iron gave a hollow rumble.'

A further feature which was beginning to seem characteristic was the practice of ascribing human emotions and attitudes to animals and plants. A kite, seen flying past with a measured beating of wings, suddenly poises in mid-air 'as though meditating on the boredom of life'. Another passage shows a link between man and nature lower on the biological scale:

'The grass, half dead and already doomed, was trying to persuade someone piteously and earnestly, that it was not to blame, and that it had been unjustly scorched by the sun. It was asserting its passionate desire for life, saying that it was still young, and would have been beautiful but for the heat and drought'.

After this it is not surprising to find a curly, ashen-grey stormcloud, which 'exchanged glances with the steppe, as if to say "I'm ready", and frowned'.

The delights of *The Steppe* are not by any means confined to nature descriptions. Against the rich background Chekhov recounts a series of minor but memorable incidents which show that he could bring human beings to life quite as well as animals and plants. The story was accordingly received with great enthusiasm by his Petersburg well-wishers, most of whom rarely erred on the side of the phlegmatic. Old Pleshcheev, one of the literary editors of *The Northern Herald*, wrote to Chekhov that he had been seized by a mad ecstasy on reading

The Steppe. What if it did lack a plot? There was an 'inexhaustible fount of inner content', calculated to drive poets and artists with a sense of poetry 'out of their mind'. Pleshcheev noted also the abundance of most subtle psychological touches, and was so carried away that he asked Chekhov to name his own fee without ceremony.

II

UKRAINE, CRIMEA AND CAUCASUS

The Steppe was finished and dispatched by the end of February, and it was natural that Chekhov should follow it with a visit to Petersburg in the following month. With Suvorin there was much to discuss, for the success of *In the Twilight* made it desirable that a further collection of Chekhov's published work should be produced in book form by *New Time*. An agreement was reached about the contents of the new volume, which included *The Steppe* and *The Kiss* among other items, and had the title *Stories*. After this, volumes of collected stories by Chekhov appeared almost yearly, and often ran into several editions.

Chekhov had not been in Petersburg long when he was carried off to stay in Suvorin's house. The Suvorins lived a life of luxury; Chekhov was given his own study with an elegant writing table, but thought his privacy would be infringed by his status as a guest, since he could not very well bring his friends back, or return on occasion slightly the worse for drink. However, the arrangement had its compensations, for it saw the beginning of increased intimacy with his host. Hitherto this friendship had developed slowly, partly owing to the twenty-six years' difference in age between Chekhov and Suvorin, but now they began to have long conversations in true Russian fashion, walking up and down the study, and 'philosophizing'. Chekhov was very popular with the children, who regarded him with awed admiration because he had written *Kashtanka,* a children's story, of which Suvorin was now preparing a separate *de luxe* edition. One result of his growing friendship with the family was an invitation to visit their Crimean *dacha* in the summer.

Plans for the summer were the chief thing that occupied his mind after he returned to Moscow. Michael and Mariya, who had fallen in love with Babkino, refused to hear of any alteration in the usual programme, but their parents were longing to revisit their native south Russia. Paul Chekhov was beginning to feel an old man, and to talk of taking a last farewell of his native land. It was in favour of this plan that Chekhov gave his casting vote. As usual the main arrangements for the summer were made by him, and it was difficult to find a *dacha* to suit everyone's taste. There had to be quiet and shade for the old people, company and good walking for the young. Fishing was, of course, one of the things which chiefly interested Chekhov himself, and he also insisted that they must not be too far from a post-office. He had spent some time during his travels of the previous year prospecting for a suitable *dacha*, but had not been successful, and in the end he took one which he had not seen, near the town of Sumy in the Poltava district of the Ukraine. It was near a river, the Psyol, believed to be rich in fish; it had a pond of its own, full of carp, and stood at the foot of a hill, surrounded by woods. Moreover, there was said to be 'an abundance of young ladies' in the neighbourhood, and the Lintvarev family, who owned the place, sounded by all accounts worthy successors to the Kiselevs. No sooner had Chekhov made final arrangements to rent the *dacha* than he began to bombard his Petersburg friends with invitations to join him. Pleshcheev was among those who accepted, and there was some hope of Suvorin. One of Chekhov's new friends, the playwright and popular novelist Shcheglov, managed to hold out, in spite of a series of letters in which Chekhov ranged from threats to cajolery in an attempt to uproot him. How could Shcheglov call himself a writer, and refuse to move from Petersburg, where he could learn nothing of Russia at all?

In May, when the Chekhovs arrived, Sumy turned out to be all that they had hoped. The Lintvarevs were an excellent family, consisting of an old mother, three daughters and two sons. They were intellectual and gifted people, whose kindness contributed much to the enjoyment of the Chekhovs' stay, and the holiday went entirely according to plan. Fish were caught in quantity. The venerable Pleshcheev turned up as arranged, and was soon surrounded by an admiring court of young ladies. He was followed by other guests. There were musical evenings at the big house where the Lintvarevs lived, and many excursions around the neighbouring countryside. Sumy was in the heart of the Gogol country, and Chekhov, who, like most educated Russians, knew his Gogol almost by heart, was fascinated by visits to nearby fairs at Sorochinsty and Poltava. He found South Russia a place of warmth, life and colour, by comparison with which Moscow and Petersburg seemed drab and featureless.

Having seen his family well settled at Sumy, and having rested there for several weeks, Chekhov started on the second stage of his summer travels, and visited the Suvorins at their *dacha* near Feodosiya in the Crimea. Feodosiya was so hot that there was nothing to do except lie on the beach and bathe. You could live a thousand years on the beach and not get bored, said Chekhov. Suvorin and he took up talking where they had left off in Petersburg, and Chekhov was sure that they would die of inflammation of the tongue and vocal chords. Between them they 'decided all questions, and marked out a host of new ones which had never been raised before'. Chekhov was beginning to admire more and more Suvorin's keen instinct and independence of judgment.

Pleasant as life was in Feodosiya, it soon struck Chekhov as enervating, and was beginning to seem like a waste of time. The next step was a voyage by steamer to the Caucasian coast, followed by a journey across the mountains to Baku, undertaken with one of Suvorin's sons. This was Chekhov's first visit to the most exotic region of the Russian Empire, and it produced a whole succession of unforgettable impressions. The larger towns were sordid. Batum had 'nothing special, except a superfluity of brothels'; Baku impressed him with its drinking water that tasted of salt, and the mud saturated with oil that squelched beneath his feet. However, the countryside was the most wonderful thing he had seen. 'If I lived in Abkazia even a month I think I'd write about half a hundred fascinating fairy tales' he wrote to one friend, and he told Leykin 'if you haven't ridden along the Georgian military road, then pawn your wives, children and *Fragments*, and go. It's sheer poetry; not a road, but a fantastic and miraculous tale told by a demon.' It was proposed to cross the Caspian and continue travelling in Bokhara and Persia, but Suvorin's son was recalled for family reasons, and Chekhov decided not to proceed alone. By mid-August he was back in Sumy, pleased to think that he had bathed in both the Black Sea and the Caspian that summer, and determined to buy a farm of his own in the south of Russia. Suvorin was prepared to advance the bulk of the money, and Chekhov was confident that he could soon work off the debt by intensive writing. He picked his farm, but the deal did not go through, owing to a disagreement over the price, and in September he returned to Moscow.

III

CHEKHOV'S 'TENDENCIES'

IN spite of the chorus of praise which greeted *The Steppe*, and the enormous advance in Chekhov's literary reputation which it marked, complaints began to be made against his writing, often by very influential critics. Their chief objections did not relate to purely literary matters. Most Russian intellectuals —the sort of people who subscribed to the literary monthlies— tended to left-wing views, and these publications had an anti-Government policy, which they took very seriously, though they were not able to express it openly. Accordingly, Chekhov's association with the conservative and pro-Government paper *New Time* had now become more of a handicap than a help. He had realized from the start that his reputation with the intelligentsia would suffer from the linking of his name with Suvorin's paper, which took a violent nationalist line, involving it in offensive attacks on the Jews and minority populations of Russia. Now that Chekhov was accepted by the *Northern Herald* he was expected to give up *New Time*, and annoyed many people by refusing to do so. It was not that he had any sympathy for its politics, but he could not see that politics should be allowed to affect his relations with Suvorin, who was becoming his closest friend; in any case he felt that he owed Suvorin a debt of gratitude for helping him along his literary path. He was annoyed with people who criticized him for contributing to *New Time*. Why should anyone dictate to him where he placed his work? He said that he would write on a window-sill provided that people would read him.

Another common criticism of Chekhov was linked with a more general question of aesthetics which exercised many Russian minds during the nineteenth century: how far should literature be a guide to life? One view, which never made very much headway in Russia, was that a writer ought to create 'beauty' without commenting on life, since any attempt to do so would spoil his writing as a work of art. This attitude came to be expressed in the formula 'Art for Art's sake', and in Russian literature it later made some contribution to the philosophy of the Symbolist movement. Although it had few adherents in the 'eighties, it was beginning to be advocated in a small way by a group of poets. P. S. Kogan, in a book on Chekhov published

in Russia in 1929, quotes as a typical profession of policy by
this group an article of the poet Minsky, who was already claiming that 'to demand from poetry anything more than aesthetic
pleasure is like asking an eye to hear or smell as well as see.'
Not many Russians in Chekhov's day would have gone as far
as this, but many of them were beginning to feel that literature
should not necessarily be harnessed to a definite programme or
system of ideas.

Although such views were gaining ground, most critics and
readers continued to regard the interpretation of life as one of
the chief functions of literature. In Russia fiction, literary
criticism and even poetry provided a platform on which rela-
tively free public discussion of non-literary matters was possible, and an imaginative writer could often air social and political opinions which would have been banned as obnoxious to
the Government if expressed in more direct form. Consequently
Russian literature had often been valued for what it taught,
especially in the 'sixties, when many critics, poets and novelists
seem almost to have regarded themselves as propagandists, and
certainly believed that aesthetic values were of secondary importance. Among these were Nekrasov, Chernyshevsky and Dob-
rolyubov. Even an ideologically neutral novelist like Goncharov
sometimes found that critics had assigned to him political and
social views which he was not himself aware of possessing.
Moreover, the two most important novelists of the nineteenth
century, Tolstoy and Dostoevsky, were not always concerned
simply to reproduce life, but usually had something which they
considered important to contribute to its interpretation.

Chekhov's early serious work was rather disappointing to
those who believed that literature should contain a message. No
such element seemed to be present in most of what he wrote,
and accordingly it began to be said that he was a writer 'without principles', and that his writings lacked any 'tendency' or
'sense of direction'. This was the burden of many critical articles
published about Chekhov in the Russian press, and the complaint
also reached him in private letters. Pleshcheev recorded the
general feeling on the subject when he wrote to Chekhov: 'People
complain that your writings do not make clear your sympathies
and antipathies', and said that he missed in them an element of
protest. Pleshcheev's letter, written in 1888, confirmed what
Chekhov had already heard earlier in the year from the critic
Mikhaylovsky. Mikhaylovsky, who enjoyed tremendous prestige

as an arbiter of literature, was a man of firm political and philosophical convictions. He wrote a long letter to Chekhov which, though complimentary, was full of complaints about his aimlessness. As he read *The Steppe*, Mikhaylovsky said, he seemed 'to be looking at a giant, who walks along a road without knowing where he is going or why he is going there; who, unconscious of his own strength, now plucks a shoot, now tears up a tree, roots and all—both with equal ease, and without seeming to notice any difference between the two acts'.

Chekhov's immediate reaction to such complaints was one of impatience. He hadn't got a tendency, and didn't want one. 'I am afraid of those who look between the lines for a tendency,' he wrote to Pleshcheev, 'and who insist on seeing in me either a liberal or a conservative. I am not a liberal, or a believer in gradual reform, or a monk or an indifferentist. All I should wish to be is a free artist.' How could he express any definite message in his work without having yet achieved a settled outlook on life? 'I have as yet no political, religious or philosophical outlook', he wrote in another letter of the period. 'I change every month, and so shall have to confine myself to a description of how my heroes love, get married, have children, die and of how they speak.'

Chekhov was not disposed to agree with critics who thought that nobody could write well without a philosophy of life. On the contrary, he thought that freedom from preconceived ideas was a good basis on which to build for it enabled him to write with objectivity, a quality on which he had come to set great value. Again and again he said that one must feel 'cold as ice' when sitting down to a story; he reserved his right to describe things as he saw them, without striking any sort of attitude. This was a point on which he continually found himself at odds with his literary friends. His story *The Horse-stealers* led to a typical argument, which gave him a further opportunity to explain his position. He wrote to Suvorin: 'You find fault with my objectivity, calling it indifference to good and evil, an absence of ideals and ideas, and so forth. You want me when I describe horse-thieves, to say "The stealing of horses is an evil". But after all, that's long been known without me showing it. Leave it to magistrates to condemn them. My job is simply to show what they're like ... Of course, it would be pleasant to combine art with sermonizing, but for me personally that is exceptionally difficult and almost impossible.'

As some of these extracts suggest, Chekhov tended to be slightly embarrassed by abstract speculations. This was a characteristic most unusual among nineteenth-century Russian intellectuals, whose fondness for making heavy weather over the fundamental questions of philosophy has often been commented on—by Chekhov himself among others. The hero of his story *Ariadne*, for example, notes that when Englishmen or Germans meet, their conversation is usually about the price of wool, the harvest, or personal affairs, whereas Russians prefer to talk about abtruse problems of philosophy. To Chekhov these problems were important, but he thought that many people made too much of them. Not long before his death he wrote to a friend: 'Don't take such a complex view of life. It's probably much simpler than you think. We don't understand life—and does it really deserve all those torturing ratiocinations with which our Russian minds wear themselves out?'

There were few things that irritated Chekhov more than the suggestion that he ought to be ready to supply answers to complicated questions, which, so far as he could see, no one ever had answered satisfactorily. 'You complain,' he wrote to Suvorin, 'that neither the conversation about pessimism, nor the heroine's story decide the question of pessimism' (the subject under discussion in the story *Lights*). 'It seems to me that it is not fiction-writers who ought to decide such questions as pessimism, God etc. The fiction-writer's function is purely to describe who talked or thought about God or pessimism, how, and under what circumstances. The artist must be, not the judge of his characters and of what they say, but merely a dispassionate observer. My business is only to be able to distinguish important evidence from unimportant, to be able to illuminate the figures, and to talk in their language. Shcheglov holds it against me that I finish the story with the phrase "You can't make sense of anything in this life". In his opinion the artist-psychologist *must* make sense of things—that's what he's a psychologist for. It is time that writers, especially if they are artists, recognized that you can't make sense of anything in this world, just as Socrates once recognized it, and as Voltaire used to recognize it. The crowd thinks that it knows everything and understands everything; the more stupid it is, apparently, the wider its horizons. But if the artist, in whom the crowd believes, takes it upon himself to complain that he does not understand anything he sees, then this very fact constitutes an important piece of knowledge in the sphere of thought, and a great step forward.'

Though Chekhov often snapped his fingers at people who expected him to have a definite philosophy of life, and to express it in his work, his attitude in this matter cannot be easily dismissed. It was not completely thought out and self-consistent in the late 'eighties, nor would he himself have claimed that it was. In the same year as that in which he boasted of his freedom from any settled outlook he admitted to Suvorin that 'it has long been known that a reasoned life without a definite outlook is not a life, but a burden and a horror'. It was in this year too that Chekhov told Pleshcheev that he disclaimed any sort of 'tendency', and yet in another letter of 1888, also to Pleshcheev, he expressly lays claim to one: 'Is it really true that there isn't a tendency even in my latest story?' (apparently *The Party*) 'You once said that my stories lack an element of protest, and don't show my sympathies and antipathies ... but in my story don't I protest from beginning to end against falsehood? Isn't that a tendency? Surely it is.'

Chekhov was usually prepared to admit criticism of life as a legitimate function of literature. This point of view is stated in one important passage from a letter to Suvorin, perhaps the most representative summary of Chekhov's aesthetic position: 'In demanding from the artist a conscious attitude to his work you are right, but you confuse two concepts: *The solution of the problem and the correct presentation of the problem.* Only the latter is obligatory for the artist. In *Anna Karenina* and *Evgeny Onegin* not a single problem is solved, but they completely satisfy us because they present all their problems in the right way.'

In spite of his dislike for the more pretentious forms of speculation, Chekhov—like any other intelligent person—could not help thinking about the purpose of life, and the place occupied in it by the work on which he was engaged. Though he sometimes wrote stories of outstanding merit in which these thoughts do not occupy a very prominent place, what may be called the 'philosophical content' of his fiction became increasingly significant as he approached literary maturity. It is tempting to say that without this element he would never have become one of the major figures in world literature. Chekhov would never at any time have claimed to have solved the problem of life, but his views did eventually settle down sufficiently to form a fairly consistent picture. The late 'eighties were a period of mental

ferment and puzzled search for something which was very difficult to find. Some of his intellectual excursions at this time
proved quite unsatisfactory, and contributed nothing permanent
to his thought. However, the foundation of his mature outlook
was already being laid. At any rate it was becoming increasingly clear that he started with the attitude usually described as
'materialist'. He was unable to accept any religious explanation
of life, for he found that his mind could only cope successfully
with the tangible and concrete. He sometimes expressed his
unwillingness to leap ahead of concrete evidence by quoting
the quaint Russian proverb 'The eyes do not grow higher than
the forehead', which neatly emphasized his distrust of anything
mystical or metaphysical.

IV

CHEKHOV AND TOLSTOYISM

THOUGH Chekhov objected so strongly to the suggestion that
fiction ought to contain a message, some of his work during the
late 'eighties nevertheless does show a definite attempt to teach
a way of life. This is particularly noticeable in a small group of
stories designed to spread the moral doctrines of Tolstoy—one
of the least successful episodes in Chekhov's literary development, but a most interesting illustration of the way his mind
was working. It was the one occasion in his life when he was
seriously attracted by any of the numerous movements of
thought in contemporary Russia. He summarized the influence
of Tolstoy on his ideas in a letter to Suvorin written in 1894,
by which time he had outlived this influence, and had taken up
an attitude hostile to it. In the letter Chekhov told Suvorin
that Tolstoy's philosophy 'deeply affected me and possessed me
for about six or seven years'. It is difficult to determine exactly
which these six or seven years were, but they certainly included
the period 1886-8, during which a number of Chekhov's stories
give evidence of a strong interest in Tolstoyism.

As is well known, Tolstoy's work falls into two main parts,
vastly differing one from the other, and separated by the mental
crisis which came to a head in the late 'seventies, and was described in *Confession*—written in 1879. Before this date Tolstoy
had been primarily a literary artist, and it is to the earlier
period that the bulk of his important fiction (notably *War and
Peace* and *Anna Karenina*) belongs. After 1880 Tolstoy became
absorbed, almost to the exclusion of everything else, with the

problem of how man should live, and devoted the rest of his life to working out the answer on paper and in practice. The creed which he began to preach in the 'eighties was one of rational Christianity. He believed that the life of Jesus Christ was a revelation from God, and that it represented the only workable ethical programme. In order to realize this programme it was necessary to disentangle Christ's essential teaching from a mass of irrelevancies superimposed on it by the Christian Churches. These were, in particular, all the supernatural elements in Christian belief—the miracle stories, the doctrine of the Resurrection and the belief in personal immortality. Tolstoy decided that he must go back to first sources if he was to purge Christianity of the perversions of theologians, and he subjected the Bible—especially the four Gospels—to a detailed examination in the original languages. The core of Christian teachings, as revealed by this process, was comprised in five commandments: (1) Do not be angry. (2) Do not indulge in illicit sexual intercourse. (3) Do not promise anything on oath. (4) Do not resist evil by violence. (5) Do not judge or go to law.

When Tolstoy and his followers began to practise these principles it was seen that they ran entirely contrary to accepted modes of human behaviour. The doctrine of non-violence involved a rejection not only of war and military service, but also of all property, including money, which Tolstoy interpreted as a means of enslaving the poor. Hence the belief in 'simplification' which gained so much notoriety for him and his followers. Tolstoy began to wear peasant dress, to clean out his own room, to make his own boots, and to work on the land. He was soon accused of inconsistency, since even he, with all his strength and stubbornness, was unable to carry out his own precepts to the full. His attempt to dispense with property led to a series of painful clashes with his wife, and a number of compromises with his principles, which caused him acute suffering.

Like Tolstoy's wife the Russian Government viewed the new prophet with suspicion. It is probable that only his world-wide celebrity saved him from persecution and exile, since he taught that the state was an evil, condemned its whole juridical and administrative apparatus, and preached a thorough-going anarchy in which love should replace force as the chief motive power in human conduct. Tolstoy's teaching gained a wide following in the Russia of the 'eighties, a period when the oppressions of the state weighed especially hard on sensitive people,

G

and when the prevalence of social injustice aroused a widespread feeling of frustration. In this atmosphere the moral self-perfection of each individual, recommended by Tolstoy, made a strong appeal. It was an energetic and thorough-going programme, implying a complete change of habits and outlook, and it did not involve the dangers attendant upon a more active attempt to influence the structure of society. Tolstoyan 'colonies' were set up, both in Russia and abroad, but the master himself never took part in any of these experiments, which seem to have been uniformly unsuccessful.

It is doubtful whether Chekhov had the opportunity to make a detailed study of Tolstoy's theoretical works, since their publication was banned in Russia for the time being. Numerous hectographed copies did circulate illegally, and it is likely that Chekhov read *Confession* and some of Tolstoy's later theoretical work in this form. In any case he would have become familiar with Tolstoy's ideas by word of mouth, for they were always being discussed, and were part of the intellectual atmosphere of the time. As a result of what he learned Chekhov became, not one of the inner ring of Tolstoy's more fanatical adherents, but one of the wider circle of intellectuals who were attracted and impressed by the teaching without being drawn into definite allegiance. There were many aspects of Tolstoy's creed which had little appeal for Chekhov. He was not tempted to wear peculiar clothes, or to give up smoking and drinking. Asceticism was always repugnant to him, and he clung to various features of civilized life which Tolstoy abjured; he liked soft carpets, and in women prized above all the quality of beauty, as he once remarked himself when discussing Tolstoyism. Thus it came about that in 1888, a year in which Tolstoy's influence on him was apparently at its height, he wrote the satirical fable *A Story Without a Title,* which, in attacking asceticism, was opposed to one of Tolstoy's cardinal propositions. Another point on which Chekhov was unable to meet Tolstoy was the religious basis of his faith. From the point of view of the orthodox Christian Tolstoy had made a fairly clean sweep of the mystical and supernatural elements of religion. His creed was uncompromisingly rationalist, with the important exception of the initial act of faith which led him to regard the teaching of Christ as a piece of divine revelation—and this Chekhov was unable to accept. With these reservations, however, there was much in Tolstoy's exposition of Christianity for which he had the highest respect. In particular the forbearance and tolerance enjoined in the precepts 'Do not be angry' and 'Do not judge' were a habit of mind with him.

Under Tolstoy's influence Chekhov wrote a few stories which have a definite message, and therefore stand outside the general trend of his work during this period. Tolstoy's *Popular Tales* served to some extent as a model. These were simple stories published in cheap editions in the middle 'eighties, and intended to appeal to as wide a public as possible. Having completely turned his back on the highly complicated art of *War and Peace* and *Anna Karenina*, Tolstoy was now concerned only to spread his new faith in homely language, intelligible to the barely literate. The success of these fictional sermons was tremendous. Tolstoy had developed an inimitable and delightful technique of telling simple stories, in which he completely triumphed over the rather unpromising limitations he had set himself. Where Tolstoy had succeeded, however, Chekhov failed. At any rate there is general agreement that his didactic stories of the late 'eighties are among his least successful work, a fact which he himself recognized by implication when he excluded several of them from the first collected edition of his works.

These didactic stories of Chekhov's are not very numerous, and he produced them simultaneously with many stories in other styles, quite free from any attempts to preach. Some of his Tolstoyan stories are devoted to the theme of compassion and forgiveness, including *A Misfortune,* which describes an official who has lost his job after a five-day drunken debauch. He arrives home expecting trouble from his wife, but the loving forgiveness with which she in fact greets him gives him the courage to begin a new life. Another example of compassionate sympathy is illustrated by *The Beggar,* where a lazy tramp accepts the job of chopping some wood. He is so work-shy that the cook has to help him out, and her kindness and co-operation finally lead to his moral regeneration. In 1888 another Tolstoyan theme appeared—the vanity of earthly goods, which was illustrated by two fables, *The Bet* and *The Shoemaker and the Devil.*

The aspect of Tolstoyism which seems to have interested Chekhov most of all was the doctrine of non-resistance to evil. In *The Meeting* he preached a sermon on this theme. Here a peasant, travelling from village to village in order to collect money for the rebuilding of a church, is robbed by a fellow-traveller, but refuses to report the incident to the police, or indeed to make protest at all. Meanwhile the thief turns gradually from blustering to penitence, and finally runs true to Tolstoyan psychology by returning what he has stolen. The theme of non-resistance turned up in various forms in other stories, among the most interesting being *Excellent People*, which contains a debate between a brother and sister on the question. The brother is an interesting figure, being the writer of articles for the intellectual press, the type of parasite on culture for whom Chekhov felt something of Tolstoy's disdain. His sister, an enterprising and intelligent woman doctor, had the misfortune to lose her husband very soon after her marriage, and in her distress made an unsuccessful attempt at suicide. For a time she was stunned by the blow, but as she recovered her interest in life, it began to seem to her that her brother's literary activities, which she had once greatly admired, were rather a waste of time. 'It seems to me,' she told him, 'that if all we thinking people devoted ourselves to the solution of big problems, then all those petty questions which you rack your brains over would decide themselves.' When he refused to drop his literary work in order to explore the doctrine of non-resistance, which was one of the big problems his sister had in mind, a coldness grew up between the two. Angered by his indifference to social issues she decided to leave her home and devote herself to medical work among the peasants. Here there is none of the overt moralizing atmosphere of *The Meeting*, but Chekhov by no means holds the scales even between the two parties. Clearly his sympathies were on the side of the sister. In the person of the literary brother he was perhaps holding himself up to criticism, though the projection was a very distorted one. Perhaps he ought to abandon his writing and the comforts of civilization for a life of self-sacrifice among the poor. The idea must have struck him repeatedly during these years, and the thoughts which inspired *Excellent People* probably played their part in persuading him to go to Sakhalin in 1890—an episode which no doubt surprised those who imagined that he was shutting himself away from life in literature.

V

ETHICAL SYMPATHIES IN CHEKHOV'S STORIES

ALTHOUGH Tolstoy's views were soon to strike him as narrow and mistaken, Chekhov's Tolstoyan stories do show a strong desire to influence human behaviour. The same desire is evident, though less obtrusive, in a number of other stories written during the same period, in which he interprets life in a manner less disastrous to the quality of his fiction. This consists in recommending by implication certain principles of ordinary, decent behaviour. A long letter to his brother Nicholas, dated 1886, reveals what these were. It contains a description of what Chekhov calls 'Educated Men'. Among the main characteristics of an Educated Man (characteristics in which his brother appears to have been strikingly deficient) he stresses respect for the personality of others, a willingness to help people in difficulty, and a dislike of dirt, untidiness and laziness. Above all he emphasizes his impatience with all kinds of 'falsehood', and here he is thinking of lies which are lived, rather than of those which are spoken. Posing, hypocrisy, affectation and snobbery always were the qualities which he particularly hated, and he does some very straight talking on the subject in the letter.

Nicholas' behaviour must have been inconsiderate indeed to make Chekhov speak so plainly. Though he did not indulge in such overt preaching in his fiction (apart from some of the Tolstoyan stories), his homily on the Educated Man does throw light on an important aspect of his work. Few critics have devoted more attention to the ethical policy recommended in Chekhov's stories than V Ermilov, one of the best-known recent Soviet writers on the subject. Admitting that Chekhov is celebrated for an 'objective' way of writing, Ermilov claims that his objectivity is often only on the surface, and that beneath it, strong sympathies and antipathies are revealed to all except the most casual reader. 'In every line and every word people could discern behind the veil of restraint and objectivity a passionate love for the hard-working man, and a contempt for his enemies—vulgarity, laziness and parasitism.'

This is perhaps not very happily expressed, and 'passionate love' does not seem to hit off Chekhov's basic attitude. However, Ermilov goes on to argue his case with great success, particularly in an analysis of the story *Enemies*. His argument is too long to reproduce; the main point of it is that Chekhov presented in a spirit of apparent objectivity a quarrel between two men, Abogin and Kirilov, but that the more one studies the story the more obvious it becomes that Chekhov disliked the rich, handsome, well-fed Abogin, and approved of his enemy, the hard-working and rather downtrodden Doctor Kirilov.

Unlike Chekhov's advocacy of Tolstoyism, the important element in his approach illustrated by stories like *Enemies* did not disappear at the end of the 'eighties. He was not, as many people said, a writer entirely 'without principles', an accusation which he particularly resented. Though he never wanted to be thought of as a judge of his fellows, he rarely described human behaviour without an attitude of latent criticism, and the basis of this criticism was usually a preference for people whose standards were genuine and linked with life.

VI

THE 'CLINICAL STUDIES'

ONE group of writings in particular made people think about Chekhov's outlook on life in the late 'eighties, and incidentally included some of his best work during the period. To this group belong the play *Ivanov* and several outstanding stories.

The central character of the play, Nicholas Ivanov, is an ineffectual landowner thirty-five years old, who sits back helplessly while his estate accumulates debts. By training and temperament he is an intellectual. Five years before the action begins he had married a Jewess, Sarah, with whom he was passionately in love, and who had to give up her faith and break with her family in order to become his wife. It appears from the play itself, and from Chekhov's references to it in his correspondence, that marrying a Jewess was an eccentric thing for a Russian landowner to do. When the play begins it turns out that Sarah is very seriously ill with tuberculosis. Her doctor, a young man called Lvov, explains to Ivanov that the only hope for her is to send her to the Crimea, and that, as she is too much attached to her husband to go away on her own, he must accompany her. Ivanov refuses, admitting that he once was in love with his wife, but now—he shrugs his shoulders: 'Here are you telling me she is going to die soon, and I feel neither love nor pity, only a sort of emptiness and fatigue.' Lvov is horrified at such callousness, and he is the sort of young man who does not hesitate to speak his mind. However, Ivanov is only interested to know whether his horses are ready. He wants to spend the evening in his usual way, drinking and gambling at the house of his wealthy neighbours, the Lebedevs, leaving Sarah by herself, a lonely, dying woman. Throughout the play Ivanov acts with indifference and brutality, for which, however, he often blames himself. At the Lebedevs' he plays court to Sasha, the daughter of the house, a self-sacrificing girl who can only love a failure; his long, self-pitying tirades prove the shortest way to her heart. Doctor Lvov is continually appearing and warning Ivanov that he is hastening his wife's death by his behaviour. This is indeed true. Sarah detects Ivanov's intrigue with Sasha, and has a violent quarrel with him, in which he loses his temper, taunts her with being a Jewess, and tells her that she has not long to live. This fact has been carefully concealed from her, so that Ivanov's conduct in revealing it is especially cruel. After Sarah's death he is to marry Sasha, but his introspection shows him that he will be no happier with her than he was with Sarah, and he commits suicide on his wedding morning.

It is perhaps not obvious from such a brief summary why *Ivanov* should have puzzled so many people. That it was puzzling is shown by a large number of references in Chekhov's correspondence of 1887-9, a period during which he was continually revising the play in the hope of making his intentions plain. He admitted that it must be his own fault if people misunderstood him, and when they continued to do so he often wished he had never written *Ivanov*. He even took to calling it 'my *Bolvanov*', from the Russian word *bolvan,* meaning 'a blockhead'. A long letter to Suvorin is one of many which show how even those most closely connected with the play failed to understand it:

'The producer considers Ivanov a Superfluous Man à la Turgenev; one of the actresses asks "Why is Ivanov a blackguard?" You yourself write "One must give Ivanov some quality to show why two women hang round his neck, and why he is a scoundrel and Doctor Lvov a great man." If the three of you have understood me in this way it means that my Ivanov is worthless. I probably got all muddled up and wrote something quite different from what I intended. If my Ivanov emerges as a blackguard or a Superfluous Man, and Doctor Lvov as a great man, if it's not understandable why Sarah and Sasha love Ivanov, then obviously my play hasn't come off, and there can't be any question of staging it.'

As this passage shows, it was the moral balance of the play which people found difficult to size up correctly. Here was Ivanov behaving in a way which surely must arouse a reaction of strong condemnation in any ordinary person; Chekhov tried to show that this reaction was a wrong one by making its mouthpiece in the play (Doctor Lvov) a most unpleasant character. Lvov's moral stuffiness is no doubt a detestable characteristic, but judged by ordinary standards it is more excusable than Ivanov's attitude. Ivanov, for all his flabbiness, cruelty and selfishness, was a better sort of person than Lvov in Chekhov's eyes, and those among the audience who found it hard to swallow this went away from the theatre in a bewildered and argumentative mood.

In presenting Ivanov in such a sympathetic light Chekhov might seem to be protesting against ready-made moral judgments as an inadequate criterion of human behaviour, and to be reinforcing the lesson contained in Ivanov's remark to Lvov in the third act: 'No, Doctor; each one of us has too many wheels, screws and valves for us to be able to judge each other on one or two likely impressions.' However, though it is true that Chekhov tended to reject conventional judgments, he did not mean his *Ivanov* as a sermon on this or any other theme. His intentions did not go so far. All he was trying to do was to present on the stage 'real people' such as he had seen in actual life. Again and again he claimed that his characters were, in conception, true to life, however incompetent he might be at enprooving them on the stage. They were ordinary and typical people—a point he was especially concerned to make about his hero, claiming also that this particular type had never been described in literature before. In the long analysis of Ivanov contained in the letter to Suvorin quoted above Chekhov explicitly states the various points he had tried to bring out in the play.

After leaving the University, he says, Ivanov had settled down on his country estate with all sorts of ambitious plans. He was going to help the peasants, to start advanced schools and introduce a rational agricultural system. Before he got very far with all this he became tired and disillusioned, and soon reached the state of romanticizing his past, convincing himself that his early achievements were heroic—though in fact they did not amount to very much. According to Chekhov this was very typical of Russian intellectuals in Ivanov's position:

'There's hardly a single Russian landowner or University man who doesn't brag about his past. The present is always worse than the past. Why? Because Russian excitability has one specific feature: it quickly gives way to fatigue. In the heat of the moment, before he's hardly left his school bench, a man picks up a load he can't carry, takes up schools, the peasant and rational agriculture ... makes speeches, writes to Ministers, battles with evil, applauds good, falls in love not simply or any old how—it must be a blue stocking or a neurotic or a Jewess or even a prostitute, whom he rescues, and so on and so forth ... But he's hardly reached the age of thirty to thirty-five when he starts feeling fatigue and boredom. He hasn't even grown a respectable pair of moustaches, but he's already saying authoritatively "Don't you marry, old chap. ... Learn from my experience".'

Particularly characteristic of Ivanov's general attitude, according to Chekhov is one piece of advice he gives to Doctor Lvov in the first act of the play: 'Don't you marry Jewesses or neurotics or blue stockings, but choose something ordinary and greyish, without bright colours and superfluous noises. In general construct your life in a stereotyped way. The more grey and monotonous the background the better. Shut yourself up in your shell and carry out the small task which God has given you.'

It is fortunate that Chekhov stated so clearly what he was trying to achieve with *Ivanov*, and made it plain that he aimed at nothing more than the accurate presentation of a characteristic contemporary type, for otherwise speculation about his intentions might well have gone on to this day. Even with his explanation there remains something disquieting and unsettling about the play, qualities which it shares with a number of important stories written about the same period. These have one thing in common—they convey, with almost unbearable vividness, a condition of mental or physical ill-health. Professor Elton in his Taylorian Lecture on Chekhov, delivered at Oxford in 1929, found an admirable phrase to cover these works. He called them 'clinical studies', and said that in them it was hard to acquit Chekhov 'of feeling, and of giving, less the pleasure of a work of art than of a perfect surgical operation'. The point had already been argued at greater length by Ovsyaniko-Kulikovsky in his *History of the Russian Intelligentsia*. He claims that Chekhov looked on Ivanov with so much sympathy because he regarded him as a sick man. Ivanov is a 'neurasthenic' and the play a 'medical' tragedy; it is a diagnosis in literary form, such as Chekhov, being a doctor, was particularly fitted to produce. *Ivanov* was not the first of these, for in *Typhus* Chekhov had given an account of the mental symptoms attending the onset of disease, and his medical knowledge, combined with his genius for conveying *nastroenie*, had enabled him to make the description a very convincing one. In *The Party* he had exploited a different department of medicine with a study of the mood aroused by his heroine by her pregnancy. Chekhov's aim was to be scrupulously accurate in presenting these sensations, and it was very gratifying to him when his accuracy was confirmed. 'With my *Party* I have satisfied the ladies,' he told Suvorin, "Wherever I go they sing my praises. Really, it's not a bad thing to be a doctor and understand what you're writing about. Ladies say I have given a faithful picture of childbirth.'

Typhus and *The Party* involve mental sensations with a definite physical cause, but in *A Nervous Breakdown*—as in *Ivanov*—a more psychological form of malaise is presented. This story, again rich in the distinctive Chekhov *nastroenie*, describes with uncanny sincerity and power the effect of a visit to some Moscow brothels on a sensitive young man, who was so upset that he fell ill on his return. The most notable of all the 'clinical studies', which followed in 1889, was *A Dreary Story* —generally regarded as Chekhov's most important single achievement of the 'eighties. It is one of his longest stories, and takes the form of memoirs written by an elderly professor of medicine.

At the time of writing his story Chekhov's Professor has behind him a brilliant academic career, which has made his name famous throughout Russia.

'But the bearer of that name—that is I myself,' he complains, 'present to the world a man of sixty-two with a bald head, false teeth and an incurable twitch. I am every bit as dull and ugly as my name is brilliant and attractive. My head and hands tremble with weakness. My neck, like that of a certain heroine in Turgenev, resembles the handle of a double-bass. My chest is sunken and my back narrow. When I speak or read my mouth twists to one side. When I smile my whole face is covered with the death-like wrinkles of an old man.'

The Professor gives a full description of his family life and university work, both of which have become a source of exasperation to him. His wife had once been beautiful and he had been in love with her during most of his married life. Now she merely irritates him with her social pretensions and petty complaints about money. He used to love his daughter when she was a little girl. Now he cannot stand the way she screws up her eyes when there are men in the room. He is driven to distraction by the presence of her unsympathetic suitor in his house, and by the important air with which his wife greets this worthless young man. What right has he to take a regular place at the family table? And the meals! Before the Professor became an 'Excellency' and the Dean of a Faculty he had simple wholesome food, and enjoyed his family's company at meal-times. Now everything is spoilt by his wife's desire to keep up her station.

His work at the University arouses in him the same weary irritation. His students are stupid, his colleagues unimaginative. He used to enjoy giving lectures, but now

'through sleeplessness, and the result of an intense strugle with growing feebleness, something strange is happening to me. In the middle of a lecture tears suddenly rise to my throat, my eyes begin to itch, and I feel a passionate hysterical desire to stretch forward my arms and complain aloud. I want to shout out in a loud voice that fate has condemned me, a famous man, to capital punishment, and that in a year or two someone else will be holding forth in this auditorium.'

The Professor knows that he is a sick man who will very shortly die; but it is not the thought of death which causes his unhappiness. As he argues himself, he can look back with pride on a happy family life and a distinguished career. All that is necessary is to reconcile himself with the idea of death and to accept it with quietness and dignity. This is rendered impossible by a discovery which he has recently made about himself, and which is the chief source of his misery—his lack, as he phrases it himself, of a 'general idea'. By this he means some comprehensive faith, whether philosophical or religious, which would give meaning to life and satisfy him that it had some purpose. Chekhov develops the tragedy of his Professor's aimlessness with the most profound feeling, in such a way that a reading of *A Dreary Story* cannot fail to be deeply moving.

This tragedy is given its most poignant expression in the scene which ends the story. More than anyone else in the world the Professor loves his ward, Katya. His attachment to her has persisted long after his own wife and daughter have ceased to arouse in him anything but irritation. Katya's is a long and complicated history. Her great passion was the stage, and she had made an unsuccessful attempt to become an actress. After her failure she lost all interest in life, and fell a victim to the same sort of defeatism as had attacked the Professor. Her case is all the more pathetic because, unlike him, she is young and physically healthy. Her condition too is to be interpreted as caused by the 'lack of a general idea'. Not realizing that the Professor, so much older and wiser than she, knows just as little about how or why one should live, she turns to him for help.

' "Help me," she sobbed, seizing me by the hand and kissing it, "You are my father, my old friend. You are intelligent, educated, have lived a long time. You have been a teacher! Tell me; what am I to do?" "Honestly, Katya, I don't know." I was embarrassed and confused, touched by her weeping, and could hardly stand upright. "Let's have lunch, Katya," I said with a forced smile. ... I looked at her and felt ashamed that I was happier than she. It was only just before my death, in the evening of my life, that I had noticed in myself the absence of what my philosopher-colleagues call a "general idea", whereas, she, poor girl, had known and would know no refuge all her life.'

Almost as soon as *A Dreary Story* was written people began to feel that the old professor was to be identified in some way with Chekhov himself. This idea did not appeal to Chekhov, who wrote to Suvorin: 'When I offer you the thoughts of my Professor, take me at my word, and don't go looking in them for Chekhov's thoughts.' This wish is one which Chekhov's critics have very rightly not respected. He obviously did project into *A Dreary Story* many of his own reflections on life, in spite of the unmistakable contrast between the tired old man and himself, young and vigorous, with his main achievements still before him. It is quite clear at any rate that the Professor's chief problem was very much Chekhov's own—the lack of any co-ordinating faith (or 'general idea') which could give a meaning to the whole of life. Like Chekhov the old man had a firm belief in science. 'Just as twenty or thirty years ago,' he says, 'so now, just before my death, I am interested only in science'.

Like Chekhov too he found that a belief in science was not enough on its own to qualify as a 'general idea'.

It will be remembered that Chekhov himself freely admitted that he had no definite outlook and conceded that its absence could be very distressing when he told Suvorin 'it has long been known that a reasoned life without a definite outlook is not a life, but a burden and a horror'. This remark, which might almost be taken as a text for *A Dreary Story*, suggests that Chekhov had moods when he was not far from the general position of philosophical despair expressed by his professor. There is no reason to believe that he was very often in this almost suicidal state of mind, but at any rate he understood it sufficiently well to convey it with almost intolerable conviction. Clearly he was looking for a 'general idea' of his own—a search which was to contribute some of the most interesting chapters in his later development.

VII

THE 'CHEKHOV LEGEND'

THE prominent position occupied by 'clinical studies' in Chekhov's writings of the late 'eighties has contributed to a distortion of his reputation from which it has hardly recovered even today. These studies impressed many people as the work of one obsessed with the futility of life, and however much Chekhov might disclaim any connection between himself and his characters, it was natural that he should begin to acquire the reputation of a pessimist.

This raises a problem which has been discussed almost *ad nauseam*. Complaints of Chekhov's pessimism began in Russia during the 'eighties, simultaneously with complaints about his lack of a 'tendency'—indeed, the two qualities were usually regarded as interdependent. Skabichevsky stated a point of view typical of many other contemporary critics when he said 'it is vain to look in Chekhov's works for bright and pleasing features or comforting prospects'. A later interpreter, the philosopher Shestov, went even farther, claiming that Chekhov was only interested in people who had lost all hope. *Ivanov* and *A Dreary Story* impressed him as the most autobiographical of all Chekhov's works. 'In them almost every line is a sob, and it is difficult to believe that nothing more than a contemplation of other people's woes could make a man sob like that.' Shestov's essay (of great interest to students of Chekhov's reputation) has been translated into English, and may have contributed to the over-emphasis on Chekhov's pessimism of which English people have sometimes been accused in Russia. There is said to exist, both in England and elsewhere, a 'legend', according to which dreary resignation and melancholy are the qualities most characteristic of Chekhov.

This conception has not appealed to many of those best acquainted with Chekhov's life and work. Soon after his death protests against the 'Chekhov legend' began to appear. Ovsyaniko-Kulikovsky, writing in 1911, gave the credit for overthrowing the legend to a writer called Batyushkov, whose book on Chekhov was published in 1906, and added that his own studies had convinced him that Chekhov never was a real pessimist: 'Behind the apparent dispassionateness of his presentations lay the deep distress of an optimist, whose best feelings were offended at every step by Russian conditions, but whose hopes and happy prognoses even they could not shatter.' This is an early statement of an idea which has since been repeated innumerable times—that the depressing elements in Chekhov's work were something inherent in the society he described rather than in himself.

The amount of print devoted to refuting the 'Chekhov legend' since this opinion was stated shows at least that it is an idea which dies hard. Other champions of Chekhov's optimism were less restrained than Ovsyaniko-Kulikovsky. An essay of 1914 by Ivan Bunin suggests that many of them had already gone to the other extreme, and had become as tiresome in their own way as those who were always insisting on the opposite view. Though the more exuberant exponents of Chekhov's optimism have damaged their case by over-stating it, their interpretation seems to correspond more closely to the facts than the 'legend'. Chekhov's optimism is stressed by many responsible Soviet critics, and an essay by one of them, Korney Chukovsky, translated recently into English, must already have done something to correct the curious picture of Chekhov drawn by Shestov. There is general agreement in Russia today that Chekhov was an optimist, both in his writings and in his personal life, and this view has the important support of Chekhov himself. There was nothing which he more resented than the accusation of pessimism—in fact he often professed himself unable to understand how he could give this impression.

Chekhov's personal life does very little to bear out the 'legend'. The quality that most impressed those who knew him was a zest for living which even periods of serious illness could not remove. Though perhaps not all his friends would have gone as far as Stanislavsky, who called him 'the greatest optimist I have ever met', everyone thought of him as a person who enjoyed life. The Soviet critic Derman speaks of his fresh and active interest in everything he saw.

'The world of his impressions was extraordinarily wide. Life unfolded itself before his incomparably observant gaze with a richness which an ordinary person cannot imagine. It would be hard to indicate any sphere which lacked interest for Chekhov. Only children—and then in a most limited range— receive impressions as freshly as he. When you read his letters, written from places where the most simple life and the most ordinary natural surroundings passed before his eyes—in some places like the Psyol, or Babkino—you immediately catch that characteristic note of childlike freshness which is found "when all life's impressions are new".'

Nobody who has caught the flavour of Chekhov's life from his letters, or the memoirs of other people, is likely to find this statement exaggerated.

It is not really possible to maintain, however, that the cheerful elements in Chekhov's character were fully reflected in all his writings. The degree of pessimism in his work did of course vary considerably from phase to phase. *Antosha Chekhonte*, whatever his faults, was never likely to be charged with spreading gloom. Chekhov's most pessimistic period was undoubtedly the one which succeeded this and ended with his journey to Sakhalin in 1890. The abruptness of the change had been emphasized by some stories of 1885 published in *The Petersburg Gazette*, the first really definite sign of his retreat from light-hearted humour. Since then a note of sadness and defeatism had often been an important element in the kind of *nastroenie* he chose to represent. The sadness of some stories, such as *The Kiss*, seems not to produce a very pessimistic impression—on the contrary, the effect is somehow exhilarating. However, the 'clinical studies' unquestionably have depressed many readers, and if all Chekhov's work was like *A Dreary Story* the legend would possess more basis in fact that it actually has. Even in the late 'eighties, however, he did not concentrate entirely on 'clinical studies', but also produced *The Steppe* and a number of light-hearted stage farces, not yet mentioned—works which were not likely to strike anyone as gloomy. In the 'nineties he proceeded to a phase in which he was less disposed to analyse morbid states of mind, having ceased to be interested (as he himself announced) in presenting pathological subjects.

It is surprising to see how many people have been prepared to answer with an unqualified 'yes' or 'no' the question 'Was Chekhov a pessimist?' Perhaps the truth is that readers have usually reacted to his work as they do to life itself, which it reproduces with such amazing accuracy. If, as has been suggested, the Slav temperament lends itself to unalloyed optimism or pessimism, this would explain why two such opposite views of Chekhov have been able to co-exist in Russia, pessimists regarding him as pessimistic, and optimists as optimistic. Both sides, as represented in criticism, often seem to be revealing more about their own slant on life than about Chekhov's. It has already been noted that Chekhov would rather have seen himself summed up as an optimist than as a pessimist, but he would certainly have preferred not to be summed up at all.

VIII

THE THEATRE, THE NOVEL AND THE DEATH OF NICHOLAS

CHEKHOV'S visits to the Taganrog theatre as a boy had given him an interest which lasted all his life, and it was natural that he should think of writing for the stage quite early in his career. His first surviving attempt is the juvenile play sometimes called *Platonov*, part of which may even have been written when he was at school. It was not published during his lifetime and his one attempt to have it put on met with a rebuff, its length alone being enough to disqualify it for the stage. Chekhov left it among his papers and probably forgot about it; its defects are so obvious that he would certainly have been horrified to know that it has been published posthumously. His next effort deserved more success than it achieved, and took place in 1885, when he amused himself by making a one-act play out of his own story *Autumn*. The play was called *On the High Road*, and it too was neither staged nor published during Chekhov's lifetime. It fell foul of the censor, who described it as 'gloomy and dirty'. The chief reason for the censor's objection seems to have been that Chekhov depicted a member of the upper classes as a dipsomaniac. In the following year Chekhov wrote a short comic monologue, *On the Harmfulness of Tobacco*. He cannot have thought very much of this, for he not only refused to include it in his Complete Edition, but wrote another sketch with the same title in 1902. It is not clear whether the original sketch was ever performed, but it was reprinted several times in the 'eighties.

The years 1887-90 saw a much greater concentration on plays. Though Chekhov's dramatic achievements during this period are unimportant compared with those of the late 'nineties, when he emerged as one of the leading figures in the world theatre, they are not by any means insignificant, and they gave him a working knowledge of the stage which was to come in very useful later on.

The plays of 1887-90 fall into two groups which must be considered separately because they are so different in character. One group consists of five one-act sketches. The first of these was a dramatic version of his own story *Kalkhas* which he called *The Swan Song*. This is a very short scene, and Chekhov boasted that he had written it in an hour and five minutes. It presents the reminiscences of an old comic actor who has fallen asleep in the theatre after a drinking party, and wakes up in a mood of sentimental self-pity. The other four sketches differ from *The Swan Song* because they are uproariously farcical. They are *The Bear, The Proposal, An Unwilling Martyr* and *The Wedding*. With these must be included a one-act play in the same style, written in 1891—*The Anniversary*—the last of Chekhov's short stage farces, apart from the new version of *On the Harmfulness of Tobacco*. Chekhov did not attach very much importance to these 'vaudevilles' as he called them, and they do not belong to the important part of his achievement as a dramatist. They bear more or less the same relation to his long and serious plays as the Little Stories do to the serious stories. Chekhov often spoke of them in a deprecating tone. 'I've managed to write a stupid vaudeville, which, thanks to the fact that it is stupid, is enjoying surprising success,' he said of *The Bear*, and he described *The Proposal* as a 'scabby little vaudeville, which I've scratched out for the privinces'.

People laughed so much when they saw these sketches on the stage that Chekhov must have known that they were not really

H

to be spoken of so disparagingly. The most outrageous things happen, such as the challenging of a woman to a duel, to which the more sombre critics objected on the grounds of implausibility. The language is extremely colloquial, and includes frequent asides to the audience. The vaudevilles show how quickly Chekhov, with little experience of dramatic writing, had acquired a very good sense of the stage, and it is not surprising that, as he said of the reception of *The Bear*, 'the public is in the seventh heaven'. It was easy for Chekhov to write these short plays, because it was often only necessary to make a few minor alterations to one of his Little Stories, or to fuse the themes of several such stories, and the job was done. When he found how easy they were to write, and how successful they were, he realized that he had hit on a good way of making money. 'I'm being fed by my *Bear*,' he once remarked. On another occasion he told Suvorin 'When I've written myself out I'm going to write vaudevilles and live on them. I think I could write about a hundred of them every year. Vaudeville subjects gush out of me like oil from the wells of Baku.'

The vaudevilles provide one of the few recorded instances of any appreciation of Chekhov's literary work by his father, who returned home delighted from a Moscow performance of *The Bear*, and said 'What a wonderful thing you've written, Anton.' Most people who have seen Chekhov's farces share his father's enthusiasm. They are among the funniest things ever written for the theatre. However, it is the more serious dramatic work of the same period—the two four-act plays *Ivanov* and *The Wood Demon* which represent Chekhov's most important contributions to the stage during the 'eighties.

Ivanov was written as the result of a conversation between Chekhov and a certain Korsch, who owned a theatre in Moscow. Korsch's terms were satisfactory, and Chekhov reckoned that he could make between 600 and 1,000 roubles on the deal —which was very good, considering that he wrote the play in a fortnight. Korsch, who probably knew Chekhov as a comic writer, may have been surprised when he received *Ivanov*, but both he and the actors expressed themselves well-satisfied. Chekhov was determined to have the play acted according to his own ideas, and regularly attended rehearsals. The actors were rather a scratch team. Davydov, who took the title role, was experienced, and could be depended on to give a good performance, but some of the others were careless about learning their parts, and when the play was first performed, on November 19, 1887, many of them impressed Chekhov as inadequate. The 'best men' in the wedding scene in the last act were drunk, and many of the other actors said their lines 'with the help of the prompter and the inspiration of the moment'. Chekhov, who was painfully sensitive to the success of his play, suffered some anxious and unhappy moments during the performance. Nobody could pretend that *Ivanov* had a tame reception. The author was called on to the stage as early as the end of the second act, a thing which had never happened before in Korsch's theatre. There was unrestrained applause both for him and for the actors, and there was almost equally unrestrained hissing. By the end of the play the theatre presented a tumultuous scene, according to Michael Chekhov who says that a fight started up between approvers and disapprovers. The performance left Chekhov with very mixed feelings and he was already beginning to wish he had never written *Ivanov*.

As will be remembered, he was to express this wish many times during the next two years. As soon as he saw his play on the stage he insisted on making some alterations, a process which was repeated almost interminably, so that the final version was very different from that given in Korsch's theatre. An important episode in the history of *Ivanov* was its first performance on the Petersburg stage in the Alexandrine Theatre on January 31, 1889. This was quite a triumph for Chekhov. The play was widely and favourably reviewed by a large number of dramatic critics, and he began to feel that his work had not been altogether wasted.

The writing of his next long play, *The Wood Demon*, occupied Chekhov's thoughts a great deal during 1889. He dropped it and took it up again several times, and it was finally produced in a Moscow theatre on December 27 in that year. It was badly received. Nearly all the dramatic critics were hostile, and accused Chekhov of mechanically reproducing an ordinary and undistinguished portion of everyday life. As this criticism suggests, he was already feeling his way towards the new dramatic technique which he developed with such success in the late 'nineties, but which was too unfamiliar to be immediately understood. It was obvious to him that *The Wood Demon* would not do in its present form, and it eventually re-emerged, after a number of radical alterations had been made, as *Uncle Vanya*. This seemed to Chekhov to supersede the earlier play, which he refused to have reprinted or revived. When someone approached him in 1900 with the idea of producing *The Wood Demon*, he still felt strongly enough about it to refuse, saying that he hated the play and wanted to forget about it.

His experience with *Ivanov* had taught Chekhov that plays could not be turned out by simply sitting at one's desk. Writing for the theatre was a craft that could only be learnt in the theatre itself. Actors and producers grew accustomed to his presence at rehearsals, and soon realized that, in spite of his diffidence and shyness, he had a definite idea of how things should be done. Though he had the knack of making his points without offending them, he was usually unable to get things entirely to his liking. The conventions and traditions of the Russian stage increasingly impressed him as mistaken, and he had to wait for the theatrical revolution accomplished by the Moscow Art Theatre some ten years later before he could begin to feel satisfied.

Chekhov took part in the social life of the theatre as well, and when rehearsals or performances were over was often involved in a drinking party in some Moscow or Petersburg restaurant. During the summer of 1889 he happened to spend a few weeks in Odessa at a time when the Moscow Little Theatre company was on tour. Here too there were the usual rounds of tea, wine, vodka, songs, gossip and excited conversation with the actors and actresses. Though he thoroughly appreciated the more Bohemian side of theatrical life, Chekhov was beginning to make firm friends with such established actors as Svobodin and Lensky, who led irreproachable family lives at variance with the traditional conception of their profession. It was Madame Lensky who embarked on the somewhat unpromising role of match-maker between Chekhov and an attractive young actress called Panova, whom he met during his stay in Odessa. However, Chekhov proved, in the words of his brother Michael 'very difficult to cope with in this respect', and the plan had to be abandoned. Actors and actresses, many of them with names known to all Russia, were frequent and welcome guests in the Chekhovs' Moscow house, where they would often entertain the company with a rendering of their parts in current plays, or with improvised scenes such as had long been a favourite entertainment of the family.

The composer Tchaikovsky was one of the many interesting and important figures in Russian life whom Chekhov met during these years. Chekhov had often heard his friends at Babkino talk about Tchaikovsky, and one day the composer came to call on him; he brought with him a present—a signed photograph with the inscription: *To A. P. Chekhov from an ardent admirer, October 14, 1889.* The conversation naturally turned to music and literature, and Tchaikovsky suggested that Chekhov might care to supply a libretto for an opera, *Bela,* to be based on Lermontov's novel, *A Hero of our Time.* It is not known how Chekhov reacted to this proposal, but the opera was never written.

Chekhov was so taken up by the theatre in 1889 that he only produced two stories. He was also engaged on other long and serious work—the writing of a novel. It was almost inevitable that a writer of his standing should now make a serious attempt on what was to many Russians the most important of all literary forms. At first the work seemed to be going well. He was soon planning to take the completed novel to Petersburg in the autumn, and 'hold it up for auction' at not less than 250 roubles a sheet. On the proceeds he said he intended to enjoy himself with French girls in Paris and Georgian girls in Georgia. Before long, however, these prophecies began to seem premature, and he was announcing that the novel would not be ready for two or three years. In fact it never appeared, though a lot of work was done, and there is some evidence of its contents. He told Suvorin that it was to be called *Stories from the Life of My Friends,* to consist of a series of separate stories, closely linked together by community of intrigues, ideas and characters. 'Each story will have a special title. Don't think the novel will consist of scraps. It will be a real novel ...' Chekhov's later 'trilogy' of stories—*The Man in a Case, Gooseberries* and *About Love*—written in 1898, does in fact answer to this description, and probably represents an adaptation of the material for his novel. This trilogy answers also to Chekhov's description of the novel to Pleshcheev, where he defines its 'framework': 'The absolute freedom of man, freedom from violence, freedom from prejudice, from ignorance, the devil, freedom from passions and so forth.' Suvorin remembered another plan for a novel, considered by Chekhov. It was to follow the scheme of Gogol's *Dead Souls,* where the hero travels all over Russia, or it would describe the adventures of a man who lived for a whole century, and took part in all the important events of his age.

The form of the novel seems to have been unsuited to Chekhov, who complained that he could 'hardly cope with the technique', and made 'a mass of crude mistakes'. In fact he has left no work of novel length, apart from the early *Shooting Party*, which is not of serious literary merit. Moreover, many of Chekhov's critics complain that his longer stories, such as *My Life* and *Three Years*, which approach the length of a short novel, do not show his literary art at its best, though this is certainly not an opinion to which all Chekhov's readers would subscribe.

Disappointing as the failure of his novel must have been, Chekhov's position as a writer could not give him any serious cause for regret as he approached his thirtieth birthday in January 1890. Yet he continued to disparage his achievements, and to look forward to a big improvement in the future. 'I think that if I lived another forty years,' he wrote to Suvorin, 'and during all those forty years kept on reading, reading and reading; if I learned to write with talent—that is compactly—that in forty years' time I would blaze out at all of you from such a big cannon that the heavens would shake.'

There were many nights during these years when he lay awake, unable to sleep for his cruel and agonizing cough. At such times he must have realized that he would not be granted the forty years so necessary to him, and he must have felt that he would have to hurry if he was to say all that he had to say.

Though it was obvious that Chekhov's health was further deteriorating towards the end of the 'eighties, it was his brother Nicholas who gave most cause for alarm at this time. In the summer of 1889 he died from tuberculosis. Chekhov did everything in his power to comfort and relieve Nicholas during his last illness. He had always been very fond of him and this death, the first he had known in his family, shook him very badly indeed. When the funeral was over he found himself in a listless and unhappy state of mind. Unable to work, he toyed with the idea of travel. At one moment he would decide to take his sister to the Caucasus; then he would change his mind and plan to join Suvorin in the Tyrol or at Biarritz. He actually started out for Europe, but before he had left Russia turned back and spent a few weeks at Yalta. His profound depression was reflected in *A Dreary Story*, much of which was written shortly after Nicholas' death. When the story was finished he began to recover his spirits in the excitement of preparing for his journey to Sakhalin.

CHAPTER SIX

Sakhalin and Europe

I

PREPARATIONS FOR THE EXPEDITION

WHEN the news spread that Chekhov was planning to visit Sakhalin, his friends did not know what to think. The island, which lies off the Pacific coast of Siberia, was little more than a name to most Russians, to whom it was simply a place of deportation for criminals and political prisoners. Travelling to Sakhalin was a very different matter indeed from taking a summer trip to the Crimea or Caucasus, and the island was the last place in the world to attract a holidaymaker. The journey itself was bound to be a severe ordeal, not to be lightly undertaken even by a healthy passenger. As the Trans-Siberian railway had not yet been built Chekhov had the unenviable prospect of two months' travel under the most primitive conditions. He would have to spend at least half of this time in jolting, horse-drawn vehicles on what were said to be the worst roads in the world, and the route was known to be infested with escaped convicts, from whom no traveller's throat or purse was safe. It is not surprising that Chekhov's friends believed him to be joking when they heard of his intentions. However, his systematic preparations soon made it clear that he was perfectly serious.

Chekhov gave all sorts of different reasons for going to Sakhalin, but he would have been very impatient with any biographer who, after marshalling all his conflicting statements on the subject, accused him of inconsistency because they often contradict each other. He may not even have been sure in his own mind why he was going, but he certainly felt that it was the logical and inevitable thing for him to do at this stage of his life. To his friends he had to give definite reasons, if only to stop them asking more questions. Some of them were told that he was going because he needed a change of air. Chekhov had still not managed to reconcile himself with the literary world of Moscow and Petersburg. It fascinated him of course, but at the same time it repelled and disgusted him. All these clever people, who might have turned their gifts to some good end, and yet preferred a narcissistic contemplation of their own mental complexities! Instead of helping their readers to see the world as it is, and thus to improve it, they seemed to devote their main energies to retailing gossip and writing malicious reviews of each other's books. There were times when Chekhov wanted to run away, especially as he often felt equally disgusted with himself. It was in such a mood that he told Suvorin at the end of 1889: 'Sketches, feuilletons, stupidities, vaudevilles, Dreary Stories, masses of mistakes and incongruities, hundredweights of paper filled with writing, the Pushkin Prize—and all the time not a single line which has any serious literary importance in my own eyes.' Obviously he needed a complete holiday. He told Shcheglov that he was not going to Sakhalin for literary copy 'but simply so as to live for six months in a way in which I have never lived before'. 'Even if my journey is an empty piece of obstinate fancy,' he said to Suvorin, 'just think, and tell me—what shall I lose by going? Even if I get nothing out of it at all there are bound to be two or three days which I shall remember all my life with joy or grief.'

Chekhov usually played down the suggestion that he hoped to provide some useful service to the community by undertaking his expedition. As so many of his stories show, he believed that philanthropy, when you took a close look at it, was not such a simple thing as it seemed. However, he sometimes allowed this motive to emerge, and it certainly was one of the most important factors in persuading him to go. 'From the books which I have read and am reading,' he told Suvorin, 'it is clear that we have let millions of people rot in prison, have let them rot idly, without reasoning, barbarously. We have corrupted them, infected them with syphilis—and put all the blame on red-nosed prison overseers. In our day something is being done for the sick, but nothing for people in prison.'

Finally, Chekhov intended to use his Sakhalin experiences as a means of paying his 'debt to medicine'. He still felt rather guilty about not practising regularly as a doctor, and wanted to make amends by publishing material of serious scientific interest. The 'one or two hundred pages' which he hoped to produce after his visit were conceived as a contribution to sociology rather than to medicine, but they gave him an opportunity to undertake an assignment which had always appealed to him: to handle a research problem in a spirit of scientific inquiry. It was in this spirit that he approached the formidable task of assembling and reading all the available printed material on Sakhalin. This work absorbed him to the exclusion of everything else during the early months of 1890. He paid a special visit to Petersburg for the purpose, and ransacked the libraries for information. Mariya Chekhov and some of her friends were set the task of copying out important extracts from the literature of the subject, and after Chekhov had returned to Moscow a succession of books and articles began to arrive from Suvorin, all of them containing information on Sakhalin. 'I have to be a geologist, a meteorologist and an ethnographer,' said Chekhov, and soon he was claiming that he had found out things which everybody ought to know under pain of forty lashes. He was working as hard as he had ever worked in his life. 'In my head and in my papers there is nothing except Sakhalin,' he said. 'It's a form of lunacy. *Mania Sakhalinosa*', and before long he was signing his letters '*Homo Sakhalinensis*'.

The planning of his expedition also took up a lot of his time and energies. Steps had to be taken to see that his family had an adequate supply of money during his absence. He had also to make elaborate arrangements for the reception of his mail, and notified his friends of various points along the route to which letters could be addressed. The time-table of his journey was one of the biggest headaches; so much depended on the date on which certain huge and far-distant Siberian rivers would cease to be ice-bound, for a large proportion of his travels was to be by steamer. Before leaving civilization he had to pay much attention to his choice of kit. Warm clothing was an essential. He bought an officer's leather greatcoat and a short fur coat. A revolver was essential for use against brigands, and he also took a knife 'for cutting sausages and tiger-hunting'. Unfortunately, having no experience as an explorer, he made some mistakes in stocking up. The heavy trunk in which he carried his gear was uncomfortable to sit on, and did not stand up to the severe jolting of thousands of miles on rough roads; it was soon replaced by a leather bag. Food turned out to be one of the major difficulties, and he later wished that he had taken more tea and tinned preserves.

II

THROUGH SIBERIA

HE set out towards the end of April. A number of friends accompanied him as far as Yaroslavl, where he was to pick up a Volga steamer. As he said good-bye he was presented with a bottle of cognac—to be drunk on the shore of the Pacific Ocean. On July 11 he arrived in Sakhalin, with almost three months of travelling behind him. His experiences had been fantastic, and he had already enjoyed many times over the 'two or three days which I shall remember all my life'. He kept up a running commentary on his journey in letters posted at various stages of the route, and supplemented by a short series of articles for *New Time* under the title *From Siberia*. The dominating feature of his journey was a constant struggle with the elements and with unco-operative human beings. It was the atrocious Siberian roads which placed the severest strain on his patience, and his carriage often got stuck 'like a fly in jam' in thick and gluey morasses.

The situation was complicated by the unpredictable behaviour of the Siberian rivers, which were liable to flood the countryside without warning, often necessitating a sudden change of plan. Horses would have to be unhitched, and led through miniature lakes. Ferrymen had to be cajoled, bribed or browbeaten into crossing vast and swollen torrents, often in the foulest of weather. There was no lack of danger. Chekhov was nearly drowned while crossing the Tom, and narrowly escaped injury in the region of Tyumen, when a succession of three *troykas*, their drivers asleep at the reins, careered into his carriage. Siberian coachmen and ferrymen had no equals in the art of swearing. 'May you get an ulcer in your mouth!' is quoted by Chekhov as the only printable item in their catalogue of oaths. He found that he had to develop a rough tongue himself if he was to make any progress; his natural mildness would not have got him very far in Siberia. A sense of urgency rarely left him during the journey, for a series of steamer connections had to be made, with considerable loss of time to be expected if they were missed. All Chekhov's ingenuity and endurance were needed to get him forward. In order not to waste time he would often travel all night, humped in the bottom of his carriage in his fur coat. It was always a relief when he arrived

at some big town like Tomsk or Irkutsk, where it was possible
to change his filthy clothes, have a bath and again feel 'like a
European'. Fortunately his health was standing up to the journey better than might have been expected, and weeks in the
open air seemed to have a beneficial effect on his cough.

Though he was usually tired, with an aching back and
frozen feet, Chekhov never lost his interest in human behaviour.
The Siberian peasants impressed him as hard-working and
honest. There was no danger of robbery, and all the stories
he had heard about brigands turned out to be greatly exaggerated; he even found that he could leave his luggage in
the yard all night without anyone touching it. The peasant huts
were clean and whitewashed, with wooden floors, and did not
smell like a Russian peasant cottage. However, much of what
he saw was disquieting. He would pass a gang of convicts, clank-
ing their fetters as they went to work, and there were many
exiles, who were not serving prison sentences, but were unhappy at having to live in this cold and strange country. In the
less inclement regions some of these exiles had settled down
fairly contentedly. Chekhov noted with approval a family of
Poles who might be expected to temper the ugliness of the
Siberian population by breeding dark hair and soft features, far
away from their motherland. The Jews lived just like any
other peasants, in contrast with Russia, where they were sometimes disliked and ill-treated. Chekhov's observations on Siberian life led him to the general conclusion: 'How rich Russia is
in good people!'

Chekhov had much to say about the astounding scenery
through which he passed. The River Enisey was a powerful
and furious giant, in comparison with which even the Volga
looked tame. Soon after the Enisey began the *tayga*, the
boundless Siberian forest tract, which aroused in him a feeling
of awe, and beside which the statement 'Man is the Lord of
Creation' sounded feeble and false. Interludes of travel by
water formed the most serene and enjoyable part of his journey.
With Lake Baikal, which he crossed by steamer, he was delighted, and it was here, he said, that Siberian poetry began—
hitherto everything had been prose. The turquoise-coloured water
was amazingly clear—in parts you could look down into it a
whole mile. The mountain scenery was superb and Chekhov
described it as a mixture of Switzerland, the Don country and
Finland. The most pleasant part of the whole journey were the

twelve days on the river Amur. He now had the most difficult stage well behind him, the weather was warmer, and his spirits were high. As he stood on deck, with Russia to the left of him, and China only three furlongs away to the right, he felt at peace with himself. It would be a delightful place to settle down, he reflected. What particularly pleased him was the freedom with which people conversed in these parts. Since they were already in Siberia they had no cause to fear the police—there was no other place for them to be exiled to, and they happily discussed politics without restraint. Moreover, it was an understood thing that no one should report an escaping convict to the police. He was quite at liberty to travel openly by steamer, without fear that anyone would give him away. Chekhov could not help contrasting this free and easy atmosphere with the suspicion and stuffiness of European Russia. Meanwhile time was passing quickly. Before long he had drunk his bottle of cognac on the Pacific shore, and had telegraphed the news of his arrival in Sakhalin to his family.

III

ON THE ISLAND AND THE JOURNEY HOME

SIBERIA had of course long been a place of exile for criminals and political offenders, but Sakhalin was a comparatively new addition to the Russian penal system. The colonization of the island had begun in the 1860s, and the intention was to form a self-supporting agricultural community of convicts. By the time of Chekhov's visit this aim had been only partly achieved, for conditions made successful farming impossible, and the settlement was still being heavily subsidized by the state. Sakhalin had a wretched climate, particularly in its northern half; the sun rarely shone, and crops were sparse and unpredictable. There was plenty of timber and a few coal mines, the products of which did little to redress the economic balance. Most of the work on Sakhalin from the felling and hauling of timber to the unloading of ships, was done by convict labour. The convicts fell into various classes. On the one hand there were old lags, often with numerous escapes to their credit, and these were confined to prison, sometimes in chains. At the other end of the scale was a handful of free settlers, usually ex-convicts who had served their sentence and had decided to remain on the island. In between were various categories of prisoners and exiles, with varying degrees of privilege and freedom. Only a small number were confined to prison; the majority lived in crude huts, and farmed a miserable scrap of land or went to work in the mines. A large number were married, and marriage was one of the most interesting social institutions on Sakhalin.

The arrival of a new batch of female prisoners was always an exciting event. The women were confined to barracks in their port of disembarkation while word went round the island to such convicts as had managed, by bribery or intrigue, to get themselves put on the list for a wife. Decking themselves out in their gayest clothes these 'suitors', followed by the jeers of their friends, would make a pilgrimage to the barracks, where they were permitted to inspect the women. The process was embarrassing for both sides. The women sat round on bunks, with lowered eyes, while the men wandered around trying to pick out likely-looking partners. Deals were swiftly concluded, once conversation had started, and thus, for a large number of prisoners, family life helped to relieve the miseries of Sakhalin. This was particularly so when there were children, as there usually were, for the birth-rate on the island was high. Chekhov paid a tribute to the moral influence which children exercised on their elders.

Chekhov certainly took his self-imposed duties on Sakhalin very seriously He knew that he had only a few months at his disposal, and decided that he must get up at five o'clock every morning in order to have as long a working day as possible. During his stay he accomplished the incredible feat of conducting a census of the entire convict population. The point of this was not so much that it would provide him with statistical information unobtainable elsewhere, as that it would give him the opportunity to meet as wide a range of people as possible. He made his way into every home, carrying cards on which he had arranged for a *pro forma* to be printed locally, and accompanied by a convict guide, who carried a bottle of ink. He entered the particulars he required, and eventually collected about ten thousand cards. Much of what he discovered was horrible; the filth, poverty and hunger on Sakhalin exceeded even what he had been led to expect. It was distressing to see many of the children growing up without proper care, often ignorant of their parents' identity, and with no schooling. The huts in which most people lived were dirty and verminous, their food unhealthy and repulsive. They talked freely to Chekhov, but no doubt many of them thought of him as just another official filling up forms which would be filed and forgotten.

Chekhov was given better facilities than he had expected. General Kononovich, who commanded the island, seemed to be as humane and kind-hearted a man as one was likely to find in his position, and was apparently prepared to help. Only one reservation was made, and that an important one: Chekhov was not allowed to come into contact with political prisoners. As his researches proceeded he began to find examples of cruelty of which the General himself was apparently content to remain in ignorance. There was no systematic maltreatment of the convicts, but much severe hardship was inflicted as the result of bad administration and the brutality of petty tyrants. The warders, mostly rejects from military units stationed in Siberia, were the lowest specimens of humanity, usually entirely uneducated and unimaginative. Chekhov noted that the treatment of prisoners was arbitrary. One man might have a reasonably easy time, whereas another, who chanced to fall foul of some vindictive minor official, might find himself flogged or shackled, without any means of redress.

Chekhov was repeatedly struck by the fact that nothing whatever was done, or even contemplated, which might lead to the moral rehabilitation of the prisoners, and fit them to resume normal life once their sentences had expired. None of the prison officials seemed to be conscious that such a thing was desirable, and there were in any case two factors which impressed Chekhov as supremely horrible, and which made the re-education of the prisoners a hopeless task. These were the length of the sentences and the floggings. Many of the sentences were for life imprisonment, so that the prisoner had nothing left to live for except the prospect of escape. The floggings were unspeakably cruel. An area commander had the right to award a hundred lashes. Chekhov forced himself to witness such a flogging, and it made him feel sick. He had to leave the scene in the middle, and for three or four nights afterwards he was tormented by nightmares.

Nearly every prisoner attempted to escape at one time or another, in spite of the savagery with which such attempts were punished. During the winter months it was possible to walk across the ice to the mainland, and during the summer it was fairly easy to get across in a boat. Escape into the centre of the island was also common. Most of the escapees were picked up by soldiers, or perished from exposure and hunger. However, a large number did get away, and some were said to have reached America, either having been picked up by American whalers, or having somehow made their way to Japan. Deluded and distracted by their miseries, many prisoners made half-hearted and unorganized attempts which could only lead to their detection and punishment. Some entered into league with their warders to stage a mock break-out. The warders would bring them back, which entitled him to a reward of three roubles per escapee, this sum then being distributed among the conspirators at a prearranged tariff.

Towards the end of his stay, tired out by long hours and overwork, and depressed by the sight of so much pointless suffering, Chekhov began to long to get away. He left by the steamer *Petersburg* on October 13th, and before long his melancholy had been dispelled by an abundance of new sights and experiences. Owing to a cholera epidemic the *Petersburg* was unable to put in at Japan, as planned. A short stay in Hong Kong gave him a taste of China, and he saw enough to praise British colonial administration at the expense of Russian. In the China Sea a tremendous storm arose, and the ship heeled over at such a dangerous angle that the captain advised Chekhov to keep his revolver handy, so that if necessary he might save himself by suicide from death by drowning. The storm blew over, and the *Petersburg* was soon engaged on saving a French vessel in distress by towing it off a sandbank. In the Indian Ocean Chekhov arranged to bathe while the ship was in full career. He would dive off the prow and haul himself up on deck by a rope let down from the stern. These escapades, during one of which he found himself observed with interest by a shark, suggested some of the detail in the story *Gusev*, begun in Colombo. Ceylon was 'like paradise', and he travelled over it by train, lost in admiration of the palm trees and bronze-coloured women. He reached Moscow on December 9th, having travelled by way of Port Said, Constantinople and Odessa.

Reviewing his travels Chekhov decided that they had been a great success on all counts. 'I am so satiated and delighted,' he wrote, 'that I desire nothing more, and would not complain if I was seized by paralysis or carried off into the next world by dysentery.' He felt that his journey had brought about a salutary readjustment, and had enabled him to see things in true proportion: 'Before I went the publication of Tolstoy's *Kreutzer Sonata* was a tremendous event to me, but now it makes me laugh and seems pointless.'

IV

OTHER TRAVELS

THE Chekhovs had now left the house in which they had spent the last few years and were living in Little Dmitrovka Street, a comparatively aristocratic neighbourhood. Quarters here were still rather cramped, particularly when it turned out that Chekhov had invited a Mongolian priest, his companion on the voyage from Sakhalin, to take up residence, and had also brought with him several tame mongooses. Christmas was much less pleasant than usual this year. Chekhov was suffering from heart trouble, and after Sakhalin and the tropics Moscow life seemed 'so vulgar and boring that I am ready to bite'. His friends were growing tedious with their interminable questions about Sakhalin, and he hastened off in January to Petersburg, where these impositions were even more of a burden. 'I am surrounded by a thick atmosphere of ill-feeling,' he wrote. 'People give me dinner and sing tawdry dithyrambs in my honour, and all the time they are ready to eat me. Why? The devil only knows. If I were to shoot myself I should afford the greatest pleasure to nine-tenths of my friends and admirers. All this is terribly stupid and boring. They're not human beings, but a sort of mildew.'

It was in this mood that Chekhov grasped at an invitation from Suvorin to join him and his son in a tour of Eastern Europe. This meant further delaying his literary work, and would obviously lead to additional expense, but Chekhov had become an incorrigible traveller. Besides, he realized that the journey would fill a big gap in his experiences. A first visit to Europe was always a time of importance for a Russian writer, and Chekhov must have felt his could be put off no longer. The journey lasted about six weeks, most of which were spent in Italy. The party first halted in Vienna, which made a tremendous impression on Chekhov, who said that he there realized for the first time that architecture was an art. His enthusiasm increased when he reached Venice, of which he spoke in terms of extravagant praise. Everything was delightful—the museums, the picture galleries and, above all, St Mark's Cathedral. The

weather was good, and Chekhov never tired of wandering down
the narrow alleys and gliding along the fabulous canals in a
gondola. No other Italian city made such an impression on
him, partly because a period of rainy weather set in, and
Chekhov found that Italy without the sun was like a man's
face in a mask. He paused in Florence and Rome (which he said
was 'like Kharkov') and then went on to Naples. Naples Bay
filled him with the proper degree of admiration, and reminded
him of Hong Kong. He paid a visit to Pompeii, followed by an
arduous scramble up Vesuvius. All this time he was worried by
the expenses he was incurring, and the loans he was forced to
make from Suvorin. Italy was a cheap country, and he could
have done the whole trip on his own for 300 roubles, but
the Suvorins as usual insisted on living in grand style, 'like
doges and cardinals', and before very long Chekhov's expenses
had run into four figures.

The weather was still bad when the party crossed over into
France, making a stay at Nice, followed by a visit to Monte
Carlo. Here Chekhov tried his luck at the Casino, where the
tense atmosphere and the piles of gold on the gaming tables
intrigued him. He and the younger Suvorin made a few trial
flutters, after which Chekhov convinced himself that he had
evolved an infallible 'system', with the result that he lost 900
roubles next day. All the same he had an exciting time, and did
not regret the loss. His first transports at the sight of European
civilization were giving way to a more critical mood. The railway trains were immeasurably inferior to the Russian; the
splendour of Monte Carlo reminded him of a luxurious water-
closet. His observations of contemporary French art convinced
him that Russian painters were more serious, and that Levitan
was head and shoulders above his French rivals. When the time
came for his return to Russia he quitted Western Europe without much regret. However, he had thoroughly enjoyed his
holiday, and was annoyed to hear of certain stories connected
with it which were being told in Russia when he got back. He
was said to have taken one bored look at the Piazza San Marco
in Venice, and to have remarked how nice it would be to lie
down in the grass somewhere in the countryside near Moscow.
Chekhov had said nothing of the sort, but he never tended to
express wild enthusiasm at anything he saw. What did people
expect him to do, he asked. Howl with delight, or break shop
windows?

I

Almost immediately on his return he joined his family at a
dacha near the town of Aleksin, about a hundred miles south
of Moscow. They were near the river Oka, with plenty of fishing, and the countryside was very much to Chekhov's liking. Unfortunately the *dacha* was too small for comfort, and before
very long they moved to a large eighteenth-century house at
Bogimovo, about six miles away. Chekhov was working very
hard, but this did not stop him from enjoying the various forms
of relaxation which made *dacha* life worth while. As usual guests
came and went. This year they included the beautiful Lika
Mizinova, on whom Levitan danced attendance. Suvorin made a
short stay, and there was a welcome visit from the youngest of
the Lintvarev sisters from Sumy. Chekhov found a relief from
his cares in mushroom-picking, and in fishing for carp and perch
in the pond. His one surviving mongoose had joined the party,
and was a centre of attraction, particularly on one walk when it
gave the company an expert exhibition of how to deal with a
snake. Remembering Monte Carlo, Chekhov installed a roulette
board, and acted as croupier; the maximum stake was a copeck,
and the profits were devoted to financing picnics.

His return to Moscow, which took place in September, emphasized his growing dislike of city life. He was continually
complaining of an 'absense of personal freedom'. His experiences
abroad had made him even more acutely conscious of the
restrictions which he had always detested in Russia. 'How
amazing to be able to read everything and say what you like,'
he had written from Vienna. Moscow seemed to hem him in.
'Oh, my friends, how bored I am,' he now wrote. 'If I'm a
doctor I need patients and a hospital. If I'm a writer I need to
live among the people, and not in Little Dmitrovka Street with
a mongoose. I need at least a small fragment of social and political life, if nothing more than a tiny fraction, but this life within four walls, without nature, without people, without a mother-
country, without health and appetite—it's not life at all.'

Lack of money seemed to be infringing on his freedom more
than ever before, and so far as his income from writing was
concerned he was living almost entirely on the past. Luckily
the various collections of his stories were already running into
several editions, and some of his plays continued to bring in
very welcome contributions. However, he had a large debt to
Suvorin as a result of his travels in Europe, and was constantly
finding himself without funds. He began to day-dream about

money. If only someone would leave him 200,000 roubles, so that he could retire to the country and read novels, and, above all, so that he could taste that personal freedom which he had come to prize above all things on earth. Lured by the attraction of sudden wealth he began to buy lottery tickets for himself and the family.

Money was all the more necessary to him now that he felt less inclined to ignore the troubles of others. In 1891 he began to be seriously engaged in charitable work. During the early part of the year he devoted much energy to arranging the dispatch of school books for the children on Sakhalin, but as winter came on his attention was attracted by disasters nearer home. A serious famine had broken out in many country districts of Russia. Chekhov helped to organize the production of a book of collected stories, to be sold in aid of the famine victims, and played a more direct part by starting a subscription together with his friend Egorov. Egorov was an official who lived in the heart of one of the famine areas, in the district of Nizhny Novgorod. Here the peasants were selling their horses at low prices in order to buy food, and it was obvious that without horses they would be unable to till the land during the following year, so that there was a prospect of an even worse famine to come. Egorov and Chekhov had decided to buy the horses, to feed them during the winter, and to return them to the peasants at ploughing time next year. Chekhov collected subscriptions in Moscow, and planned to help Egorov with his work on the spot. However, a severe attack of influenza confined him to the house during part of October and November, and he had to put off his visit to Nizhny Novgorod until the following year.

His failing health underlined yet another of the disadvantages of city life, and made him take active steps to effect a plan which had long lain at the back of his mind. 'If I don't move to the provinces,' he wrote, 'and if for some reason I don't succeed in buying a farm, I shall play the role of a great evil-doer in respect of my own health.' He realized that it was necessary to change radically his way of life, and intended to live for nine months of every year in the country. The remaining three months must be spent in Moscow and Petersburg, for he did not forget that he would have many literary and social contacts to keep up. His decision to move to the country shows how much his attitude had changed. Five years earlier he could not have contemplated leaving Moscow, but now, as his friends and family were beginning to notice, a life of strain and overwork was beginning to make him wish for rest and quiet. He continued to cultivate ignorance of his tubercular condition, but the unpalatable truth was forcing itself nearer to the level of his conscious mind. Knowing that there was something seriously wrong, he tried to explain it as the onset of old age, adding 'if it's not old age, then it's something worse'. He already feared that his health would never be fully restored, and felt that it was time he began to lead a more settled existence.

V

THE STORIES OF 1890-1891 AND *Sakhalin Island*

CHEKHOV meant what he said when he claimed that he was not going to Sakhalin for literary copy, and he might have made the same claim about his visit to Western Europe. It is characteristic of him that he made very little use in his later fiction of his strange and unusual experiences during these two years. They helped to contribute part of the background in less than half a dozen stories, and that is all. The fact was that ordinary Russian life, seen through his particularly penetrating eyes, provided him with as much strange and unusual material as he could digest.

Little need be said of the four stories written during 1890 and 1891. *The Horse-stealers* is the most outspoken, but not the most successful, of his fictional manifestos in favour of freedom, a subject on which he was to have more to say later in the decade. The story fully reflects his impatience with petty and conventional living; as has been remarked, it might well pass as the work of Gorky—which is enough to show that it is not one of Chekhov's more characteristic works. On the other hand *The Duel*, also written during this period, is characteristic, and is one of Chekhov's longest and most important stories. In the central character, Laevsky, Chekhov presents another 'clinical study', but with a rather significant difference. Laevsky had left Petersburg for a small Caucasian town on the Black Sea coast, with the idea of working on the land. Affected apparently by the Tolstoyan belief in 'simplification', he expected to derive moral uplift and happiness from the fulfilment of his vague, but strenuous programme. In order to help him in his labours, and deviating in this particular from Tolstoy's teaching, he ran away with another man's wife. When the story begins Laevsky and his mistress have been living in the Caucasian town for some time, but their ambitious programme does not at all look like being realized. Laevsky has found himself a sinecure in some government office, in which he occasionally appears to sign papers without reading them. He walks around the town in slippers, spends most of the day drinking and playing cards, and is heavily in debt. To make matters worse, he has fallen out of love with his mistress, and is preparing to desert her, though he knows quite well that she is completely dependent on him. She too is fast degenerating. As the only young and attractive woman in the place she takes great delight in the disturbing effect of her presence upon the men in Laevsky's circle. She wears flashy clothes, behaves in a provocative and flirtatious manner, and even embarks on a short-lived and nasty liaison with the local chief of police. Laevsky's flat is always untidy, with unwashed dishes and dead flies on the table.

Laevsky and his mistress are intensely disliked by a certain zoologist, Von Koren, a very different sort of person. He claims that they are corrupting the morals of the local inhabitants. Before Laevsky came they didn't gamble or drink vodka, but now these two diseases are sweeping the Black Sea coast as a result of his influence. Previously men lived with other people's wives secretly, but now Laevsky has lent the authority of an educated and cultivated man to the open flaunting of illicit unions. Von Koren says that he regards Laevsky as a noxious insect, which should be extirpated by society. Asked whether he would decree this extirpation if he was ever in a position to do so, he replies, 'my hand would not tremble'. Circumstances eventually do put him in such a position when he is involved in a duel with Laevsky, and only an unexpected interruption at the last moment prevents him from shooting down his enemy.

The Duel presents certain obvious parallels with *Ivanov*, notably the antagonism Laevsky-Von Koren, which reproduces the Ivanov-Lvov relationship in more convincing form. However, the end of the story provides an interesting contrast with the play. Ivanov, seeing no hope of escape, had put an end to his life, whereas Laevsky undergoes moral regeneration. He settles down with his mistress to a life of hard work, in the hope of paying off his numerous debts. Even Von Koren is impressed, and realizes that he has been too harsh. Accordingly *The Duel*, although it in some ways deserves to be regarded as a 'clinical study'—and one of the best examples of the type—does at any rate end on a comparatively optimistic note, and is thus symptomatic of a general trend in Chekhov's work which became more pronounced later in the 'nineties.

The Duel has not found favour with all Chekhov's critics, but many readers would agree with one of his friends, who wrote to him shortly after its publication: 'In spite of double-faced and only half-favourable reviews *The Duel* is the best thing you've written yet.' It is perhaps most remarkable for the sureness with which Chekhov handles character, and this applies as much to the minor characters as to the two protagonists. The story bears no trace of the impatience Chekhov felt while he was writing it. He did not want to write stories at all at this time, and only did so because he needed money; he would have preferred to spend all his time on the book which he was preparing about Sakhalin.

The writing of this gave him a lot of trouble, and it did not appear in print until 1893, when it began to be featured as a series of articles in the magazine *Russian Thought*. It had taken him several years to digest his material and to present it in a form which satisfied him. Further research in Petersburg was needed to reinforce some of his findings, and Chekhov was determined that his book should be a really authoritative scientific work. He spent some time struggling with this unfamiliar form of writing, and it was not easy to hit the appropriate tone. His first drafts did not satisfy him, because 'it looked as though I was trying to teach people'. Finally he managed to achieve an objective presentation of the subject which was entirely consistent with sound scholarship without being arid or austere. Apart from some passages, such as those listing the geographical and economic particulars of large numbers of settlements, the book is extremely readable, and is at the same time a creditable specimen of Chekhov's literary workmanship and a shining example of what a research thesis can be. It certainly achieved one of its author's major aims—that of bringing home to educated Russians certain unpleasant facts, of which they had hitherto preferred to remain in ignorance.

The book, which had the title *Sakhalin Island*, was the talk of Petersburg and Moscow, and it had considerable influence both in Russia and abroad. Foreigners were amazed that it had passed the censorship, but it had done more than that. It had even impressed the Department of Prison Administration, which dispatched a special mission to Sakhalin, with the result that

Chekhov's findings were fully confirmed. Unfortunately this commission was not followed by any sweeping or effective prison reform. However, Chekhov could feel that he had done something to open people's eyes, and that he had made a definite contribution to human welfare. So far as his 'debt to medicine' was concerned, after the publication of *Sakhalin Island* Chekhov felt that he had repaid it, and he said he was glad that this 'rough convict's smock will hang in my literary wardrobe'.

CHAPTER SEVEN

Melikhovo

I

CHEKHOV BUYS A FARM

By the end of 1891 the idea of acquiring a country house had almost become an obsession in Chekhov's mind. Hearing of a suitable property in the village of Melikhovo, about fifty miles south of Moscow, he immediately sent Mariya and Michael along to conduct as thorough an inspection as was possible in the heart of the winter. The house made a cheerful impression, its bright green and red paintwork standing out in pleasing contrast against the background of snow. They liked the look of it, and Chekhov was in such a hurry to become a landowner that he concluded the deal straight away, without even having set eyes on the place himself. In spite of all this hurry the choice turned out a fortunate one, and provided him with a happy and congenial home during the next seven years. Though there were many distractions and interludes, the general background of his life remained quiet and even during this time, so that he was able to concentrate as never before on his literary work. One after another there appeared stories and plays, almost all of them on his highest level, with the result that the Melikhovo years are regarded as marking the peak of his achievement as a writer.

The property cost him thirteen thousand roubles—twice as much as he had originally thought of giving—and incidental expenses added on another thousand. He was able to provide only a third of this money out of ready funds, and had to borrow the rest. Calculating and recalculating his financial position, he decided that it was reasonably sound. The terms of the loan were easy, and he should be able to pay it off in a few years from the proceeds of his literary work. Moreover it was a relief to be spared the usual outlay on rented apartments in Moscow. Though he tried to comfort himself with such arguments he could not help feeling some uneasiness, and was perhaps predisposed to worry by memories of his father's disastrous excursion into property-owning in Taganrog some fifteen years earlier. What would happen to his dependants, he kept asking himself, if he were to die before the loan had been paid off? One day, no doubt, Melikhovo would be put up for auction to pay his debts. He felt more deeply involved than he had ever intended, and ruefully compared himself with a man who had gone into a restaurant for a modest beef culet, but 'meeting some boon companions fell to swilling and guzzling like a pig, and ended up with a bill for 142 roubles 75 copecks'.

The family moved in at the beginning of March 1892, and Chekhov soon found his worries dispelled by the delights of his country home. He strode around the estate, which he called his 'dukedom', with the eager pride of a new proprietor. It was exciting to find oneself the owner of a well with an iron pump, and of a henhouse 'constructed in accordance with the latest findings of science'. Observing through his study window a hare, motionless on its hind legs in the high-piled snow, he asked himself how he could ever again be content with city life. He had little time for self-congratulation, however, for there was work to be done. The house needed redecorating, and the family was soon busy with paint-pots and wallpaper. Chekhov, who said that he couldn't even knock a nail in straight when he started, managed to turn himself into a tolerable handyman. There were also jobs to be attended to outside the house. At first it was chiefly a matter of clearing paths and dumping loads of snow in the ponds. As spring approached and the snow began to disappear the Chekhovs began cultivating the land. They were ambitious, and had decided to have ornamental gardens, kitchen gardens, and even to run a small farm, for all of which there was plenty of scope, since the ground covered about five hundred acres.

None of them had much experience of tilling the soil, but the advice of neighbours and a study of text-books did something to make up for their ignorance. Michael put himself in charge of the farm and began ploughing the fields. Mariya concentrated on the kitchen-garden, which became the most successful department in the family economy; her radishes, artichokes and potatoes were soon the pride of the household. Home-grown vegetables and fruit were a constant delight to Anton, but the supreme joy was picking mushrooms on his own estate. All this produce

was used liberally by Evgeniya Chekhov, whose talents as cook
were more than ever in demand, for her children regularly came
in from their open-air work with enormous appetites. When not
cooking she was constantly bottling, pickling and preserving. Paul
Chekhov assisted Anton in clearing paths, and also branched out
into Evgeniya's sphere by brewing certain mysterious cordials
from the buds of birch trees. Religion still engrossed his mind.
He had now retired after a life of hard and unrewarding labour,
and was free to devote himself even more conscientiously than
before to his favourite occupation of reading the Bible and singing psalms. At night, after everyone else had gone to bed, the
quiet droning of his voice could often be heard as he intoned
a prayer in his room. Among his duties was the keeping of a
'Melikhovo Diary', a curious document, which has been preserved. Though he recorded all the comings and goings of his
family and their guests, it was in a style so laconic that very
little can be inferred from the Diary about Anton's projects and
ideas. Typical entries are 'Anton ill' or 'Suvorin arrived'. Sometimes the old man allowed himself to be slightly more expan-
sive, but usually on themes of limited interest, such as that
Evgeniya Chekhov had had a dream of a 'goat on an earthenware
jar' or a 'goose in a skull cap'. Anton occasionally amused himself and the family by making entries of his own, in which he
faithfully copied his father's style.

His own particular province on the estate was the care of
trees. Rising sometimes as early as four o'clock in the morning,
he would swallow a hastily-brewed cup of coffee, and go into the
garden. Here he would spend hours wandering from tree to
tree, pruning a little here and there, or squatting down to
examine the bark. There were some quite good trees already
growing on his land—including a picturesque grove of limes—
and he was anxious to increase their number. He began to cultivate tiny firs and poplars from the seed, and ordered apple- and
cherry-shoots by the hundred, determined, as he said, to turn
Melikhovo into a source of pleasure and profit to his descen-
dants. He also planted flowers and watched carefully over his
narcissi, tulips and roses.

It was only to be expected that one who was such a keen
angler should take steps to provide himself with sport on his
own premises. As the result of his efforts in stocking the two
ponds Chekhov was soon able to claim that all Russian fish except pike were represented at Melikhovo. Further projects and

acquisitions took in other departments of the animal kingdom. He amused himself with the idea of keeping bees on a large scale, though he never carried it out. Horses were bought for farm-work and for pulling the trap in which he conveyed his friends to and from the railway station. He acquired a cow or two, and was pleased when a grateful villager sent him a pig in return for medical treatment. As a farmer he could not feel complete without dogs, and very much welcomed the present of two terrier-pups, 'Bromide' and 'Quinine', from his old friend Leykin.

II

CHEKHOV AND THE COMMUNITY

CHEKHOV'S estate took its name from the small village of Melikhovo in which it was situated. The villagers may have watched the new 'masters' move in with feelings of mistrust, but the ice was soon broken to everyone's satisfaction. For the Easter celebrations of 1892 Paul Chekhov was reinstated in his old role of choir-master, and under his direction the family, together with some guests, sang the anthems in Melikhovo church. This made a favourable impression on the villagers, who were even more delighted when they heard that the new owner of the estate was a doctor. Doctors were scarce in Russian country districts, and as the news spread ailing peasants began to arrive in large numbers. Many of them were brought in carts by relatives, and a long queue often formed outside Chekhov's gate.

He was very soon made a member of the Sanitary Council in the nearest large town, and events began to move in such a way as to engulf all his energies for a time in medical work. In 1892, and again in 1893 he was put in charge of anti-cholera precautions in an area of twenty-five villages, an important task, for a serious epidemic was approaching from the south-east. Fortunately Chekhov's area was spared. However, there were plenty of claims on his medical skill in the ordinary course of village life. His reward was the gratitude and appreciation of the peasants. They bowed and smiled their greetings as his carriage passed them in the road, and when he was picking his way across the fields the village women were always eager to show him the best path, and to stop the dogs from barking. It appears that Chekhov is still remembered in Melikhovo. His biographer Ermilov mentions an incident which took place in 1944 when a Chekhov Museum was opened in the village. An old villager, now a collective farm official, made a speech in which he went so far as to blame himself and his fellow-villagers for Chekhov's early death. They had been so insistent on their demands on him, the old man remembered, as to impair his health.

Chekhov soon found that all sorts of other new responsibilities devolved on him as squire of Melikhovo. He became a prominent figure in local government, organizing the construction of a road from Melikhovo to the nearest railway station, and devoting much attention to improving educational facilities. During his stay in Melikhovo he built three village schools, for which he provided most of the money, and which he helped to plan. His public-spiritedness involved him in a wide variety of other activities, ranging from administration of justice in the local courts to the organization of a trip for children to the Nizhny Novgorod fair.

His charitable and educational activities went far outside the Melikhovo area. Impoverished writers were helped with money or, perhaps, a letter to Suvorin asking him to find them work on *New Time*. When he heard that his Taganrog cousin Vladimir wanted to study medicine he offered to pay his way at Tomsk University. The promoters of a new medical journal *The Surgical Chronicle* turned to Chekhov for help when their project showed signs of failing. He took up their cause with enthusiasm, and did not drop it until he was successful. As he himself said, 'In order to save the journal I am ready to visit anybody, and I don't care whose ante-room I have to wait in. If I succeed I shall breathe with relief and pleasure because saving a good surgical journal is just as useful as doing 20,000 successful operations.'

Chekhov also extended his benefactions to his own home town. His interest in Taganrog had considerably revived in the 'nineties, and he determined to do what he could to improve its library. He dispatched a very large number of books, some from his own shelves, and some which he bought in Moscow or abroad. He conducted prolonged negotiations by letter with the Mayor of the town and stated his willingness to go to any lengths in helping the library. He wanted to see a good reference department established, and was soon recommending that a new library building should be put up, a suggestion which was eventually carried out on the plans of his friend, the architect Shekhtel.

III

THOUGHTS ON MARRIAGE

THOUGH still a young man, Chekhov had moments when he was unpleasantly aware of the passage of the years, and this feeling was increased by various family events. Uncle Mitrofan died in Taganrog. Ivan and Michael got married, and Anton's friends were soon urging him to follow their example. He was disposed to agree, and debated the theme of marriage quite frequently, coming to contrary conclusions in different moods. Sometimes he expressed himself content to live out his days as a bachelor, and for a very long time seemed likely to carry out this intention. On other occasions he would remark that he had no objection to marrying even a pock-marked widow, but he did not have recourse to this extreme when he eventually got married in 1901.

Among his speculations about marriage during the Melikhovo years are a number of characteristic passages which show how far he was from any element of romanticism in his attitude to the subject. 'All right, I'll get married if you want me to,' he wrote in one letter. 'My conditions: everything must be as it has been hitherto. That is to say she must live in Moscow and I in the country, and I shall visit her. I can't stand happiness which lasts all day, from one morning to another ... I promise to be a marvellous husband, but give me a wife who is like the moon, and won't appear in my sky every day. I shan't write any better for being married.'

Another of his meditations on marriage raises issues which are obscure, but have an important bearing on his life: 'I am afraid of a wife and of family routine which will hamper me, and which somehow don't link up in my imagination with my disorderliness. All the same they are better than tossing around on the sea of life and braving the storm in the fragile barque of profligacy. I don't love my mistresses any more, and in my relations to them am gradually becoming impotent.'

It would be a mistake to treat this passage as an authentic glimpse into Chekhov's private life, for his habit of filling his letters with humorous inventions means that they must always be treated with caution as a source. However, this is a question on which almost any indication is of value in the almost total absence of evidence. In general Chekhov's life is well documented, often down to the minutest detail, such as the names and habits of his domestic pets or his methods of catching mice. It is disappointing to find a comparative lack of information on his relations with the women who must have played a big part in his life before his marriage. So little information is available that his biographers have practically nothing to say on the subject. Chekhov himself was the last person to flaunt details of his private affairs, and his family may well have been unwilling to make public, after his death, material which might appear to compromise his respectability.

Chekhov was a person of temperate nature, and it would seem that he found his own level somewhere between the rigidity of his parents and the freedom current among the more Bohemian of his nearer contemporaries. A colourful member of the latter group was the artist Levitan, of whom Chekhov remarked: 'Levitan has been worn out by women. These charming creatures bestow love, and they don't take much away from a man! Only his youth! ... If I were a landscape painter I would lead an almost ascetic life.' Chekhov, of course, was not a landscape painter, and the asceticism which he prescribed in the rather special case of Levitan does not seem to have been the policy which he invariably adopted himself. Perhaps the most straightforward evidence on this side of his life is that provided by Nemirovich-Danchenko in his memoirs.

'I believe,' he remarks, 'that Chekhov had great success with women. I say "I believe" because neither he nor I liked gossiping on this theme.' The passage which follows contains some confidences, supplied by Chekhov in a rare moment of frankness, and relating to an affair between himself and an anonymous married woman. Nemirovich-Danchenko goes on to say that Chekhov never had any firm or long-standing attachment, and that, shortly before his marriage, he revealed that 'none of his liaisons had lasted more than a year.'

Chekhov's correspondence contains no love letters, except those to his wife. Of his other letters to women the most intimate to have been published are addressed to Lika Mizinova. Here, however, the language is not that of a lover. The tone is one of affectionate banter, rather than of passion, and Chekhov retains the use of the more formal 'you' as opposed to the 'thou' required by intimate relationships. Lika had long been a friend of the Chekhov family, into which she had originally been introduced by Mariya. Anton and his brothers were not likely to forget her first arrival in their Moscow flat. They had all come out on to the first floor landing to have a look at her as she took off her coat in the hall. She was very beautiful and very shy. The unconcealed admiration of the young men made her hide her face in the clothes which hung on the hall-stand. Since then Lika had become a favourite visitor both at Moscow and Melikhovo. For many years she and Chekhov maintained an attitude of sparring flirtatiousness. His letters to her were playful and teasing. After addressing her as 'Golden-haired Lika' and professing his undying adoration, he was liable to inform her that he had removed her tearstains from his jacket with the aid of benzine. There are many such cryptic references to incidents which had passed between the couple, but the letters do not reveal much about the inner side of their relationship. Lika's letters to Chekhov, which have recently come to light, have been explored by Russian biographers in the hope of illuminating this question. They show that she was very much in love with him, but that his attitude to her did not go beyond affectionate friendship. She sought consolation in her disappointment by having affairs from time to time with one or other of his friends. The omnivorous Levitan made her the target for one of his lightning and remorseless courtships; after this she was taken up by the writer Potapenko, with whom she apparently had an affair in Paris. Chekhov regarded these events with amused detachment, and remained on friendly terms with all three parties.

IV

VISITS TO MOSCOW AND ELSEWHERE

LIKA, Levitan and Potapenko were among the most frequent guests at Melikhovo. Others included Chekhov's three brothers who had all set up establishments of their own elsewhere. Michael and Ivan would bring their wives to stay, and Alexander would arrive from Petersburg with his family, giving his mother an opportunity to observe the antics of her three grandchildren. It was also pleasant for the Chekhovs to be able to return country hospitality given to them in the days when they were city-dwellers. When members of the Kiselev and Lintvarev families came to Melikhovo, conversation often turned to happy holidays spent in earlier years at Babkino and Sumy. Suvorin, of course, came frequently, and, on the occasion of his first visit, caused some consternation by turning up his nose at Chekhov's new home. Possibly the amenities of the house, which lacked a water closet in the early days, were insufficiently luxurious for this frequenter of expensive hotels and lover of good living.

Some of the visitors were less welcome; they arrived in large numbers, often without invitation, overflowed into the barn or slept four to a room. It was sometimes hard to discover exactly who they all were. Hunting parties, consisting of chance acquaintances and total strangers, would announce their intention of staying the night, and on one occasion a woman who was quite unknown to any of the Chekhovs installed herself for a whole week. Intruders like these made inroads on Anton's time, and reminded him vividly of some of the disadvantages he had hoped to escape by his flight from Moscow, where unwanted visitors had so often fatigued and exasperated him. It was beginning to seem a law of nature that he should always be surrounded by clamour and uproar. After some years at Melikhovo he conducted a further retreat by building a small three-roomed cottage away from the house in the middle of an apple-orchard. This proved an ideal place of refuge, particularly when the weather was warm, and it was here that he retired to write *The Seagull* in the autumn of 1895.

Though Melikhovo provided Chekhov with a real home, such as he had never had before, he showed no sign of wanting to bury himself permanently in the country. When he felt the need of a break it was always possible to get away to Moscow. Though he rarely gave notice of his arrival, the news spread with amazing speed. 'Anton Pavlovich has come,' passed from mouth to mouth, and he was soon overwhelmed with visitors. Invitations to parties, theatres and literary gatherings were showered on him.

With one group of Moscow intellectuals in particular he maintained close and sympathetic relations throughout most of the 'nineties. This was the circle associated with the liberal magazine *Russian Thought*. Liberal writers were continually protesting against the lack of freedom under the Tsarist autocracy and one of their ambitions was to see the establishment in Russia of a constitution which would afford more rights to the citizen. Though they were regarded with hostility by the Government, they were nevertheless allowed to publish periodicals in which they could advocate such aspects of their policy as were not too aggressively oppositionist.

Hampered in the public expression of their views, they often laid down the law in private with an intolerance which Chekhov regarded as typical of politically-minded people. During the late 'eighties he had been particularly opposed to their way of talking, and drew the conclusion that a victory of liberal policies would not lead to any great improvement in Russia. He once went so far as to describe his dismay at such a prospect in violent language: 'Under the flag of science, art and . . . freedom of thought we shall have such toads and crocodiles ruling Russia as were unknown even in Spain at the time of the Inquisition.'

In 1890 Chekhov had been involved in a quarrel with the liberal sponsors of *Russian Thought*. Finding himself described on their pages as a 'devotee of unprincipled writing', he had reacted with surprising vigour by sending a furious letter to one of the editors, V. M. Lavrov. He said that he regarded the review as a piece of insulting slander, and that he wanted to have no further relations with the magazine or its staff. Two years later the quarrel was patched up as the result of a letter from Lavrov asking Chekhov to forget the incident and to contribute stories to the magazine. Chehov was extremely pleased and described the reception of this letter as a sensational piece of news. He gladly accepted the offer of reconciliation and was soon on the most cordial terms with Lavrov and his colleague, Goltsev. The same year Chekhov's *Ward No. 6* appeared in *Russian Thought* which throughout the 'nineties continued to publish his work, including a very high proportion of his best stories.

Visits to Moscow were not enough to satisfy an inveterate traveller like Chekhov, who was always planning to go to such distant parts of the globe as Tahiti, Chicago and South America. However, Western Europe was as far as he got during the Melikhovo years. In 1894 he again travelled with Suvorin, and the itinerary of three years earlier was more or less repeated. The most interesting of his journeys was one which did not take him far from Melikhovo. It had long been obvious that Chekhov must sooner or later pay a visit to Tolstoy at his home in Yasnaya Polyana. Though he knew that Tolstoy was interested in his work, and very much wanted to see him, Chekhov kept putting off the visit, apparently frightened by Tolstoy's immense reputation. When, in 1895, he at last made the plunge he found that there was nothing to be frightened of. He spent a day and a half at Yasnaya Polyana, and went away deeply impressed.

K

With Tolstoy he felt completely at ease from the start, as indeed those who knew both men had predicted.

Chekhov's attitude to Tolstoy at this time was rather mixed. For Tolstoy's personality and literary powers he had an almost unlimited admiration, and in speaking of them often abandoned his habitual reticence for the language of enthusiastic praise; a survey of his references to Tolstoy throughout the 'nineties and early nineteen-hundreds shows that he must have regarded him as the greatest living Russian. For Tolstoy's doctrines, however, he had no longer very much respect; indeed, his early sympathy for Tolstoyism had now given way to a pronounced hostility. Some echo of their disagreements is to be found in Tolstoy's account of this first meeting, in which, after recording his high opinion of Chekhov's talents and good heart, he goes on to regret his 'lack of a definite point of view'. A lack of philosophical harmony did not, however, prevent the two men from liking each other and forming a firm friendship, which lasted until Chekhov's death.

v

The Seagull IN PETERSBURG

THE reception of his last two full-length plays, *Ivanov* and *The Wood Demon*, had temporarily discouraged Chekhov from writing serious drama, and it was not until 1895 that he made his next attempt. Most of the work was done in the late autumn of that year, and by November he had a draft ready for typing. The new play was *The Seagull*, which marked a great advance on anything he had previously written for the stage; its fortunes and misfortunes were to have large-scale repercussions both on Chekhov himself and on the development of the Russian theatre. While engaged on the play he let fall characteristically diffident remarks about its quality. He described it negligently as containing 'many conversations about literature, little action and a hundredweight-and-a-half of love', and said that in it he offended most terribly against the rules of the theatre. On re-reading the work after its completion he remarked that he was more dissatisfied than satisfied, and had decided that he was not a dramatist at all. He would have been more dissatisfied still if he could have foreseen what would happen at the first performance.

Early 1896 was devoted to revision, alterations and negotiations with the dramatic censor, whose moral susceptibilities were

offended by certain features of the plot. By August these difficulties had been smoothed out, and *The Seagull* was accepted
for production by the Petersburg Alexandrine Theatre. Very
little was done with it until about two months later, when a
sudden decision was taken to put it on at short notice. This
was the result of a request by the actress Levkeeva, who was
due for a benefit performance on October 17th, and had taken
it into her head that the première of a new Chekhov play was
the choice most calculated to ensure the success of her evening.

There were only nine days left for rehearsing, but producer
and cast set to in a businesslike fashion. Rehearsals were
strenuous, and were often interrupted by heated argument on
interpretation, for *The Seagull* represented something quite unfamiliar in the way of dramatic writing. After a few days Chekhov himself turned up in Petersburg, and began to attend the
theatre, so that the actors had at any rate the benefit of explana-
tions from the most authoritative source. 'The main thing, my
dears', he told them, 'is not to be theatrical ... Everything must
be simple ... Completely simple ... The characters are all
ordinary, simple people.' He does not seem to have been very
satisfied with the way things were shaping, and after a few
visits wrote to his sister that 'so far *The Seagull* is going tire-
somely'.

In choosing the play for her benefit night Levkeeva herself
unintentionally affected its reception in a way she can hardly
have intended. She was a popular comic actress with a large
following among the rowdier section of the theatre-going public,
and as *The Seagull* was completely unsuited to her style of acting she had to be left out of the cast. The result was that
her admirers, who filled the theatre, having paid the usual high
prices charged on benefit nights, conceived a violent prejudice
against Chekhov's play as soon as they set eyes on the programme.
Russian audiences were never slow to give vocal expression to
their views in the theatre, and the trouble started near the
beginning of the play with a monologue not calculated to appeal
to these particular hearers. It began: 'Human beings, lions,
eagles, partridges and horned deer. ...' This was greeted with
jeers and derisive guffaws so that the actress who pronounced
it burst into tears on making her exit, under the impression that
she was the cause of the trouble. As the play proceeded the uproar increased, so that the actors were often inaudible. There
were certain moments, such as the appearance of one of the

characters with his head bandaged—in accordance with the stage directions—when the laughter, hissing and cat-calls were so loud that veteran theatre-goers claimed never to have witnessed anything like it, even in a Russian theatre.

After the second act Chekhov could not stand it any longer. He ran out of the theatre, and soon his disappearance was causing alarm to his sister and the Suvorins. A series of telephone calls failed to trace him, and it was only at two o'clock in the morning that he arrived back after wandering the streets of Petersburg for hours. Suvorin went to condole with him, but Chekhov asked him not to put the light on. 'I don't want to see anyone,' he remarked, 'and I only want to say one thing: Let people call me a——(apparently a very rude word) if I ever write anything else for the stage.' Next morning he left by an early train for Moscow. He told a friend, who accompanied him to the station, that he would never write another play if he lived for seven hundred years. At the station he fobbed off a newspaper-seller with a cry of: 'I can't read,' and remarked of him to his companion: 'Look what a kindly face he's got, while all the time his hands are full of poison. In each paper there is a review.'

Chekhov was not mistaken in thinking that the Petersburg papers would make the most of his downfall. A considerable section of the press had always adopted a grudging attitude to his work, and was bound to greet the *Seagull* incident as an opportunity for rejoicing. The more ill-mannered of these detractors began to gloat over what they regarded as a clear demonstration of Chekhov's 'lack of talent'. Some of them even broke into verse in an attempt to be witty at his expense.

Before leaving for Melikhovo Chekhov sent word to the management asking that *The Seagull* should be taken off. His request was disregarded, for the producer realized that conditions on the first night had been abnormal and wanted to give the play another chance. It is easy to imagine the nervousness of the actors as the curtain rose on the second performance. In spite of their fears the play was fairly well received, and two further performances which followed were equally encouraging. *The Seagull* seemed to be gaining ground when the directorate of the theatre, apparently under the influence of a delayed reaction to the initial scandal, intervened and removed it from the repertoire. However, a sufficiently good impression had been created in some quarters for letters of appreciation to reach Chekhov in Melikhovo. One of them, written by the well-known jurist A. F. Koni, was particularly kind and far-sighted. Koni reminded Chekhov of the initial failure and subsequent success of Glinka's opera *Ruslan and Lyudmila*, though even the orchestra had joined in the hissing at its first performance. He also quoted the similar history of Bizet's *Carmen*.

Chekhov wrote back expressing his appreciation of Koni's letter, but for some time it was very difficult to approach him on the subject of *The Seagull*, which was now associated with one of the most bitter experiences of his life. He reluctantly allowed *Russian Thought* to publish the play in December, after which he did his best to forget the whole incident. However, *The Seagull* was not to be forgotten; indeed, its adventures had hardly begun.

VI

A WINTER IN NICE

IN March 1897 there occurred a crisis in Chekhov's health which completely altered his plans for the future. He collapsed one evening, just after he had sat down to dinner with Suvorin in a Moscow restaurant, and he was immediately removed to Suvorin's room, where he spent the whole night coughing. It was only towards morning that the flow of blood from his lungs began to abate. One of his doctor friends was called, and immediately ordered his removal to a clinic where he spent the next few weeks; there he was at last subjected to a thorough diagnosis, which established beyond all doubt that he was suffering from tuberculosis. Weak and Ill, Chekhov lay on his back, hardly able to move or to speak. Mariya and Ivan hurried to his bedside, and he gave them strict instructions that the nature of his illness should be concealed from his mother and father. Other visitors came with flowers and books, but were not allowed to stay long. Tolstoy, who arrived full of his theories of art, which he was in process of publishing, managed to defy these instructions. Chekhov, in spite of his condition, could not help contesting Tolstoy's thesis that art was only legitimate in so far as it was assimilable by the most uneducated *muzhik*. The excitement of the argument was too much for him, and brought on a further attack, which retarded his recovery. However, his strength gradually began to return and he took to wandering up and down the ward in his dressing-gown. The diagnosis had been a great shock to him. 'How could I fail to have noticed it?' he kept reproaching himself.

On his doctors' advice Chekhov left for France in September. He settled down for a short time at Biarritz, but rainy weather drove him away, and he made a more permanent headquarters in the Russian Pension at Nice. Here he spent a pleasant winter. The weather was warm, and he did not have to put on his goloshes or heavy coat during the whole time he was there. The company of his fellow-lodgers was congenial to him, especially that of M. M. Kovalevsky, a biologist of international repute, who had been dismissed from his professorship in Russia because of his free-thinking views. Kovalevsky was active and successful in France, holding lectures from time to time in Paris. Chekhov and he planned a winter voyage to Tunis and Algiers, but this had to be abandoned owing to Kovalevsky's ill-health. Other Russian friends who occasionally arrived at the Pension for a short holiday included Potapenko, with whom Chekhov made frequent expeditions to the tables at Monte Carlo.

On the whole he was fairly contented during his stay in Nice. His health showed no signs of further deterioration, and at one time he noticed with satisfaction that he was beginning to put on weight. His cough abated, but he realized that there was not much chance of any rapid improvement in his condition, and that he must reconcile himself for the time being with the status of semi-invalid. After the turn of the year he began to express dissatisfaction with Nice. His friends had left the Pension, and had given way to other guests whom he found rather unpleasant. He began to long for the sight of a Russian village, and was already looking forward to the onset of warm weather in Melikhovo, which would make his return possible. At Nice, Chekhov was not inactive, and continued to write stories. None the less, he had the feeling that there were 'going sour in his brain' many subjects which he could have turned to better account in front of his own desk at Melikhovo.

In spite of his restiveness he took great interest in his country of exile, noting with satisfaction the unfailing courtesy of all classes of French people, and contrasting it with a comparative coarseness of behaviour current in Russia. He had made considerable progress with the French language, though he never claimed to be much of a linguist. What little German he remembered from school had enabled him to express himself in Vienna, though he said that it made people laugh; as for French, travelling from one Paris station to another reminded

him of playing blind man's buff. In an attempt to improve
matters he had begun to study seriously in Biarritz. His teacher
was a nineteen-year-old French girl, as he told Lika, adding that
she must not be jealous. At Nice he was sufficiently fluent to
indulge a growing taste for French literature. Voltaire was an
author who particularly attracted him, and it is interesting to
note that he contemplated making a translation into Russian
of Maupassant, who is generally regarded as his only serious
rival in the art of the short story.

During his stay at Nice, Chekhov allowed himself to be drawn
into the controversy over the Dreyfus Case. The unjust condemnation of this French-Jewish army officer on a charge of
treason, had become the talk of Europe. While Dreyfus lan-
guished on Devil's Island the French government was widely
criticized for its apparent eagerness to hush up a legal blunder,
and for its reluctance to order a re-trial. The intervention of
Emile Zola, whose study of the case had convinced him of
Dreyfus' innocence, and Zola's own trial, following the publication of his outspoken letter *'J'accuse'*, had enveloped the affair
in a blaze of publicity. Everywhere people were taking sides;
arguments raged and tempers were lost. The controversy acted
as a touchstone of the political and psychological make-up of the
participants, dividing them into the two main camps of accepters
and rejecters of the existing order. People of an authoritarian
turn of mind were indignant at Zola's championship of Dreyfus,
and were detested by their opponents for their conservative,
militarist or clerical views, which were often tinged with anti-
Semitism. Zola's supporters, on the other hand, belonged mostly
to the political and psychological left wing.

Chekhov felt that the spokesmen of both sides tended to make
snap judgments, based on superficial and emotionally-coloured
reactions. A close study of the case convinced him of Dreyfus'
innocence and disgusted him with the behaviour of the other
side. The distortions of the press infuriated him, and it was particularly aggravating when he received in Nice copies of *New
Time* containing virulent anti-Dreyfus articles, which often
seemed to be based on a deliberate twisting of the evidence.

Chekhov had disliked the politics of *New Time* even in the
'eighties, when he had professed complete neutrality on political
subjects. In the 'nineties he had begun to adopt an attitude of
increasing sympathy with left-wing views, and it was partly for
this reason that he stopped writing for Suvorin's paper in 1893.

However, he managed for several years to keep his personal relations with Suvorin quite distinct from his opinion of *New Time*. The Dreyfus Case, on which he felt so strongly, made such a position no longer tenable and led to a crisis in this long-standing friendship. The occasion was an extremely blunt letter to Suvorin in which Chekhov forcibly protested against the campaign of calumny conducted against Zola on the pages of *New Time*.

'The great point about Zola,' he wrote, 'is that he is sincere; that is, he founds his judgments on what he sees, and not on phantoms, like other people. Even sincere people can make mistakes—that is undeniable—but such mistakes cause less harm than calculating insincerity, prejudices and political considerations. Even if Dreyfus were guilty, Zola would still be right, because it is the function of a writer not to accuse and persecute, but to champion even the guilty, once they have been condemned and are undergoing punishment. People will say: "What about politics? What about interests of state?" Great writers and artists must take part in politics only in so far as it is necessary to put up a defence against politics. There are enough prosecutors and gendarmes already, without adding to their number.'

Chekhov said that Zola's intervention had given him the right to lead a peaceful old age and to die with a clear conscience. This was the way in which a writer ought to behave, said Chekhov, and he reinforced his argument by quoting Korolenko's championship of a minority tribe in Russia, the Multans, whom he had saved from persecution by the police. He might also have compared his own work for the convicts of Sakhalin. For the rest of his life Chekhov hardly ever spoke of *New Time* except in terms of furious indignation, referring to it, for example, as 'not a paper, but a menagerie, a pack of hungry jackals, engaged on biting each other's tails'. Relations with Suvorin were not permanently broken off after the quarrel, but they never regained their former cordiality.

In spite of Chekhov's keen interest in French life and culture, his exile showed no sign of weakening his ties with Russia. He was continually asking his friends to send copies of Russian magazines for the use of himself and his fellow-countrymen. Taganrog public library continued to interest him, and he dispatched from France over three hundred volumes of French literature. On his way back to Russia he conducted negotiations with the sculptor Antokolsky, who worked in Paris, and who agreed to provide a huge monumental statue of Peter the Great to be set up in Taganrog. His family were as much in his thoughts as ever, and he wrote regularly to Mariya. He sent his mother flowers from Nice on her name-day and bought his father a hat in Paris; he sent to Melikhovo a special brand of candles sold in France, which were claimed to be an efficient gnat-deterrent. Thoughts of his garden filled his mind, and he was continually giving assignments to his sister. Had she transplanted the poplars near the gooseberry bushes in the park near the pond? Would she put a row of sticks around the peonies so they wouldn't get trampled on? Would she leave the pruning of the rose-bushes until his return? He was longing to be back, and throughout April 1898 waited in Paris for a telegram from Mariya telling him that the weather was warm enough for his return.

He returned in May 1898 and stayed until September, remaining in reasonably high spirits. When autumn came on he realized that he must again move south, and this time chose to winter in Yalta.

CHAPTER EIGHT

Chekhov's Review of Russia

I

THE LATER STORIES AND THEIR POSITION IN CHEKHOV'S WORK

THE year 1892, in which Chekhov moved to Melikhovo, can conveniently be regarded as a literary as well as a biographical turning-point. This date, which happens to fall halfway through the twenty-four years of his career, marks the beginning of a more settled period of short story writing than anything which had preceded it during the eventful journey from irresponsible farce to literary maturity. Accordingly the entire body of Chekhov's fiction written between 1892 and his death will be taken as a single group. It contains altogether forty-two stories, and, as this figure reveals, the quantity of fiction written by Chekhov during the last twelve years of his life falls very much below that which had preceded it. In the latest Russian complete edition seven volumes are assigned to the earlier, and only two to the later period, but this ratio by no means corresponds with their relative importance. Indeed, one main feature of the later short stories, as opposed to their predecessors, and to all other sections of Chekhov's work—not excluding even the four last plays—lies in the dominant position which they occupy in his achievement. They are, in fact, generally agreed to form his main contribution to Russian literature, and have often been spoken of as the finest collection of short stories in any language.

The period which begins in 1892 shows, apart from a higher literary standard, the emergence of an approach to fiction which was new, though it had been latent in Chekhov for some years. He began to abandon the approach of a comparatively dispassionate observer, and to handle his stories in a manner more consistent with the demands of those who looked to fiction for a comment on life. Social problems began to feature more prominently, and though Chekhov's attitude to them never became tendentious enough to satisfy all his critics, he did begin to show his own sympathies more openly, and to express protests, often extremely vigorous, against trends and theories which impressed him as undesirable. For this reason the later stories can most suitably be grouped in accordance with the problems which they illustrate, in an attempt to establish the main features of Chekhov's outlook during the 'nineties. The result will be to focus attention on about a dozen stories which stand out because of their particular value in this investigation, and which also happen to be among the finest from a literary point of view.

II

Ward No. 6

THE first of the later stories to be considered is *Ward No. 6*, in which Chekhov seems to be serving notice of his new approach, and which is generally agreed to produce a more powerful impression on its readers than any other example of his work. It is said to have been the most popular of his stories during the 'nineties, with the possible exception of *Peasants*, written later in the decade, and has been called 'the most terrible production in the whole of Russian literature'. The scene is set in a small and unbelievably squalid provincial hospital. When Doctor Ragin arrived to take charge, he found that he could hardly breathe for the stench in the wards, corridors and courtyard. Hospital servants and nurses slept in the wards together with the patients. Other typical features of the place were that it was overrun with cockroaches, beetles and mice, that there were only two scalpels and not a single thermometer, and that potatoes were kept in the baths. The hospital officials regularly robbed the patients, while Ragin's predecessor was said to have sold medical stores on the sly, and to have set up a harem among the nurses and patients. Ragin had a great love of intelligence and decency, but had not enough character to create intelligent and decent conditions of life around him, so he left the hospital as it was. He soon worked out a satisfactory routine for himself—conducting an occasional perfunctory examination of his patients, but spending most of the day in his room, where he would read or meditate with a vodka bottle at his elbow.

Among his patients were five lunatics, housed in Ward No. 6, which partook to the full of the general squalor. It had a vile ante-room, where on a pile of decomposing rubbish, the warder

Nikita usually sprawled with his pipe in his mouth. He was a retired soldier with a passion for discipline, and limited the discharge of his functions almost excusively to beating his six patients. The ward itself was like a zoo, with iron grilles on the windows, and distilled the inevitable smells of beetles, ammonia, and sour cabbage.

Among the five lunatics imprisoned in the ward was a young man called Gromov, who suffered from persecution mania, and indulged in wild ravings.

'He talked about human baseness, about the violence which tramples on justice, about the beautiful life which will some day exist on earth, about the bars on the window—a permanent reminder of the obtuseness and cruelty of his ill-users. Whatever you talked to him about, he always brought the conversation back to the same point: that life in the town was stifling and boring; that society had no higher interests; that it led a dim, senseless existence, to which it lent variety by brutality, coarse debauch and hypocrisy; that crooks were well fed and dressed, while honest men fed on crumbs; that there was a need for schools, a local newspaper with an honest policy, a theatre, public lectures and a unification of intellectual forces.'

It was not Doctor Ragin's normal practice to visit Ward No. 6, which he was content to leave to the harsh jurisdiction of Nikita. When he did happen to go in one day he was met with a furious onslaught from Gromov. 'So the doctor's come!' he shouted. 'At last! Gentlemen, I congratulate you! The doctor is honouring us with a visit. You vile vermin!' he shrieked at Ragin. 'Kill the rat! No, killing's too good for him. Drown him in a lavatory!' Distressed by this reception, Ragin inquires gently what he has done to deserve it. Gromov says that the lunatics are on an immeasurably higher moral plane than Ragin and his staff, and ought to be allowed to go free. He says it is illogical that they should be imprisoned. Ragin replies that this is not a matter of morals or logic, but of pure chance. After all, since prisons and asylums exist, somebody has got to occupy them. Moreover, to a truly enlightened man the external conditions of life are a matter of entire indifference.

This attitude exasperates Gromov, as well it might. It is all very well for Ragin, who has spent most of his life sitting on a comfortable chair in a warm study, to say that one should be indifferent to circumstances. 'You despise suffering,' he tells the doctor, 'but if you pinched your finger in the door I'll bet you'd shout your head off.' When Gromov is told that meditation could convince him of the insignificance of external things, he retorts: 'I only know that God created me of warm blood and nerves. Organic tissue, if endued with life, is bound to react to every stimulus. And I do react! To pain I reply with shouts and tears, to baseness with indignation, to vileness with revulsion.'

Ragin enjoys Gromov's conversation, although it is chiefly devoted to discrediting him. His frequent visits to Ward No. 6 become the talk of the hospital, and eventually come to the ears of the town administration. Foreheads are tapped significantly, especially when the doctor begins to announce that he has found the one intelligent man in the town to be a lunatic. Soon Ragin is asked to resign, and is left without private means or pension. Everyone says that he is ill, and ought to allow himself to be treated. In the end a careerist doctor, who has taken his place as head of the hospital, tricks the old man into paying his first visit to Ward No. 6 since his resignation. The door snaps to, and the brutal Nikita tosses his former master a filthy hospital dressing-gown with a horrible odour of stale fish. As Gromov had predicted, Ragin's philosophy proves an inadequate defence against real suffering and very soon he is protesting himself. His demands for release are only met with a savage beating by Nikita for insubordination. Shortly after this Ragin dies of an apoplectic fit, with all his theories of passivity and indifference completely overthrown.

Ward No. 6 has lent itself to a wide variety of interesting interpretations in Russia. One contemporary reviewer, who regarded it primarily as an exposé of conditions in Russian provincial hospitals, was not emphasizing an aspect of the story which would strike many readers as especially important. A more common tendency has been to conceive it as an attack on Tolstoyism because of certain parallels between this doctrine and the philosophy of the discredited Ragin. These are, in particular, Ragin's preoccupation with moral self-perfection and the element of non-resistance to evil involved in his deliberately cultivated indifference to outside conditions.

Chekhov's attitude to Tolstoyism had altered considerably since the days when he had occasionally tried to propagate it in his fiction. By the time of the expedition to Sakhalin his sympathy had evaporated, and his subsequent correspondence contains a number of actively hostile references, including, in particular, one passage from a letter of 1894.

'Tolstoy's philosophy affected me powerfully and held me in its grip for about six or seven years. ... But now something in me protests; reason and justice tell me that there is more love for humanity in electricity and steam than in chastity and abstention from meat. War is an evil, and law-courts are an evil—but that doesn't mean that I've got to walk around in peasant boots and sleep on a stove with a workman and his wife. However, it isn't a question of *pro* or *contra* but of the fact that, somehow or other, Tolstoy has now sailed away. So far as I am concerned, he no longer has a place in my heart.'

It is hard to say how far this antagonism to Tolstoy's philosophy really was in the forefront of Chehov's mind when he created Doctor Ragin, and for an unmistakable refutation of Tolstoyism his readers had to wait until *My Life*, written four years later.

A different aspect of *Ward No. 6* was stressed by the large number of Russian intellectuals who were appalled by the backwardness and mismanagement of their country. They regarded Chekhov's hospital as a symbol of Russia as a whole, and were impressed by the strong psychological affinities between the warder Nikita and the Tsarist police. This interpretation has encouraged one Soviet critic to describe the story as a 'hammer-blow against autocracy', a description which would probably have surprised Chekhov. Though he had no love of autocracy it is doubtful whether he had consciously intended *Ward No. 6* as an attack on the régime, but it makes very interesting reading if regarded as such.

Another fascinating speculation is one which links the story with the internal processes of Chekhov's mind. It has already been suggested that his stories can often be plausibly interpreted as artistic projections of his own mental conflicts. On this interpretation Ragin must be regarded as a symbol of the indifference to social problems which had tended to dominate Chekhov during the 'eighties. Gromov, on the other hand, represents the active interest in society's welfare which had helped to send Chekhov to Sakhalin, and which increasingly affected his approach to literature after his return. It is for this reason

that Gromov's debating victory over Ragin forms a fitting introduction to the last phase of Chekhov's work.

It is always interesting to find in Chekhov's correspondence
confirmation of the ideas which he expressed in his fiction, and
an important passage from a letter to Suvorin, written shortly
after the publication of *Ward No. 6*, shows that he no longer
believed that a writer could afford to be aimless.

'Remember that those whom we call "immortal", or simply
"good" writers, and who intoxicate us, have one most important feature in common: they are going somewhere, and are
calling us there, and one feels, not with one's mind, but with
one's whole being, that they have some goal, like the ghost of
Hamlet's father, which didn't come and stir up people's imaginations just to pass the time of day. Some of them—it depends
on their calibre—have immediate aims: serfdom, the liberation
of their country, politics, beauty or simply vodka ... others
have distant aims like God, the life hereafter, human happiness and so on. The best of them are realist and describe life
as it is, but because every line they write is saturated with the
consciousness of a goal, one senses, in addition to life as it is,
life as it should be, and that grips one.'

Chekhov goes on to say that an inability to see beyond life
as it is seems to him one of the faults of his own generation of
writers. He had tried to do something to remedy this fault in
Ward No. 6, but perhaps he felt that he had not been entirely
successful. Although the philosophical message of the story does
suggest the feeling that Chekhov has a 'goal', its general tone has
naturally led many critics to class it among his pessimistic
works. It really forms a bridge between the earlier 'clinical studies'
(among which Professor Elton very naturally classes it) and the
social criticism of the stories which were to follow.

III

THE CAPITALIST

AFTER stating a general philosophical position in *Ward No. 6*,
Chekhov descended to a more specific level in many of the
stories which followed. Among the special problems of Russian
society which he illustrated, the first to be considered is the rise
of capitalism, on which his chief contributions are contained in

three important stories: *A Woman's Kingdom, Three Years* and *A Doctor's Visit*. Though the Industrial Revolution had reached Russia later than the countries of Western Europe its development had been swift, and by the time these stories were written it was well enough advanced to have created a class of poverty-stricken workers, the sordid misery of whose lives is strongly emphasized by Chekhov. However, the workers themselves serve only as a background to his stories, and it is the psychology of the owners on which he concentrates. He makes the point that, so far as peace of mind and contentment are concerned, they are not necessarily any better off than anybody else.

Each of the three stories contains as central figure a wealthy person who is a capitalist by inheritance, and not by inclination. These three characters are not heartless exploiters, but sensitive and bewildered people, too conscious of the absurdity and injustice of the whole situation to derive anything but unhappiness from their position. They are embarrassed by their wealth, and do not know what to do with it. Anna Akimovna, the factory-owning heroine of *A Woman's Kingdom*, would rather have been a worker. The trappings of ownership were alien and distasteful to her, including her big house, full of candelabra and pictures, her servant Mishenka, with his tail-coat and velvet moustache, and the innumerable people who kept pestering her for money on some pretext. Laptev, the hero of *Three Years*, also loathed his wealth because of the way in which it was obtained, and said that, if he had had a farthing's worth of will and courage, he would long ago have thrown it all away and started to earn his own living.

The factory in *A Doctor's Visit* was a more modern concern than the establishments owned by Laptev and Anna Akimovna. Among the amenities enjoyed by the workers were stage performances, lantern lectures, and an excellent canteen. All the same Doctor Korolyov could not help being depressed on the occasion of a professional visit to the owners. Korolyov had only the vaguest knowledge of industrial life, but whenever he saw a factory, he always contrasted its outward appearance of order and calm with what he imagined to exist inside—impenetrable ignorance, the blind egoism of the proprietors, the dreary and unhealthy labour of the workers, scuffles, vodka and insects. However many entertainments, lantern lectures, canteens and factory doctors there might be, the workers he had met that day on his way from the station did not look much different from those he had seen long ago in his childhood before such improvements came into fashion. As a doctor accustomed to prescribe for chronic ailments, the basic cause of which was incomprehensible and incurable, he thought of factories as something rather similar. He did not think that improvements in the life of the workers were unnecessary, but compared them to the palliative treatment of incurable diseases. After a talk with his patient, Liza Lyalikov, a young woman who was one day destined to inherit the factory, Korolyov realized that she agreed with him in regarding it as no better than a prison. Indeed, the depression aroused by the prospect of becoming a factory-owner seemed to be the chief cause of the breakdown in her health which had occasioned his visit.

The story gives Korolyov further opportunities for talking about capitalist conditions. To him the Lyalikov factory seems to be the work of an unknown force which determines the relations between weak and strong—relations to which weak and strong alike fall victims.

'Fifteen hundred or a thousand factory-workers,' he comments, 'labour without rest in unhealthy surroundings on the production of bad cotton. They lead unhealthy lives, and only occasionally sober up from the nightmare of their lives by getting drunk. The work is supervised by a hundred-odd people, whose existence is entirely given over to oaths, injustice and the listing of punishments. Only two or three individuals—the so-called masters—enjoy the fruits, although they don't do any work at all and despise bad cotton. But what are the fruits, and how do they enjoy them? Liza and her mother are so unhappy that one can only feel sorry for them, and the one person who derives satisfaction from life is Liza's governess, an aged and stupid spinster who wears pince-nez.'

The only positive result of all this chain of misery is in fact to provide one governess with the opportunity to eat sturgeon and drink madeira.

When Liza complains of her dissatisfaction, and says that she cannot sleep, Korolyov congratulates her:

'It's better than if you were satisfied, slept soundly and thought that everything was splendid. Your sleeplessness does you credit. ... It is a good sign. The sort of conversation we are having now would have been unthinkable for our parents. They didn't talk at night, but slept soundly. People of our generation sleep badly. We get tired, do a lot of talking and keep trying to decide whether we are right or not. But for our children or grandchildren this question ... will already have been decided. It will be clearer to them than to us. Life in fifty years' time will be good, and the only pity is that we shan't live to see it.'

IV

THE PEASANT

An Artist's Story saw Chekhov giving his first considered treatment of Russian village life, which he found just as baffling as the world of the factory. The story contains a debate on the peasantry between two members of the wealthier classes. One of these is a young woman, Lida Volchaninov, who lives in a country house, and devotes her whole energies to social service. She teaches in the village school, takes an active part in local government, and is especially eager to improve medical facilities. Her fanaticism in these matters leads her to view with contempt her younger sister's suitor, an artist, whose profession makes him a useless member of society from her point of view. The artist returns Lida's disapproval, and claims that all her schools, libraries and hospitals serve only to add further links to the chains which bind the peasantry. When Lida quotes the case of a village woman whose life she was able to save by means of medical aid, he retorts that this is not important. What does matter is that this woman and people like her spend all their days on back-breaking work, that they live and die in filth and squalor, and that their children have nothing better to expect in the future. Lida replies that one's highest duty is the service of one's neighbours, but this does not impress the artist, who contrasts the size of the evil she is trying to cure with the insignificant and superficial character of her remedies. She might as well expect the lamp in the drawing-room window to make daylight in the garden. He says that she must first free the peasants from hard physical work, so that they do not have to spend their whole lives in the fields. 'Make this coarse, animal labour unnecessary,' he tells her, 'let them feel free—and then you will realize what a mockery your books and dispensaries are.'

The artist's opinion of superficial remedies in the village corresponds closely with Korolyov's attitude to industrial problems in *A Doctor's Visit*. Korolyov and the artist both state their conviction that the situation is too serious to admit of solution by short-term methods. What is really needed is some far-reaching change, though neither of them is able to specify exactly what form this should take. In this they both express a point of view very close to Chekhov's own, and this is particularly true of Korolyov, who, while frankly admitting his bewilderment, definitely believes that the problem will be solved in the future.

After writing *An Artist's Story* Chekhov produced a number of direct studies of Russian village life, two of which in particular—*Peasants* and *In the Ravine*—rank among his most influential works. In these stories he was again treading on controversial ground. Many Russian intellectuals of his day tended to approach the peasant in a spirit of idealism, endowing him with all sorts of virtues which more hard-headed observers professed themselves unable to detect. Among those who were determined to see the peasant in the rosiest possible light were Tolstoy's adherents and the Populist or *Narodnik* branch of the socialist movement.

To their attitude Chekhov's stories were a direct challenge. In his eyes the Russian village was a sink of brutishness and ignorance, and the villagers an object of pity, not of admiration. In *Peasants* he stresses the miseries and coarseness of life in a poor family. There was much quarrelling and beating amid the inevitable smells, dirt and insects. Food was bad, and their one pleasure, the drinking of tea, very restricted in scope, for the tea always tasted of fish and its consumption stopped entirely when the village elder impounded the samovar because of unpaid taxes. Chekhov's general conclusions on village life are summarized in a passage near the end of the story:

'At times it seems that these people live worse than cattle ... They are coarse, dishonourable and drunken. Holding each other in mutual disrespect, fear and suspicion, they are always at loggerheads and never stop quarrelling. Who keeps the inn and makes the people drunk? The peasant. Who squanders and drinks away the funds of community, school and church? The peasant. Who steals from his neighbour, commits arson and perjures himself in court for a bottle of vodka? Who is the first to take up arms against the peasantry? The peasant.'

This plain speaking on a controversial subject by a major Russian author could not be expected to pass unnoticed, and according to one recent Russian critic the publication of *Peasants* produced the effect of an exploding bomb. It was discussed with animation all over the country. Though the Populists were indignant, the other main section of the socialist movement took a very different view. The Marxists, whose influence was rapidly increasing in the mid-'nineties, were not disposed to endow the peasantry with any unduly creditable qualities and their attitude later came to be expressed in the formula 'The idiocy of rural life'. They were convinced that big changes in society must spring from the urban proletariat, and expected little help from the agricultural classes, which they regarded as backward and politically unripe. Chekhov's presentation in *Peasants* therefore suited them very well.

As the Marxists themselves realized, Chekhov was an accidental ally. He was simply describing things as he saw them, and was not committed to any particular body of thought. In any case he was only vaguely acquainted with the Marxist viewpoint, as the history of his next important village story shows. At Gorky's suggestion *In the Ravine* was given to the magazine *Life*, and it was only after he had sent it off that Chekhov learned that *Life* was a Marxist publication. He immediately wanted to withdraw it, not because of any objection to Marxism, but as a matter of courtesy, because he thought that the line he had taken ran contrary to Marxist thought and would therefore prove an embarrassment to the editor. In fact he was entirely mistaken, for his new story was even more acceptable to Marxists than *Peasants* had been.

In the Ravine is a study of a comparatively wealthy household, which gives Chekhov an opportunity to observe the spread of capitalism in the village. The old man in the story keeps the village shop and deals in illicit liquor; one of his daughters-in-law builds a brick factory, and exploits the labour of her fellow-villagers. They are both grasping and unscrupulous, and are the type of rich and predatory peasant known as the *kulak*—the Russian word for 'fist'. *In the Ravine* is regarded in Russia as a classic treatment of the rise of the *kulak*, and, like *Peasants*, is one of Chekhov's finest stories.

V

THE INTELLECTUAL

As evidence of Chekhov's later views, *My Life* is especially valuable. Though Tolstoy's name is not quoted in it, the story contains Chekhov's most deliberate and devastating criticism of Tolstoyism. The chief aspect of this teaching selected for demolition here is the doctrine of 'simplification'. It will be remembered that Tolstoy considered most sorts of higher cultural or intellectual pursuit an immoral and unnecessary luxury. He thought that people capable of such complicated activity would do better to simplify themselves by sharing the labours and experiences of the common man. In *My Life* Chekhov allows his readers to observe a test case of simplification. The central character of the story, Misail Poloznev, had never been able to settle down in the sort of job he was expected to do as the son of the leading architect in a provincial town. His father was exasperated by his shiftlessness, and complained that Misail's behaviour was inconsistent with the family's social position. It was incredible that Misail should talk of becoming an ordinary labourer, though fully aware that his great-grandfather had been a General, and his grandfather a poet and Marshal of Nobility. Misail maintained that what his father called social position was nothing more than privilege based on capital and education. Poor and uneducated people had to earn their living by physical labour, and he saw no reason for making an exception of himself. Though his father wanted him to do mental work, thus keeping alive what he called the sacred flame of the intellect. Misail knew very well that this only meant sitting in a stuffy office and turning himself into a writing machine. He decided to defy his father, and soon got himself taken on as a house-painter.

Misail's early adventures as a labourer lead to an argument with his friend Doctor Blagovo which contains the philosophical core of the story, and in which Chekhov uses Blagovo to show why he thought Misail was mistaken. Blagovo begins the debate by paying a tribute to the energy and courage shown by Misail in carrying out his arduous programme. 'But now tell me,' he continues, 'if you directed your will-power, efforts and potentialities to some other end—for example, to turning yourself into a great scholar or artist—don't you think that your life would become broader and deeper, and that it would be in all respects more productive?' Misail replies by stating his belief in a moral law—that physical labour should be divided equally between all men, irrespective of their intellectual capabilities, since it is necessary at all costs to stop the strong from enslaving the weak. Blagovo retorts that if the intellectual élite is to waste time crushing stones and painting roofs, human progress will be seriously endangered.

'Where is the danger?' counters Misail. 'After all progress lies in acts of love, and in the fulfilment of the moral law. If you do not enslave anyone, and if you are not a burden to anyone, then what more progress do you need?' 'Look here!' Blagovo answers, 'Supposing a snail in its shell occupies itself with perfecting its own character and plays around with moral laws—do you call that progress?'

When Misail accuses him of living, without knowing definitely what he is living for, Blagovo replies:

'All right! But my ignorance is not so dull as your knowledge. I am climbing the staircase which is called Progress, Civilization and Culture. I go on and on, without knowing definitely where I am going, but in fact this wonderful staircase alone makes life worth while.'

Events which follow Misail's marriage further emphasize the bankruptcy of Tolstoy's programme. Masha Dolzhikov did not look much like a potential Tolstoyan when Misail first met her, for she wore expensive clothes, and was tall, blonde and beautiful. However, she was sufficiently attracted by Misail and his philosophy to settle down with him on a farm, eager to share his life of manual labour. Their experience of Russian village life soon made her revise her ideas. The behaviour of the villagers, who were unbelievably dishonest and ignorant, was on the low moral level familiar from Chekhov's other peasant studies. When Masha decided to build them a school they took to stealing the materials which she had collected for the purpose, and another of their exasperating habits was to gather outside her house and make a noise until supplied with vodka. Masha could not see that the Tolstoyan way of life was making much headway, and began to think again about Simplification, with the result that she decided to leave Misail. Before going away she summed up the result of their joint labours, and her remarks supplement the earlier arguments of Blagovo against Tolstoyism. She claims that, though Misail and she may have achieved something in the realm of self-perfection, they have had absolutely no effect on the surrounding milieu. Dirt, ignorance and drunkenness are as prevalent as ever. It is clear, in fact, that they have worked only for themselves, and that if they were to continue in the same way until the end of their lives it would be impossible to make any impact on such elemental forces as famine, cold and degeneracy. What was needed here was a much more bold and enterprising approach to the problem. 'Leave the narrow circle of ordinary activity,' she told her husband, 'and try to influence the masses directly! The thing most required is a loud and energetic appeal.' Misail realized that Masha had outlived his narrow ethic, that it was merely a phase through which she had quickly passed, and that she would now go on to fresh and new experiences. He felt that she had a broad, free and energetic character, whereas he himself was limited and uninteresting. Chekhov leaves him confirmed in his routine, pursuing without any enthusiasm a menial job as the foreman of a gang of painters.

In summing up the case against Tolstoyism presented in *My Life*, it must be realized that Chekhov had few quarrels with Tolstoy's exposé of the evils in Russian society. For the conventional snobbery of Misail's father and for the misdirected activities of many other people who regarded themselves as cultured and intellectual, Chekhov had much of Tolstoy's contempt. Similarly, as his industrial and peasant stories reveal, he shared Tolstoy's indignation at social and economic injustice, especially at the use of money by one section of the community to enslave another. Such indignation is frequently voiced by Misail in *My Life*. 'We've got rid of serfdom,' he says, 'but have got capitalism growing in its place,' and he goes on to point out that, in spite of much talk about freedom in Russia of his day, 'the majority still feeds, clothes and protects the minority, while itself remaining hungry, unclothed and defenceless, just as at the time of the Mongol invasion.'

Chekhov himself certainly thought that this was fair criticism of Russian society. The trouble with Misail's creed was that it did not look like ever bringing about any change in the system which it condemned. So far as Chekhov could see it simply did not work. On the outside world Tolstoy's followers did not seem to have any effect at all, except to make a few people smile and shrug their shoulders. In any case Tolstoy's standards did not impress Chekhov as particularly worth pursuing. They turned life into something drab and circumscribed, whereas he hankered after an intangible element which he could not describe, except to call it broad, enterprising and free. If Tolstoyism was an explanation of life he preferred to leave it unexplained.

Intellectual and cultural activity, of the type which Tolstoy renounced, seemed to Chekhov to contain the chief hope for the future. This point must be borne in mind when considering the numerous representatives of the intelligentsia studied in his later fiction. Chekhov did not approve of all intellectual activity, irrespective of its quality, and many of his stories contain harsh criticisms of the various aberrations to which the intellectual often succumbed. He might simply submit to the vulgarity of his surroundings for the sake of making money, or of leading a drab and undistinguished family life. Two particularly striking examples of such renegades from the intelligentsia are the doctor Ionych in the story of the same name and Andrew Prozorov in the play *Three Sisters*. Ionych, who started out as a young energetic and sensitive doctor in a provincial town, gradually subsided into a condition of flabby and unimaginative affluence. Prozorov, who was expected to become a professor, ended up as a minor official, overwhelmed by his card debts and the influence of a vulgar and stupid wife.

Another variety of intellectual disapproved of by Chekhov was the talkative type which seemed incapable of making any genuine contribution to the community. Characters like the engineer in *The Wife* and Vlasov in *Neighbours* have retained much of their mental vigour, but their constant philosophizing tirades are little better than a nervous trick, directed principally to the evocation of self-pity. Similarly Chekhov disliked the 'arty' section of the intelligentsia, which he described in scathing terms in *The Grasshopper,* and which seems to have impressed him as a useless froth on the surface of society. The picture conveyed in such studies is reinforced by the numerous outbursts against the intelligentsia to be found in Chekhov's correspondence. 'I don't believe in our intelligentsia,' he wrote in 1899. 'It's hypocritical, false, hysterical, uneducated and lazy.'

In spite of the violence of such condemnations Chekhov firmly believed in the value of the right sort of intellectual who, from his point of view, was usually the person who cultivated his own special qualities for the service of the community. It was perhaps natural that the subjects of his more sympathetic studies should often have been doctors. For example, he used Doctor Blagovo in *My Life* to refute the false philosophy of Misail, and Doctor Korolyov to express his views on factory conditions in *A Doctor's Visit*. Another of his doctors was Dymov in *The Grasshopper*—a brilliant medical research worker, ignored by his flighty wife, who thought her interest in landscape-painting made her a much more important person than he. Doctor Astrov in the play *Uncle Vanya*, an energetic country practitioner with a keen interest in forestry, has sometimes been taken as Chekhov's attempt to portray a positive hero embodying his own ideals. Since education occupied a central part in Chekhov's theory of progress it was natural that he should approve of hard-working and devoted school-teachers, such as the heroine of *The Schoolmistress*. Chekhov stresses the unpleasantness of her life, and the fact that her efforts go entirely without recognition, but he felt that the future of Russia depended on the labours of thousands like her. Stories such as these suggest that Chekhov's views on the intellectual were accurately summed up when he wrote in his *Notebooks*: 'The strength and salvation of a country lies in its intelligentsia—in that section of it which thinks honestly and is capable of work.'

VI

FREEDOM

CHEKHOV was usually chary of large and airy generalizations, and felt more at home among individual facts and observations. He departed from his normal practice in this matter when talking about freedom. To him freedom represented something of fundamental value, for which he was always yearning in his own life, and which he found lacking in many of the people around him. It was not merely the oppressiveness of the Russian government and the absence of political freedom in Russia to which he objected. So far as he could see individuals were often as big a menace to their own freedom as any government, because of a tendency to accept from others, or to impose on themselves, unimaginative and stultifying patterns of behaviour. It has been seen that Chekhov regarded Tolstoyism as a pattern of this sort, and that one of his charges against it was the fact that it restricted the freedom of its devotees, and made their lives uninteresting.

Lack of freedom could take many other forms, as Chekhov proceeded to show in three stories, all published in 1898, *The Man in a Case*, *Gooseberries* and *About Love*. These stories were intended to be read as a group, and are accordingly sometimes referred to as a trilogy. The Trilogy has three narrators, who each tell a story to one or both of the others. In each case the characters described by the narrators lack the kind of freedom which Chekhov considered necessary, and the narrators themselves express a critical attitude closely allied to Chekhov's own. This is a feature of all three stories, although in the last one narrator and central character are the same person.

As an example of a person smothered in self-imposed restrictions, Belikov, the schoolmaster described in *The Man in the Case*, is outstanding. Belikov always wore goloshes and carried an umbrella; even in the summer he was never seen without a warm overcoat. He kept everything in some kind of case or holder, including his face, which he concealed in an upturned coat collar. He was always praising the past, and taught the classical languages, 'which were just another form of goloshes and umbrella in which to hide from real life.' Belikov was always trying to have things prohibited, and whenever any new proposal was made he used to shake his head and say, 'It's all very well, of course, but—let's hope nothing comes of it.' According to Chekhov's narrator, Belikov had a deadening effect on the whole town. Ladies were afraid to organize private theatricals in case he got to know, and the clergy did not dare to play cards. As a result of his influence people were afraid to talk in a loud voice, to send letters, make friends, or even to read books.

Belikov was so set in his ways that it was a great surprise to everyone when he was almost persuaded to become engaged to Barbara Kovalenko, the sister of another master at the same school. As might have been expected, he found it difficult to make up his mind to propose. 'Marriage is a serious step,' he kept saying. 'One must weigh up one's impending responsibilities.' He was still undecided when he happened one day to see his prospective fiancée and her brother riding bicycles together in the town. Feeling it his duty to protest at such a flagrant offence he later called on Kovalenko and pointed out that there was nothing in the regulations permitting teachers to ride bicycles. 'If the teacher rides a bicycle, what can one expect his pupils to do?' he asks. 'Walk on their heads, I suppose!' As for Barbara, 'A woman or girl on a bicycle—horrible!' Obviously it was only a matter of time before this disgraceful affair reached the ears of the Headmaster and the school governors. Kovalenko was offended at this complaint, and in the quarrel which developed, told his visitor to mind his own business. On his way out Belikov said that he must warn Kovalenko of one thing: 'In order that people may not give a wrong interpretation of our conversation, and in order that nothing may come of it, I shall have to report its substance to the Headmaster.' 'Go ahead and report!' shouted Kovalenko, who was so annoyed that he shoved his visitor downstairs. At the bottom Belikov had just righted himself, and was looking to see if his glasses were intact, when he caught sight of Barbara, who had entered the house with two ladies in time to witness the end of his fall. Seeing his goloshes and rumpled coat, and not realizing what had happened, she burst into ringing laughter. This was terrible. Now the matter was sure to reach the Headmaster and the Governors. Something, in fact, was bound to come of it, and Belikov could see himself as the laughing-stock of the town.

This occurrence put an end to Belikov's prospective engagement, and, incidentally, to his existence on earth. He was so upset that he worried himself into an illness, and died four weeks later. Of the funeral Chehhov's narrator remarks that, though nobody liked to show it, the burial of Belikov was really quite a pleasant business. It gave everyone a feeling familiar from childhood, 'when the grown-ups had left the house and we ran about the garden for an hour or two, enjoying full freedom. Oh, Freedom, Freedom! Even a hint, even a faint hope of its possibility gives wings to the soul.'

Though Belikov was dead, it was a disturbing thought that there were still many other Belikovs left alive. One of these was the hero of *Gooseberries*, Nicholas Gimalaysky, whose history is told by his brother Ivan. Nicholas had always been a poor man, and had been forced to earn his living by taking a job as a clerk in a government office. He hated town life, and early in his career had conceived the ambition of buying himself a country estate to which he could retire. For some reason an integral part of this obsession became a desire to eat gooseberries grown from bushes on his own land. His whole life was devoted to saving money which would enable him to achieve this wish. He denied himself all pleasure, married an old and ugly widow for her money, and contributed to her early death by stinting her of food. Finally, after a lifetime's sustained effort he had saved enough to realize his dream.

On his first visit to Nicholas in his new estate Ivan found him sitting up in bed with his knees covered by a blanket, and looking old, stout and flabby. Any moment, it seemed, he would grunt into the blanket. His character had completely changed. He was an important person now—a country squire—and he was not likely to let anyone forget it. He kept saying: 'We members of the upper class,' regardless of the fact that his grandfather had been a peasant and his father a common soldier. He took offence when the peasants failed to call him 'Your Honour!' As a government clerk he had been afraid to have any personal opinions at all, but now he delivered himself of pompous generalizations in the tone of a minister of state. Such remarks were: 'Education is necessary, but for the common people it is premature,' 'As a general rule corporal punishment is pernicious, but in certain cases it is useful and indispensable.'

It so happened that Ivan's visit coincided with the momentous occasion when the first gooseberries were plucked from his brother's bushes. Nicholas looked at the fruit with tears in his eyes, and was unable to speak for emotion. All through the night Ivan could hear him walking up and down his bedroom, taking berries from the plate one by one. Here was a happy man who had achieved his aim in life, and was entirely satisfied with his fate. However, in the light of the vast potentialities of the human spirit Nicholas and his gooseberries seem pathetic. Ivan recalls that he himself had once been happy in the same way as his brother. Like Nicholas he had made pompous remarks about freedom being necessary, adding, however, that 'we must wait for it'. Now he finds himself asking 'Why should we wait?'

'Is there any order or law in the fact that I, a live and thinking man, stand on one side of a ditch and wait for it to grow over of its own accord or fill up with slime, when all the time it is possible that I might be able to leap across it, or build a bridge over it. Again I ask, in the name of what should we wait?'

The third record of timidity and lack of freedom, contained in the story *About Love*, concerns the farmer Alyokhin, who recalls an unsuccessful love affair of his own which might have turned out very differently if he could have brought himself to act with imagination and enterprise.

Betrothed, the last story Chekhov wrote, further illustrates his views on freedom. It contains a more positive study than those in the Trilogy, for the heroine, Nadya, manages to transcend the limitations which threaten to circumscribe her life. She has always lived in a small provincial town with her grandmother and mother. It was a very ordinary sort of provincial household, in which the main occupation was the preparation and consumption of food. Listening to the bustle in the kitchen and smelling the familiar roast turkey and bottled cherries, Nadya realized that things had been exactly the same twenty years ago, and didn't look as if they would ever change.

Ever since she was sixteen she had dreamed of getting married, and now that she was twenty-three she had just become engaged to the son of a local priest. Though she was fond of Andrew, the engagement did not make Nadya particularly happy, and she found herself unable to sleep at night for worrying. The reason for her dissatisfaction was a subconscious realization that Andrew was as limited a character as her mother and grandmother, and that marrying him could only mean exchanging one form of mediocrity for another. A friend of the family, Sasha, who saw this more clearly than Nadya, did his best to explain things. He said that she should break off the engagement and leave home in order to study. The effect of this would be to change her whole life for the better, since according to him only cultured and educated people are interesting or useful, and the more such people there are the sooner

'the Kingdom of Heaven will appear on earth. By a gradual process not one stone will be left on another in your town. Everything will be turned upside down. Everything will be transformed, as if by magic. There will then arise here large and magnificent houses, wonderful gardens, extraordinary fountains and noble people.'

Nadya was more impressed by this appeal than she cared to admit, and though she protested her intention of persisting with the marriage, very soon Sasha's intervention began to make her see things in a different light. A demonstration of affection by Andrew, which followed shortly afterwards, impressed her as resembling something read in an old and dog-eared novel. The same evening she realized that her mother, whom she used to revere as something unusual, was only a very ordinary and unhappy woman. Her disillusionment was further strengthened by a visit with Andrew to the apartment in which they were to live after the wedding. Though it was well appointed, with parquet flooring and magnificent furniture, everything about it depressed her. As Andrew led her around the house with his hand about her waist, and explained the details of the plumbing, she realized that she had fallen out of love with him, and could see nothing in their prospective way of life except 'vulgarity, stupid, naive, intolerable vulgarity'. At last she decided that it was impossible to go through with the marriage, and took Sasha's advice by running away to Petersburg in order to study. After her examinations were over Nadya visited her home, feeling healthy and happy. Somehow the whole town seemed smaller and dirtier than it had been when she knew it before. Looking around her Nadya felt sure that she had done the right thing, and that human life in general would one day change in the way she had changed her individual life.

' "Oh, if only that new and bright life would soon begin," she mused. "A life in which it will be possible to look directly and fearlessly in the eyes of one's fate, to recognize that one is right, to be happy and free! Sooner or later such a life will begin." '

VII

CHEKHOV'S GENERAL OUTLOOK

IN steering a course from the pessimism and indifference of the 'eighties towards the optimism and social criticism of the 'nineties, Chekhov was following a general current in Russian thought as assessed by all authorities on the period. P. S. Kogan expresses the usual view on this subject in his biographical sketch of Chekhov. He says that 'the 'eighties were distinguished by the predominance of melancholy moods ... of an indifference to social matters, and of a heightened interest in private spiritual experiences'. To illustrate the change which followed he goes on to quote a typical description of the 'nineties by a contemporary observer, who claimed that the general mood had completely altered, and that 'New men had appeared, men of confidence and conviction'.

Chekhov's later stories show that this mood was increasingly communicating itself to him, but he would probably not have gone so far as to call himself a 'man of confidence and conviction'. Still less would he have subscribed to the grandiloquent phrases which the more excitable of his fellow-countrymen began to apply to him. 'A Champion of Freedom' was one of these. As Nemirovich-Danchenko notes in his memoirs, this may have been an approximately true statement of fact, but the choice of words sets entirely the wrong tone for a description of Chekhov. Nemirovich-Danchenko goes on to suggest what Chekhov might have said if he had chanced to hear such a description: ' "Good Heavens! Me a champion!" he would have remarked, placing his hands in his trouser pockets, and walking about the room with long strides. "I won't shake hands with him for talking such nonsense," he would have added with reference to the author of the remark, adjusting his pince-nez with emotion.'

Unwilling though he may have been to have himself thought of as any sort of champion, Chekhov repeatedly expressed in his later work a most vigorous condemnation of the patterns of life evolved in Russian society. He saw the community as divided into two main sections, the one a privileged minority, and the other an unprivileged mass, which worked to support the minority. This diagnosis did not lead him into regarding either section as the villain of the piece. He thought of the whole business as a muddle which produced nothing but frustration and unhappiness in all quarters. So far as the unprivileged group was concerned he drew a picture of ignorance, squalor and brutishness —the result of long, exhausting and underpaid labour. On the other hand the privileged class, in spite of its higher standard of living, seemed to Chekhov to be equally far from achieving any sort of contentment. His factory-owners were miserable, and did not know what to do. Though his stories contain few studies of the Russian landowner, various representatives of this class in the later plays show that to Chekhov it appeared every bit as liable to frustration and maladjustment as its industrial counterpart. As for the intermediate section of society, represented by professional men and intellectuals, the position was not very much better, and Chekhov tended to emphasize its distress and bewilderment in face of the general chaos.

Although pictures of frustration and depression did not entirely disappear from his work, the longer his life lasted the more hopeful did he seem to become. It is no accident that, of the stories here selected for discussion, the more cheerful in tone belong to the latter part of the period, such stories being in particular the Trilogy and *Betrothed*. The forecasts of Nadya and Sasha in *Betrothed* find many parallels elsewhere in predictions of a future paradise on earth. Such predictions were included among Gromov's ravings in *Ward No. 6*, and there were hints in the same direction from Blagovo in *My Life* and Korolyov in *A Doctor's Visit*. Prophecies of a better time for humanity also figure largely in the last three plays, each of which contains a character with a confident faith in the future.

There is much evidence that Chekhov himself shared this faith. Kuprin in his reminiscences quotes him as making speeches in the style of his more optimistic characters. He recalls an occasion when Chekhov screwed up his eyes with pleasure as he looked at his garden, and said 'Before I came this place was a waste-plot with ugly ditches, all covered with stones and thistles. Well, I came along and turned the wilderness into a beautiful cultivated place. Do you know,' he went on—according to Kuprin, 'in a tone of deep faith'—'Do you know, in three or four hundred years the whole earth will turn into a blossoming garden, and life will then be extraordinarily easy and comfortable.' There are many passages in Chekhov's correspondence where he expresses a similar belief in human progress, though in words usually more sober and less prophetic than those attributed to him by Kuprin or those used by his fictional mouthpieces. Chekhov remained as reluctant as ever to preach, and it is perhaps for this reason that he has endowed some of his prophets of the future with qualities designed to soften the didactic impact of their pronouncements. Gromov, to take an extreme example, is a raving lunatic. Others are patently ineffectual, like Trofimov in *The Cherry Orchard* who, when not proclaiming his faith in the future of humanity, is liable to be worrying about his lost goloshes. Other exponents of the faith, such as Korolyov and Astrov, are comparatively normal and balanced people. Whatever their individual degree of eccentricity, all these characters can plausibly be regarded as interpreters of Chekhov's own viewpoint.

Two well-established elements in Chekhov's philosophy are, accordingly, a strong condemnation of existing conditions and an underlying hope of improvement. However, the gap between the evil present and the glorious future was discouragingly wide, and the problem of bridging it was one which Chekhov never solved, though he gave it much thought. His explorations produced a number of interesting suggestions, and he was able to examine other people's ideas and to show why they seemed to him unsatisfactory. It has been seen that most of them impressed him as superficial attempts to cure a deep-seated malady. Chekhov felt that something more drastic was required. Though he could not say exactly what form the change should take, he could indicate some of the conditions most likely to conduce to it. Prominent among these was freedom from external restrictions and from the kind of limitations which people tended to impose upon themselves. A willingness to work and the spread of education were further important elements, and another was the development of scientific processes. An interest in scientific development is a well-established feature of Chekhov's outlook which found little expression in the stories, but which is much in evidence in his correspondence. 'He liked looking at new buildings of original construction and at large sea-going steamers,' Kuprin recalls in his reminiscences of Chekhov: 'He took a lively interest in all the latest technical inventions, and was not bored by the company of specialists.'

To the above contributions towards a better future Chekhov would have added that he placed his hopes, not in political parties or groups of people but in enlightened individuals. To the Three Sisters, who come into this category, his character Vershinin says:

'There are only three like you in the town at the moment, but in future generations there will be more—ever more and more —and a time will come when everything will change to your way and people will live like you; then you too will grow old and people will be born who will live better than you.'

A parallel passage in one of Chekhov's letters, dated 1899, shows how close Vershinin is to expressing Chekhov's own opinion on this point:

'I believe in individual people; I look for salvation to individual personalities, scattered here and there throughout Russia, whether they are intellectuals or peasants. It is in them that strength lies, though they are few in number. The individual personalities of which I speak play an unobtrusive role in society; they do not dominate, but their work leaves its mark. Whatever else may be going on, science keeps moving forward and social consciousness is growing.'

VIII

RELIGION AND POLITICS

ON Chekhov's religious opinions it would be difficult to find any helpful pointers at all in his literary work. He accepted the Orthodox Church as a feature of Russian life, and, in the portraits which he drew of religious people maintained an attitude of such tolerance and detachment that they might easily be mistaken for the work of a believer. This was particularly true of *The Bishop*, one of his finest stories, in which he drew a most sympathetic picture of a member of the clergy. None the less, Chekhov's personal outlook was completely free from any religious element. 'I have long ago lost my faith, and can only look with consternation on any intelligent man who is a believer,' he remarked in one letter, written after the turn of the century, and, though he speaks here of losing his faith, there is no evidence that he ever entertained serious religious beliefs. A longer passage from a letter of about the same period shows his low assessment of religion as a potential contributor to the future of humanity:

'One may say of the educated portion of our society that it has abandoned religion, and that it is retreating farther and farther away from it, whatever people may say, and however many religio-philosophical societies may hold their meetings. I won't take it on myself to decide whether this is a good or a bad thing, and I will only say that the religious movement ... is one thing, and that all modern culture is another and quite different thing. It is impossible to place the latter in causal relationship with the former. Modern culture is the beginning of work in the name of a great future, work which will perhaps continue for tens of thousands of years, so that humanity may learn, if only in the distant future, the truth of the real God—that is, not guess it, or look for it in Dostoevsky, but realize it with as much clarity as it has realized that two and two make four. Present-day culture is the beginning of work, while the religious movement is a thing of the past, almost the end of something which has become obsolete or is becoming so.'

Chekhov's literary work is much more richly furnished with clues to his political tendencies than to his religious opinions. Here also, however, the picture can only be completed with the help of additional information. The evidence shows that he retained throughout his life some of his early prejudice against politically-minded people, and at no time regarded himself as the adherent of any political party. None the less it would be correct to say that his political views were constantly developing, in the sense that he was reaching, independently of political parties, positions on individual questions coinciding more and more with the views of the Left Wing.

It will be remembered that Chekhov abandoned the
~~tive~~ paper *New Time* in the early 'nineties, and that,
~~tling~~ his quarrel with *Russian Thought* in 1892, he
principally in the liberal press. This did not mean that he ~~...~~
now become a liberal, any more than that he had previously
been a conservative, though the move was symptomatic of his
general trend. He could agree with the liberals on certain points,
particularly in opposing the autocratic system of government
and requiring greater freedom of expression for the country. It
appears also that Chekhov shared with the liberals a wish to
supplant autocracy with a constitution on Western lines. Kuprin
says that one of his favourite phrases in conversation, often
introduced without apparent relevance to the subject under discussion, was, 'In ten years we shall have a constitution in Russia.'

The chief reason why Chekhov could not side wholeheartedly
with liberalism was that it committed itself to the type of gradual
change which he regarded as insufficient. He did not of course
object to the alleviation of social ills, as is shown by his own
efforts in promoting medical and educational improvements at
Melikhovo and elsewhere. What he objected to was the frame
of mind which regarded such remedies as adequate to the situation. In any case Russian liberalism often impressed him as a
kind of self-intoxication with high-sounding words by people
who seemed willing to acquiesce in practice with the abuses
which formed the subject of their theoretical denunciations.
After attending a dinner held by his liberal friends to com-
memorate the Emancipation of the Serfs, Chekhov wrote in his
diary of 1897: 'Boring and silly. To dine, drink champagne,
make a lot of noise, hold speeches on national self-consciousness,
freedom etc—when all the time slaves in tailcoats are darting
around the table, no different from the old serfs, and in the
street coachmen wait in the frost.'

Chekhov's view that only drastic measures could save Russia
raises the question of his relations with the revolutionary socialism. This is a particularly interesting point, since the majority of
serious attempts at interpreting Chekhov have been made by
Soviet critics. An indication of their general approach to
Chekhov's politics will serve as an illustration of his attitude to
socialism.

Soviet critics admit that Chekhov could at no time be described as a direct and conscious supporter of any section of the
socialist movement. He did not have the kind of mind which

sees problems from a political angle, and accordingly did not take pains to inform himself very thoroughly on the details of the socialist case. It is pointed out, however, that there is a remarkable coincidence of views between Chekhov and the Marxist wing of socialism on a large number of individual points. This has not led any Soviet writer to claim Chekhov as an adherent of Marxism. On the contrary it is usual to quote a passage from a letter of 1900 in which he appears to express some distaste for this movement. Writing from Nice he says that one of the advantages of this town from his point of view is the fact that you never run across Russian police officials or 'Marxists with their arrogant physiognomies'.

Some of the points on which Chekhov's views tallied with Marxism have already been mentioned. Particularly noticeable is his view that capitalism divided society into the two classes of exploiters and exploited, and his use of the word 'bourgeois'. 'The bourgeoisie,' he once wrote, 'is very fond of novels with so-called "positive types" and with happy endings, because they comfort it in the thought that it is possible to accumulate capital while preserving one's innocence, to be a brute without forfeiting one's happiness.'

In his approval of the material advantages achieved under capitalism, especially by the application of scientific technical processes, Chekhov was again at one with Marxist thought. Indeed, a remark already quoted from one of his letters, to the effect that 'there is more love for humanity in electricity and steam than in chastity and abstention from meat' reads almost like a Marxist slogan. His belief in hard work is a further point on which his views approached those advocated in present-day Russia. Finally, one most important point of contact lies in the 'scientific attitude' to life which underlay Chekhov's philosophy, involving him in a hard-headed empirical approach to society and a marked hostility to all forms of religious speculation and metaphysics.

The problem naturally arises as to whether Chekhov foresaw a Russian revolution, and the general conclusion drawn by Soviet critics is that he did not. One of his few direct references to revolution is unfortunately contained in a letter written in 1888, at a time when his views were considerably farther to the right than in his later life. He wrote on this occasion that one of the characters in *Steppe*, Dymov, seemed to him a potential revolutionary but 'There will never be a revolution in Russia and

Dymov will end up by drinking himself to death or getting into prison'. By contrast with this Chekhov's later work contains many passages which lend themselves to interpretation by Soviet propagandists as predictions of the future of Russia. One of these already quoted is Korolyov's claim in *A Doctor's Visit* that social problems would be decided in the next two generations, and that 'Life in fifty years' time will be good and the only pity is that we shall not live to see it'. An even more remarkable passage is Tusenbach's speech in the first act of *Three Sisters*.

'An avalanche is moving down on us all. There is brewing up a mighty, health-giving storm. It is on the move, it is already near at hand, and it will sweep all laziness, indifference, distaste for work and rotten boredom out of society. I shall work and in another twenty-five or thirty years everyone will have to work. Everyone!'

All the same it seems unlikely that Chekhov believed in the imminence of a socialist revolution in Russia. His main difference with the socialists was that he had a less exact idea of the kind of society he would like to see, and no precise conception of the tactics required to produce it. Soviet critics do, however, claim that if Chekhov had thought out the logical implications of his position he would inevitably have become a supporter of revolution.

Had the natural expectation of life been fulfilled in Chekhov's case he would have witnessed the 1917 revolutions, and it is natural to ask what his attitude would have been. Soviet critics are able to adduce evidence that he would have been likely to support the Bolshevik side, but this is a question which can never be decided, and on which individuals will normally pronounce in accordance with their own political views. Whatever his initial reaction to the overthrow of the autocracy might have been, Chekhov's attitude to later developments in Soviet Russia (had he lived to witness them under Lenin and Stalin) is less a matter for speculation. It is unlikely, to put it mildly, that he would have been favourably impressed.

CHAPTER NINE

The Moscow Art Theatre and Yalta

I

THE IDEAS BEHIND THE MOSCOW ART THEATRE

THE foundation of the Moscow Art Theatre in 1898 makes this year one of the most important dates in the history of the Russian stage. The new theatre was to affect the whole of Chekhov's subsequent life and literary development, changing him from a writer of experimental plays with limited appeal into one of the leading dramatists of modern Europe, and incidentally providing him with a wife.

The Moscow Art Theatre was created by two men of about the same age as Chekhov, Konstantin Stanislavsky and Vladimir Nemirovich-Danchenko. Their intention was to bring about a complete reform of the Russian stage, and there was certainly plenty of room for change. In the theatre as they found it too much attention was paid to a few star actors, who often laid down the law to the producer, and attracted an undue share of the limelight. Stanislavsky and Nemirovich-Danchenko were determined that in their theatre the producer should be the absolute master; he must, however, be a benevolent despot, who could carry his staff with him as a disciplined and enthusiastic team. Each production must be a unified, imaginative and conscientious work of art, in which full weight should be given to all elements, including acting, dress, scenery, properties, the behaviour of the audience, choice of incidental music and design of programmes. These were all matters which were more or less unsatisfactory in the existing theatre. The character of the two reformers was enough to ensure that there should be no lack of daring and experiment in the choice and presentation of plays, but the main thing they intended to insist on was a natural and sincere way of acting. They were determined to do away with the over-theatrical gestures and intonations which they felt were turning the drama into a dead art.

Stanislavsky and Nemirovich-Danchenko have both spoken at
length in their reminiscences of the founding of their theatre.
These reminiscences were written many years later at a time
when their efforts had long been crowned with the most outstanding success. Not only had their theatre become the foremost
in Russia, but their standards had set the tone for the post-
revolutionary Russian stage as a whole. So enormous had their
prestige become that it was difficult to believe that their early
struggles had been so hard, and that there had been a time
when even some of their well-wishers regarded them as cranks.
It is impossible not to be infected by their exhilaration in
describing the early days. In Moscow no suitable theatre was
available for rehearsals, so the whole company moved to the
country, and worked in a large shed a few miles away from
Stanislavsky's property at Lyubimovka. Stanislavsky and
Nemirovich-Danchenko lived at Lyubimovka, while the rest of
the company were disposed in various nearby *dachas*. It was an
arduous life, for rehearsals went on all day, and in the absence
of servants everyone had to turn a hand to cleaning duties when
not wanted on the stage. The weather was unpleasantly hot,
and the novelty of the whole enterprise led to some misunderstandings and difficulties. However, general enthusiasm proved
equal to all obstacles, and there were many exciting interludes
to compensate for discomfort. At one point Stanislavsky, with
characteristic élan, borrowed a train, and together with other
members of the company conducted a raid on the markets of
such medieval Russian towns as Rostov-near-Yaroslavl. At such
places and at the celebrated Nizhny Novgorod fair he was
successful in acquiring valuable old fabrics for use in historical
plays. A night spent in Ivan the Terrible's castle at Rostov gave
everyone the right atmosphere for the play *Tsar Theodore* by
A. K. Tolstoy, and was made all the more horrific by one of the
company who pretended to be a ghost.

In the repertoire of ten plays which had been chosen for the
opening season *Tsar Theodore* occupied pride of place, and was
to be given at the inaugural performance of the Art Theatre,
scheduled for October 14, 1898. A. K. Tolstoy's play, which
was a historical drama in verse, had been written some thirty
years previously, but had only just been released by the censorship. It provided Stanislavsky with full scope for his love of
the spectacular. Other items on the repertoire included Sophocles'
Antigone and Shakespeare's *Merchant of Venice*. In choosing

more modern authors preference had been given to playwrights with a fresh and unusual slant on the stage, such as Hauptmann and Maeterlinck. Finally, Chekhov's *Seagull* was included, in the face of strong opposition, on the insistence of Nemirovich-Danchenko.

II

The Seagull IN MOSCOW

NEMIROVICH-DANCHENKO had been on terms of intimacy with Chekhov for some years before the founding of the Moscow Art Theatre, and took great interest in his friend's work for the stage—indeed *The Seagull* had been written partly at his suggestion. The failure of this play at its first performance in Petersburg had been yet one more proof to Nemirovich-Danchenko of the inadequacy of the existing theatre. He conceived a most extravagant admiration for *The Seagull* and was one of the few people who refused to join in the general chorus of condemnation in 1896. Now that he had a theatre of his own one of the first things he wanted to do was to show that a fresh and intelligent approach could make a success of the play. However, a lot of persuasion was necessary before Chekhov would agree to release it, and Nemirovich-Danchenko had opposition to overcome in the Art Theatre itself, for Stanislavsky and many of the actors were less appreciative than he of the new qualities which Chekhov brought to the stage. Fortunately Nemirovich-Danchenko possessed a talent for communicating his enthusiasms, and was able to win his colleagues over.

The play was given adequate rehearsals—twenty-six in all—and Chekhov managed to attend one of them before leaving to spend the winter in Yalta. His visit seems to have been a slightly disappointing occasion for the actors. Perplexed by the novelty of the play they hoped for some hints from the author, but his answers to their questions tended to be obscure. To a request for guidance on the interpretation of his Trigorin he replied, 'Why, he wears check trousers!' as though that made everything clear, and when asked how to play another part, he replied, not very helpfully, 'As well as possible.' There was at first a feeling of awkwardness between him and the actors. He looked at them, sometimes with a smile, sometimes with an expression of unexpected seriousness, plucking his beard and jerking his pince-nez. Owing to his reticence he did not always create a good initial impression, and Stanislavsky has even recorded that

Chekhov at first struck him as 'arrogant and insincere', owing to a way he had of throwing back his head when speaking to people. However, such impressions never lasted very long.

Before leaving Moscow, Chekhov managed to attend one other rehearsal of the Art Theatre. This time the play was *Tsar Theodore*, and he was particularly pleased and attracted by Olga Knipper, the actress who played the part of Irina. 'If I'd stayed in Moscow I'd have fallen in love with that Irina,' he remarked in one letter written soon after his arrival in Yalta.

The first performance of *The Seagull* was fixed for October 17, exactly two years after the memorable fiasco in Petersburg. Everything combined to make the occasion a tense experience for all concerned. The new theatre was not doing well. *Tsar Theodore* had been a great success, but the plays which followed were disappointing. *The Merchant of Venice* was a complete failure, and a worse disaster followed when Hauptmann's *Hannele* was suddenly banned on the instigation of the Metropolitan of Moscow. Things had moved in such a way that the success or failure of *The Seagull* on the 17th apparently meant success or failure for the theatre. *The Seagull* had not been intended by the directors to bear this load of responsibility. They were relying more on some of the other plays to establish the theatre, feeling that Chekhov's work was too unorthodox to catch on at once. The intervention of Mariya Chekhov contributed to the general nervousness. Better than anyone else she knew how the original failure of the play had upset her brother's health, and, fearing that a second failure might have an even worse effect, appealed at the last moment for the cancellation of the performance. Nemirovich-Danchenko had to take responsibility for refusing her request. Stanislavsky, who always saw things in rather glaring colours, has given his impression of the feeling in the theatre just before the curtain rose: 'Standing on the stage we listened to an inner voice, which whispered to us: "Act well; act magnificently; achieve success and triumph. And if you do not, then know that on receipt of your telegram your beloved author will die, the victim of your own hands. You will become his executioners." '

Under these circumstances the first act was a harrowing experience to the players. Everyone had taken valerian drops, and Stanislavsky had great difficulty in controlling a nervous twitching of his foot. At the end of the act there seemed to be no reaction from the audience, for the curtain came down in dead silence. All the actors looked at each other in horror and, according to Stanislavsky, Olga Knipper had to repress hysterical sobs. Suddenly, however, the applause broke out in a way that left no doubt at all of the audience's enthusiasm. The curtain was raised in answer, and took the actors by surprise, for some were turned half away from the audience and others were sitting down. Everyone was too overcome to bow. It did not matter, for the situation was saved, and Stanislavsky was not the only one who celebrated by executing a wild dance in the wings. The rest of the play went splendidly and on the demand of the audience a telegram was sent to Chekhov in Yalta assuring him of a really memorable triumph.

The success of *The Seagull* had surprised everybody, including even Nemirovich-Danchenko, and the rival Moscow Little Theatre was reported to be 'ready to bite' with enraged envy. So far as Chekhov was concerned the performance made it clear that Russian audiences could appreciate his dramatic technique, and that the Art Theatre was his ideal interpreter. For the rest of his life he maintained a close association with the Art Theatre, which even came to be known by the alternative title of 'Chekhov's Theatre'. His plays have formed a staple part of the repertoire ever since their first performance, and his importance to the theatre was signalized by the adoption of a seagull as its permanent emblem. This emblem has been retained to this day in the Art Theatre, and is to be seen on the curtain, programmes and attendants' uniforms.

III

CHEKHOV'S LIFE IN YALTA

THE success of *The Seagull* was wonderful news for Chekhov, but unfortunately he was in no mood to give it his undivided attention. Five days previously a telegram had arrived in Yalta announcing his father's death. The old man had injured himself by lifting a heavy case, and had been hurriedly removed from Melikhovo to Moscow, where he died after an unsuccessful operation. Chekhov was especially grieved, for he felt that he might have been able to save his father's life if he had been on the spot himself. 'It seems to me,' he reflected sadly, 'that after Father's death things will never be the same in Melikhovo, as though the course of Melikhovo life had been cut short together with his diary.'

Chekhov decided to provide a new home for his mother and sister in Yalta, and though it was a wrench to part with the Melikhovo property, on which so much care had been expended, no other course seemed possible. It was likely from what the doctors said that Chekhov himself would be regularly marooned in the south during the cold weather, and his mother had lost all wish to live in Melikhovo after her husband's death. Accordingly Chekhov bought a plot of land near Yalta soon after his father's death, and borrowed money to pay for the building of a house. Though there was a picturesque view of sea and mountains, the site had its disadvantages, and Mariya Chekhov is even said to have burst into tears when her brother took her to see it for the first time. It was twenty minutes' walking distance from Yalta, next to a Tartar cemetery, was outside the sewage and water-supply system of the town, and, being overgrown with wild vines, looked wild and neglected. However, Melikhovo had shown that Chekhov was capable of transforming his surroundings, and he lavished all his enterprise and skill on the Yalta property. Together with his architect he worked out the plans for a most original and charming villa, which eventually became the admiration of visitors to Yalta, with its small, square tower, terraces and glass veranda, all constructed on a most unusual design. The house was ready for habitation by August 1899. It was one of the most prominent buildings on the coast, and for some reason Chekhov joked that it would be the first to be shelled when the British fleet attacked Yalta. From the outset the garden claimed much of his attention. It was thrilling to find that roses would bloom in December in the Crimea, and he quickly ordered a hundred bushes. Trees were planted methodically, and included—now that the sub-tropical climate enabled him to increase his range—mimosa, cypress, camelias, palm-trees, fig and eucalyptus.

Chekhov did not shut himself up in his new property, but took a prominent part in the life of the town. He became a familiar figure on the sea-front, and made a friend of a certain Sinani, who kept a bookshop there. A bench outside Sinani's shop was a regular rendezvous for the exchange of gossip between Chekhov and his Yalta acquaintances. Many of these were themselves celebrities in Russia, and Sinani kept a book in his shop for the purpose of recording their signatures. A cult of Chekhov quickly developed in Yalta, and he complained that he sometimes had to hide his face behind a newspaper on the front so as to escape unwelcome attentions. He was much sought after by members of the opposite sex, so that a special name—*Antonovki*—was evolved to describe his lady-admirers. Since *antonovki* is the Russian name for a brand of apples, the expression may be translated into English as 'Chekhov's pippins'.

As at Melikhovo, Chekhov found himself accepting various local responsibilities. He was appointed governor of the local girls' high school—'giving me the right to wear the uniform of an official of the sixth grade,' he remarked with amusement. Moreover, his educational work earned him a decoration from the Government—the Stanislav medal, third class—an award which he seems to have carefully concealed from his friends. The chief cause to which he devoted himself in Yalta was the assistance of the sick. Consumptive patients were flocking to the Crimea in large numbers from all parts of Russia—in some cases they came from as far away as Siberia. They were often extremely poor and in desperate need of help. Chekhov could not help contrasting their miserable condition with the gaiety and glitter of wealthy visitors who came to Yalta for the season. He spent much time organizing subscriptions all over Russia, and became the member of a committee which equipped a tubercular sanatorium in Yalta.

In spite of the active part which he took in the life of the town, Chekhov very soon came to regard his enforced stay in Yalta as an exile. During his first few weeks there in September 1898 he was quite enthusiastic, writing to Suvorin that he preferred the Crimean coast to the French Riviera. This mood gave way to disillusionment before long. During each successive winter for the rest of his life Chekhov was compelled to spend some months in Yalta, and his references to the town became increasingly bitter. He called it 'my warm Siberia', a place so dull that he interpreted such benefits as it bestowed on his health by the fact that 'here even bacilli fall asleep'. He referred with distaste to the 'tedium, gossip, intrigues and most shameless slander' current in the town, and once said that there were many young ladies, but no pretty ones, many writers, but none talented, and much wine, but none of it drinkable. He was never tired of thinking out picturesque similes to describe his position, comparing himself to a balloon which has lost its moorings, or to a tree which has been transplanted and shows every sign of an unwillingness to take root in new soil.

IV

THE FIRST COLLECTED EDITION

AT the beginning of 1899 Chekhov began to take energetic steps to regularize his financial position by selling the copyright of his entire published works. Suvorin's firm had already started to produce a complete edition, but Chekhov was dissatisfied at the inefficient and untidy way in which the job was being done. He complained that Suvorin's people lost his manuscripts and left his letters unanswered. At the present rate of progress, he told his sister, the edition was not likely to be ready until 1948. Accordingly he asked Suvorin to discontinue, and opened negotiations with the publishing firm of A. F. Marx. A contract was signed on the following terms: In return for 75,000 roubles Chekhov made over the copyright of all his work published before the signing of the contract, with the exception of his plays. He was bound to furnish Marx with a copy of all his work, while retaining the right of excluding from the new edition such stories as he himself did not want reprinted. Stories written after the signing of the contract could be published once in the press and Chekhov could receive fees for them in the usual way. Thereafter the copyright of such stories passed in perpetuity to Marx, who was to pay for them at the following rates: 250 roubles a 'printed sheet' (about 6,000 words), then, after five years, 450 roubles a 'printed sheet'—and so on, with additions of 200 roubles every five years. If Chekhov survived into old age these accumulations were likely to yield considerable sums, and he joked that he had promised Marx by telegram not to live to be more than eighty.

He remarked that he had now become a 'Marxist' for the rest of his life, and felt greatly relieved once the contract was signed. One of the main reasons for his pleasure was the feeling that Marx would produce a really good edition of his works, such as he could handle with pride in his old age. He also realized that he had done something to safeguard the future of his dependants in the event of a complete breakdown in his health. Finally, it was good to be free from the obligation of supervising the unco-ordinated collections of his stories which had been appearing in numerous editions over a number of years. Marx's terms seemed advantageous at the time, but many of Chekhov's literary friends felt that he had been rash in concluding the deal so quickly. In

one letter he himself admitted that the sale would probably turn
out to be a bad bargain, and events proved this prediction to be
correct. The demand for books was rapidly increasing in Russia,
and shortly after the signing of the contract there was a general
rise in the level of fees obtained by writers. By the year 1903
it became evident that Marx had already managed to recover
several times over the sum expended on the purchase of the
copyright, and Chekhov seemed to have made a poor deal. Accordingly a number of his friends, including the writers Leonid
Andreev and Maxim Gorky, composed a letter to Marx appealing
for an annulment of the contract. They hoped to collect a large
number of signatures to the letter throughout Russia, but the
project broke down because Chekhov somehow got to hear of it,
and asked that it should be dropped. He felt that he should
stick to his bargain.

Chekhov's agreement with Marx immediately involved him in
the troublesome task of tracing all his early stories. He had not
realized how hard this would be, and seems to have forgotten
many of the details of his early writing career; when he started
collecting his work together he could not even remember in what
year he had written for the *Petersburg Gazette*—not to mention
such insignificant magazines as *Onlooker, Dragonfly* and *Alarm-
Clock*. He remarked in despair that Marx might as well ask him
to list all the occasions on which he had ever caught fish in his
life. The job was all the more difficult now that he was confined
to Yalta, and had to delegate the examination of old newspaper-
files to friends in Moscow or Petersburg. As samples of his
very early work began to arrive in Yalta, Chekhov realized that
he had forgotten how bad it was. 'What awful tripe!' he exclaimed. 'Reading it through I remember how boring it was to
write.' He scored certain items through in red pencil before
supplying them to Marx. These were stories which could not
be very well destroyed as they had once appeared in print, but
which Chekhov would certainly have burnt if they had remained
in manuscript. Chekhov said that biographers and critics could
collect them if they wanted to, in order to shed light on his
literary development ('After all, they like to spend their time on
such trifles')—but they must never be offered to the public.

Since Chekhov attached so much importance to the edition of
his works which Marx was preparing, he devoted much energy
to editing and improving the material which he did consider
worthy of inclusion. The result was the appearance during the

years 1899-1901 of the first comprehensive edition of his works, in ten volumes. In 1903 it was reprinted with certain supplementary volumes including the plays, and was for many years the standard edition of Chekhov's work. Apart from its lack of completeness this edition had the other disadvantage that the material was not arranged in chronological order, and that no indication was given of the year in which the various stories had been written. It was not until 1933 that the first scholarly and critical edition of Chekhov made its appearance in Russia, but this is not an entirely satisfactory publication, particularly as the paper is of very inferior quality. A new and better edition, with fuller notes and commentaries, has now begun to appear (Moscow 1944). When it is completed it will be the first really good complete edition of Chekhov's work. His prediction that readers would have to wait until 1948 for such an edition has come surprisingly near to being fulfilled, but it must be noted with regret that the text of Chekhov's letters in this twenty-volume edition (completed in 1951) has been mutilated from what appear to be political motives.

v

Uncle Vanya AND *Three Sisters*

CONFINEMENT in Yalta was all the more infuriating to Chekhov because he regarded constant attendance at rehearsals and performances as essential to success as a dramatist. Torn away from the stage he had little desire to write another play. For this reason the directors of the Art Theatre went to some trouble to stage a special performance of *The Seagull* for his benefit as soon as the spring of 1899 made possible his migration to the north. The theatrical season had already closed, and the performance could not be adequate, as it took place in a strange theatre and without the usual décor. It seems to have had a depressing effect on Chekhov, but he could not help being cheered by the warmth of his personal reception. After the performance the company took him off for an all-night session at the *Prague* restaurant, during which he caused some amusement by giving marks to the actors on the scale used in Russian schools. Nemirovich-Danchenko as producer deservedly got the maximum of five.

Everyone at the Art Theatre was getting to like Chekhov very much. His diffidence seemed only an additional part of his charm now that they were beginning to appreciate the keen intelligence

and lively humour which lay behind it. In spite of his exaggerated reluctance to show his feelings, the Art Theatre personnel soon began to realize that he returned their devotion.
'Oh, do not tire or grow cold,' he wrote to Nemirovich-Danchenko in 1899. 'The Art Theatre will form the best pages of the
book which will one day be written about the Russian theatre.
This theatre is your pride, and it is the only theatre which I
love, although I have never been inside it.' Chekhov went on
to say that if he lived in Moscow he would willingly take on the
job of door-keeper at the Art Theatre if he thought it would help
to sustain Nemirovich-Danchenko's enthusiasm. Elsewhere he
remarked that he envied even the rats that lived under the floor-
boards.

It was natural that Nemirovich-Danchenko and Stanislavsky
should want to follow up *The Seagull* with the performance of
a second Chekhov play, and such a play was already in existence.
It is not certain just when Chekhov transformed his earlier *Wood
Demon* into *Uncle Vanya,* but the new play appears to have
been ready by 1896. Chekhov's distress over *The Seagull* in
that year communicated itself to *Uncle Vanya.* Convinced that he
was a failure as a dramatist, he began to wish that he had not
wasted on his plays subjects which might have done excellent
service in fiction. However, he allowed *Uncle Vanya* to be published, together with *The Seagull* and some vaudevilles, in a
collection of his plays which appeared in 1897. To his surprise
Uncle Vanya was taken up by several provincial theatres, in
which it seems to have enjoyed great success. Gorky wrote to
say that it had made a big impression on him in Nizhny Novgorod, where the performance had ended with an ovation. It was
inevitable that Nemirovich-Danchenko should press for the release of the play to the Art Theatre when Chekhov visited
Moscow in the spring of 1899. His answer could not have been
more disappointing. *Uncle Vanya* had been promised to the rival
establishment, the Little Theatre.

Fortunately, however, circumstances played into the hands of
Nemirovich-Danchenko. The committee which examined *Uncle
Vanya* on behalf of the Little Theatre pronounced it fit for performance, but only on condition that Chekhov would consent to
introduce certain far-reaching alterations. He was delighted at
the opportunity which this afforded him to take offence and withdraw the play, which promptly went into rehearsal at the Art
Theatre. On the evening of October 26, 1899, Chekhov retired

to bed in Yalta without realizing that this was the first night of *Uncle Vanya*, so that this time he was not in the state of tension appropriate to the occasion. He had not been asleep very long when the telephone rang, and he received the first of a series of congratulatory telegrams which continued to arrive during the night. However, he soon realized that *Uncle Vanya* had not repeated the triumph of *The Seagull* in the previous year. The actors, who followed up the first performance with the usual all-night party in a restaurant, awaited the morning papers in a slightly troubled mood. As they suspected, the reviews were mainly unfavourable and Olga Knipper sent a slightly hysterical letter to Chekhov, blaming herself for a bad performance as Elena. Chekhov wrote back consoling her and her colleagues. He said that they had been spoilt by too many spectacular triumphs and must learn to be satisfied with modest success. *Uncle Vanya* had certainly not been a failure, but its reception showed that Russian audiences were not as ripe for Chekhov as had been hoped. Nemirovich-Danchenko comments in his memoirs that: 'the broad public did not immediately understand *Uncle Vanya*, *The Three Sisters* or *The Cherry Orchard*. All these plays achieved success only with their second season, maintaining themselves thereafter without break.'

After *Uncle Vanya* everyone began to urge Chekhov to write a play specially for the Art Theatre. He was quite willing, but protested that he could do nothing until he had seen a proper performance of his existing plays. This was one of the reasons which prompted the directors of the Art Theatre to organize a tour of the Crimea in April 1900. They were a lively body as they mounted the train to Sevastopol. Many of the actors had brought their families and friends, and a well-known dramatic reviewer attached himself in the role of travelling critic. The usual songs and laughter accompanied the journey, and the excitement grew when mountainous scenery, tunnels and sea announced the approach to Sevastopol and increased the holiday spirit. The tour was a triumphant success. In Sevastopol all the seats were greedily bought up at the first opportunity, and the visit of the Art Theatre completely transformed the general mood. Nemirovich-Danchenko commandeered the illumination apparatus of the town park to improve his lighting effects, and Stanislavsky was almost crippled by an enthusiastic band of High School boys who mobbed him on his way to his hotel. Chekhov arrived from Yalta, and seemed chiefly concerned to

N

acquire a place in the theatre where he would be invisible to the public. Ensconced between Nemirovich-Danchenko and Madame Nemirovich-Danchenko, he thought himself safe, but at the end of *Uncle Vanya* peremptory shouts of 'Author!' from the auditorium forced him to appear on the stage.

The next port of call was Yalta, and the Art Theatre was given a magnificent send-off at Sevastopol harbour. The deck of the steamer was a grotesque sight, covered with all manner of scenic effects, and the general enthusiasm was such that a crowd of additional camp-followers had attached themselves in Sevastopol. Their reception in Yalta was even more memorable. The fact that it was Chekhov's home town gave the company an extra sense of responsibility, which was further increased by the presence of Maxim Gorky and Ivan Bunin, together with some less important writers. Almost immediately the whole party invaded Chekhov's house where his mother and Mariya had to produce lunch in relays. The growing friendship between Chekhov and the actress Olga Knipper could not be concealed from Olga's colleagues, and it was no surprise to them to find her helping out his mother and sister as additional hostess.

Everyone was sorry when the Art Theatre returned to Moscow at the end of April, leaving behind as a permanent memento in Chekhov's garden the children's swings used in the first act of *Uncle Vanya*. The visit did exactly what had been hoped—it made Chekhov settle down to work on a new play, *Three Sisters*. Distracted by visitors, ill-health and the revision of his complete edition he found that things progressed slowly. Chekhov's dramatic activities were now front-page news, and the papers began to print all sorts of incorrect reports and forecasts about his next play. One hostile journalist, by name Burenin, affected to regard these premature announcements as a deliberate build-up by Chekhov. According to Burenin a series of telegrams, published in the press, prefaced the appearance of *Three Sisters*:

' "First act written," "Half second act sketched out," "Three-quarters of third act finished," "Title of play is *Three Tom-tits*," "No. Title of play not *Three Tom-tits*, but *Three Aunts*," "No. Not *Three Aunts* but *Five Sisters*," "just *Sisters*," "*Two Sisters*," finally "*Three Sisters*".'

In October 1900 the play was ready and Chekhov himself brought it to Moscow where he remained until December. This

time he took a more than usually active part in supervising rehearsals. The news had leaked out that the new play contained
characters drawn from army life. In military circles it was believed that Chekhov had written some sort of satire or burlesque,
and he was anxious that the production should do nothing to
bear out this impression. Every detail of military life must be
absolutely right, and Chekhov co-opted a friendly artillery colonel
to see that it was so. 'He was anxious,' Stanislavsky records,
'that we should not turn the military into the usual theatrical
heel-clickers and spur-jinglers, but that we should play simple,
charming and good-natured people, dressed in worn and non-
theatrical uniforms, without any theatrico-military erectness of
carriage, raising of shoulders, bluffness and so on.'

Before *Three Sisters* was ready for the stage Chekhov went off
to Nice, where he spent the whole of January, sending occasional
alterations and suggestions by post to Moscow. On January 31st
the first night took place, again without the spectacular success
which had fallen to *The Seagull*. *Three Sisters* had to win its
place gradually, and in Russia today it is bracketed with *The
Cherry Orchard* as Chekhov's most popular play.

CHAPTER TEN

Chekhov's Approach to Fiction

I

CHEKHOV ON CRITICISM

CHEKHOV'S numerous comments on literature reveal an unassuming approach, very near in many ways to that of any ordinary reader. 'I divide all works into two classes,' he once wrote. 'Those I like and those I don't like. I have no other criterion.' Why did he prefer Shakespeare to the minor Russian writer Zlatovratsky? Chekhov found himself quite unable to say. He would not have wanted anyone to regard him as a person of superior aesthetic tastes, and showed as much by cheerfully admitting his inability to read poetry because it bored him. 'Is it interesting?' was one of the first questions he naturally asked about any work of fiction. He mistrusted theories of literature, especially when expressed in long words, and after one correspondent had written to congratulate him on an alleged conversion, deduced from some of his stories, to 'Anthropocentrism', confessed himself puzzled, and asked 'What does this word mean? I've never seen it in my life before.' Elsewhere he admitted to confusion at much less bizarre specimens of critical vocabulary:

'When people talk to me of what is artistic and inartistic, of what is dramatic and not dramatic, of tendencies, realism and so on, I am bewildered, hesitatingly agree, and answer with banal half-truths not worth twopence.'

A similar distaste for the approach of literary critics was displayed when Chekhov discovered that his work had been divided up by one of them into three periods. He wrote to a friend with amused irony that he had never suspected the existence of these periods himself. 'You and I didn't know it,' he said, 'but here I am in my third period. First of all there weren't any periods at all, and now, all of a sudden, there are three of them.'

Chekhov's irritation with critics dates from the mid-'eighties, when his work first became important enough to attract their attention. He retained this hostility during the whole of his life, as witnessed by a large number of stinging remarks, of which the one most often quoted appears in Gorky's reminiscences:

'Critics,' said Chekhov, 'are like gad-flies which prevent horses from ploughing. The horse works, with all its muscles drawn tight like the strings of a double-bass, and a fly settles on its flanks and tickles and buzzes. What does the fly buzz about? It hardly knows itself—simply because it is restless and wants to announce, "See here, I too am living on the earth. Look, I can buzz!" ... For twenty-five years I have read criticisms of my work, and don't remember a single remark of value, or one word of valuable advice.'

Chekhov's chief charge against critics was that they pretended to know all sorts of things which they really did not know at all. They spoke of literature as though it were a science with firmly-established laws. Chekhov, who did not know any such laws, was prepared to admit that they might one day be discovered, but was sure that the discovery had not yet been made: 'Perhaps in time, as I grow wise, I may work out some criterion,' he said, 'but meanwhile all conversations about what is artistic merely tire me, and seem like a continuation of the scholastic disputes with which people wearied themselves in the Middle Ages. If criticism knows what you and I don't know, why hasn't it yet spoken? Why does it not reveal the truth and its immutable laws?'

He had many detailed objections to make. Why must critics continually go through the tiresome and unprofitable process of comparing one work of literature with another? Chekhov once flatly refused to read a certain magazine article which he knew was devoted to a comparison of his *Uncle Vanya* with Goncharov's *Oblomov*. 'I loathe this sucking of conclusions out of one's finger-ends,' he said, 'this fastening of things on to *Oblomov* or Turgenev's *Fathers and Sons*. You can fasten a play on to anything you like, and if the reviewers had taken Gogol's *Dead Souls* or Shakespeare's *King Lear* instead of *Oblomov*, the result would have been equally profound.'

Another game of Russian critics which Chekhov found irritating was to ransack their literature for examples of character-types such as the Superfluous Man, or his near relative, the Unsuccessful Man. The Superfluous Man was the type of hero out of harmony with the society in which he lived. The first specimen was generally agreed to be Chatsky in Griboedov's play *Woe From Wit,* and successors included Pushkin's Onegin, Lermontov's Pechorin, Turgenev's Rudin and many more. Any new hero who happened to be at variance with his surroundings was liable to be branded as a specimen of the type, and to be compared in detail with his predecessors. Chekhov did not see that these methods led to any valuable results, and could not help groaning when he found that they had been applied to his work by the writer and philosopher D. S. Merezhkovsky. A letter of November 1888 shows what he thought about this. Merezhkovsky, said Chekhov, 'calls me a Poet and my heroes Unsuccessful Men—in other words he's plugging the old routine. It's time to get rid of these Unsuccessful Men, Superfluous Men and so forth, and to think up something of one's own.'

In spite of these condemnations Chekhov let fall other remarks which show that he did not believe that all literary criticism must necessarily be a waste of time, though nearly all the examples of it which he actually met seemed to come into this category. He often said that he longed for really good criticism —something which could set him on the right lines both as author and reader—and once remarked that for lack of it works of art were disappearing without trace before the eyes of his contemporaries.

II

CHEKHOV AS CRITIC

ALTHOUGH Chekhov did not himself publish critical articles, his correspondence is so full of references to literature that it is not difficult to form an impression of his tastes and interests. Naturally he was most attracted by plays and fiction, for it was fascinating and instructive at the same time to observe another man's approach to the types of writing he himself practised. He was very interested in foreign authors (whom he read mostly in translation), but had a thorough knowledge only of his own literature. With the period contemporary to himself he was particularly well acquainted, and probably missed little of importance that came out during his adult lifetime. It is, however, his observations on his outstanding predecessors in Russian literature which hold most interest as illustrations of his outlook.

Turgenev came in for the harshest treatment, though Chekhov was not blind to some of his virtues. He spoke with especial approval of *Father and Sons*, saying that Bazarov's illness at the end of the novel was so powerfully described that he felt infected with it himself. *A Nest of Gentlefolk* also had an ending which was 'like a miracle'. In spite of these excellencies, however, Turgenev was not a writer likely to make an overwhelmingly strong appeal to Chekhov. Turgenev's heroines enjoyed great vogue in Russia, but Chekhov did not like them at all. In portraying them Turgenev tended to repeat himself, with the result that almost every heroine belongs to one or other of two types. Chekhov disliked both these types, which to him were 'intolerable in their artificiality and spuriousness'. Liza (*A Nest of Gentlefolk*), Elena (*On the Eve*), and other similar heroines were supposed to be examples of pure and innocent Russian girlhood, but to Chekhov they were 'not Russian girls, but Delphic priestesses, abounding in pretences above their station'. As for the other brand of Turgenev heroine, older women, usually set in contrast to the pure and innocent variety, 'social lionesses, burning, full of appetites and insatiable'—Chekhov put them down as so much 'nonsense'. Of Turgenev's nature-descriptions Chekhov wrote, 'they are good, but one has the feeling that we are growing out of descriptions of this kind, and that what is needed is something different.' His general conclusion on Turgenev was that only an eighth or a tenth of his work would survive, and that all the rest would find its way into the archives in about twenty-five to thirty years.

On four other Russian writers of front rank—Pushkin, Lermontov, Gogol and Leo Tolstoy—Chekhov's comments were more uniformly enthusiastic. Though he said he was 'scared stiff of verse', he made an exception in favour of Pushkin, whom he described as the only poet he could read. Lermontov's *Taman*, from *A Hero of Our Time*, seemed to him a model of what a short story should be, and he once said he could die happily if he managed to do anything as good himself. He found Gogol direct and powerful. 'His *Carriage* alone is worth two hundred thousand roubles. Nothing but sheer delight. He is the greatest of writers.'

Of all writers, Russian or foreign, Tolstoy was the one who chiefly excited Chekhov's admiration, and who most consistently evoked the superlatives of which he was normally so sparing. To Chekhov, Tolstoy was 'not a man, but a Jupiter, a superman', and he said that Tolstoy would never grow old. He admired most of all the three long novels *Anna Karenina, War and Peace* and *Resurrection,* and in discussing the first of these found an opportunity for dealing a further back-handed blow at Turgenev: 'When you think of Anna Karenina, all Turgenev's heroines with their seductive shoulders fly away to the devil.' Chekhov's admiration for Tolstoy's creative gifts never wavered, but as soon as Tolstoy began to preach any sort of message he found himself making objections. Tolstoy's methods of argument often seemed to him dubious, and his treatment of evidence high-handed. Thus *The Kreutzer Sonata,* in which Tolstoy lays down the law about sex, was marred for Chekhov by what were, according to him, glaring factual inaccuracies which could have been corrected by reference to one or two standard works. All the same Chekhov thought the story a masterpiece of literary art, and it helped to widen the gap between his assessment of Tolstoy the writer and Tolstoy the thinker. A similar distinction emerges in Chekhov's criticism of the long novel *Resurrection* contained in a letter of January 1900. After paying enthusiastic tribute to Tolstoy's powers Chekhov concluded with a complaint against the end of the novel:

'To write and write, and then hang the whole thing on to a text from the Gospels—that's just a bit too theological. ... He must first make us believe in the Gospels, in the fact that it is the Gospels which contain the truth—and only then decide everything by texts.'

It was Tolstoy's air of prophetic infallibility which offended Chekhov, and it was of Tolstoy that he was thinking when he wrote to Suvorin in 1891: 'The devil take the philosophy of the world's great men. All great sages are as despotic, impolite and indelicate as generals, since they know they won't be punished. Diogenes used to spit in people's beards, because he knew he could get away with it.'

Another of these great men, and one whose philosophy Chekhov would even more willingly have consigned to the devil, was Dostoevsky. It would be difficult to name a writer less likely to appeal to Chekhov. Dostoevsky's great novels have been described as an arena for ideological conflict between characters who embody various abstract ideas—which is enough to show why Chekhov found them uninteresting. He does not appear

to have shared the admiration which Dostoevsky compels even
from those who are least impressed by his prophetic message.
In fact he hardly ever mentioned Dostoevsky, and in one of the
few recorded references set him down as 'good, but awfully long,
immodest and pretentious'.

III

'ONE MUST WRITE SIMPLY'

CHEKHOV is usually claimed to have been remarkably independent of literary influences, and even the major Russian
writers just mentioned seem to have left no important traces on
his work. Some of the early stories had echoes of Gogol, Turgenev and Saltykov, but these disappeared soon after Chekhov
took to serious writing. His mature work probably has more
points of contact with Tolstoy than with any other author. For
example, Chekhov and Tolstoy both had a capacity, exceptional
even among the greatest fiction-writers, for making a scene live
by inserting some apparently unimportant and irrelevant detail.
Another feature common to them both was the comparatively
minor role which creative imagination played in their work. It is
well known that many of the characters in Tolstoy's great novels
are portraits, either of himself, or of friends and relatives, and
that many of the scenes are pieces of autobiography or family
history. Chekhov did not draw so fully and directly on his own
personal and family background as Tolstoy, but he tended like
Tolstoy to make his own experience the starting-point of his
fiction—more so, at any rate, than writers like Dostoevsky and
Gogol, who drew heavily on their imaginations in creating plots
and characters.

It has been suggested by several Russian critics that a systematic examination of Chekhov's subject matter might profitably
be made in an attempt to give a full picture of its origins in
real life, and there is abundant evidence which might form the
basis of a very detailed study. The type of result which could
be achieved may be very briefly indicated from two instances
quoted by Chekhov's biographer Izmaylov. Walking through Yalta
one day Chekhov was impressed by a photograph in a book-
shop window, showing a certain Bishop Michael Gribanovsky,
together with an old woman. He bought the picture and made
some inquiries into Gribanovsky's life, the result of his investiga-
tions was *The Bishop*. Another story of Chekhov's, *The Grass-*

hopper, was sufficiently close to real life to lead to a quarrel with one of his best friends. In it Chekhov drew on what he knew of the relations between the artist Levitan and a married woman; when taxed with this by one of his other friends he remarked innocently that no one should have recognized Levitan's mistress in his heroine, whom he had purposely made young and pretty in order to conceal the resemblance. If this remark ever reached Levitan it no doubt increased the fury which he already felt against Chekhov for ventilating the less savoury aspects of his private life. Levitan began to talk of challenging Chekhov to a duel, but fortunately forgot his grievance as his amours pursued their usual kaleidoscopic course.

Not all Chekhov's stories can be linked as closely with actual people as *The Bishop* and *The Grasshopper,* but almost every one of them can be related in some way to its origins in his experience. Thus, to take a few further examples, such as could be indefinitely repeated and expanded, the warehouse in *Three Years* is said to be copied from the Moscow firm of Gavrilov, in which Paul Chekhov worked for several years; Belikov in *The Man in a Case* is claimed as a synthesis of the less sympathetic masters at Taganrog High School, and the general picture of village life in *Peasants* is modelled on Melikhovo. Clearly Chekhov usually proceeded by a careful selection and adaptation of things he had seen himself, and it is for this reason that his fiction almost never strays outside the sphere of Russian life of his own day. Though he did a fair amount of travelling he made the most sparing use of non-Russian scenes, and one reason for this was probably that he never got to know life outside Russia thoroughly enough to feel at home in describing it.

It must have seemed to Chekhov that other fiction-writers—even those described as realists—put life through various distorting processes before presenting it in their works. This was often revealed in their subject-matter, for they chose to write about murder, lunacy and suicide more often than the incidence of such themes in actual life might seem to warrant. Among the writers of Chekhov's day a concentration on the more gruesome sides of life was becoming fashionable, partly as a result of Dostoevsky's success in treating such subjects. Chekhov himself did not remain entirely immune from the general tendency, and gave powerful studies of madness in *Ward No. 6* and the even more horrific *Black Monk.* A sensational crime forms the main subject of his *Murder.* However, such stories are exceptional in his later work and cease almost entirely after the middle 'nineties, about which time he proclaimed that he had finished with morbid and pathological themes.

His attitude to this question may be further illustrated from Kuprin's reminiscences. Chekhov, says Kuprin, 'demanded from writers ordinary, everyday subjects, simplicity of exposition and the absence of virtuoso tricks. "Why write," he would ask with bewilderment, "that a person gets into a submarine and goes to the North Pole to seek some sort of reconciliation with humanity, while at the same time the woman he loves hurls herself from a belfry with a theatrical shriek? All this is untrue and does not happen in real life. One must write simply—about how Pyotr Semyonovich got married to Mariya Ivanovna, that's all." '

Besides choosing ordinary everyday subjects Chekhov also declined to do violence to life by twisting its material into complicated plots. So far as he could see real events rarely fall into the elaborate patterns which fiction-writers tend to weave, and he was determined to preserve in his stories the comparative shapelessness of life as he observed it, even at the cost of losing narrative interest. Accordingly, among the various qualities which sustain the reader's attention in reading a Chekhov story a wish to know 'what happens' is not likely to be very prominent. Usually very little does happen.

IV

THE VIRTUES OF RESTRAINT

THE cultivation of literary restraint was a matter of conscious policy on Chekhov's part, and had been so ever since his earliest attempts at serious writing. His letters of the 'eighties are full of passages deprecating any sort of emotional self-indulgence on the part of an author. He was particularly careful to make this point plain to one woman-writer who valued his advice, telling her that if she wanted to describe unhappy people in such a way as to move her readers' compassion, she was only likely to succeed if she remained cold and dispassionate herself, thus providing a background against which the sorrows of her characters could stand out in greater relief. She might weep and suffer with her characters as much as she liked, so long as she was able to conceal this from her readers, for fiction could only strike home in so far as it was objective. In the same spirit Chekhov discussed with another literary friend a subject which seemed to him suitable for a short story, but which was bound to fail unless it was treated with adequate restraint:

'You remember how huntsmen wound an elk. The elk looks at them with human eyes, and no one can bring himself to kill her. It's not a bad subject, but dangerous because it is difficult to avoid sentimentality—you must write it like a report, without pathetic phrases, and begin like this: "On such and such a date huntsmen in the Daraganov forest wounded a young elk. ..." If you drop a tear you will rob the subject of its austerity and of everything worth attention in it.'

The choice of titles was one matter in which Chekhov thought a writer should be especially careful to avoid affectation and unnatural pomposity. 'Why all these sub-titles like *A Psychological Study, A Genre Picture, A Novella*?' he once exclaimed in conversation with Kuprin. 'All this is mere pretentiousness. Make your title a simple one—let it be the first thing that comes into your head—and nothing more. Also make as little use as possible of inverted commas, italics and dashes—they're an affectation.'

The titles of Chekhov's own stories do in fact fulfil the condition which he insists on here, but he did not always find it possible to use the first one that came into his head, for the simplicity he sought was not always easy of attainment.

Restraint was evident in every aspect of Chekhov's work and made him concentrate above all on brevity and appositeness. In this connection Stanislavsky quoted an illuminating incident which occurred while *Three Sisters* was under rehearsal. The play contained in its fourth act a particularly fine monologue, put into the mouth of Andrew Prozorov, and devoted to an impassioned denunciation of provincial Russian wives. The actors were disappointed when a note suddenly arrived from Chekhov cancelling the entire speech, and replacing it with the simple sentence, 'A wife is a wife.' However, reflection eventually convinced them that this was a wise piece of self-discipline on the author's part, and the incident taught Stanislavsky a vital lesson about Chekhov. 'In this short sentence,' he remarks, 'if one thinks one's way deeply into it, is contained everything which had been said in the long monologue of two pages. This is typical of Chekhov, whose work was always short and full of content.' Though this story has since been shown to be apocryphal, it remains a valuable commentary on Chekhov's methods.

The excision of everything not absolutely essential was a process to which Chekhov habitually subjected his writing, and which he repeatedly urged on others. He told Gorky:

'When you read your proofs strike out where you can the qualifications of nouns and verbs. You have so many qualifications that it is hard for the reader to make things out, and he grows tired. It's easy to understand when I write, "The man sat on the grass"—because it's clear and does not hinder attention. Conversely it's hard to understand, and wearisome for the brain if I write, "A tall, narrow-chested man of medium stature with a ginger-coloured beard, sat down on the green grass, which was already trampled by passers-by, sat down noiselessly, timidly, glancing about him fearfully." That doesn't settle down straight away in the brain, and fiction must settle down immediately, in a second.'

A similar plea for simplicity is to be found in another passage of advice to Gorky. Here Chekhov deprecates Gorky's over-indulgence in a technique of nature-description which he sometimes used himself in greater moderation:

'A frequent comparison (of nature) with human beings—when the sea breathes, the sky looks, the steppe snuggles, nature whispers, speaks, grieves and so on—such comparisons make description a little monotonous, at times cloying, and at times obscure; colour and expressiveness in description of nature are only achieved by simplicity, by such simple phrases as "The sun set", "It grew dark", "It rained".'

As might easily be deduced from some of the above observations, Chekhov was not the kind of writer whose creations appeared in a mood of white-hot inspiration. Writing was to him a matter of hard and painstaking concentration. At times he seems to have regarded this approach as an unsatisfactory one, and he told Suvorin as much in a letter of 1889:

'I haven't enough passion—and, consequently, not enough talent for literature. In me the fire burns evenly and feebly without blazing and crackling. For this reason it never happens that I write twenty-thousand-odd words straight off in a single night, or get so carried away by my work as not to go to bed when I'm tired. That's why I don't produce anything either outstandingly stupid or remarkably clever.'

V

Nastroenie

THE points so far made about Chekhov's literary methods show
that in some ways he worked within a limited range compared
with many other writers of similar importance. This was due,
not to a lack of enterprise on his part, but to a wish to concentrate on something which he regarded as of overriding importance. 'Real life' was the criterion which he repeatedly applied to
literature, and accordingly the words 'such things do not happen
in real life' often have the ring of absolute condemnation when
related by him to a story or play. If he could reproduce a fragment of life with complete authenticity he did not think it
mattered very much if his themes and language were not
spectacular. The ordinary world, viewed with the right degree
of sensitivity, was more thrilling than any invented world, a
point which he allows one of his own characters to make in
Terror. 'Why is it,' this character asks, 'that, when we want to
tell some fearful, mysterious and fantastic story, we must always
take our material not from life, but from the world of visions
and supernatural shadows?' It is no answer to say that we fear
that which we do not understand. 'Do we understand life? Tell
me, do you understand life any better than the world beyond the
grave?' It was because he thought ordinary life the most interesting possible subject for fiction that Chekhov told Kuprin
that one ought to 'write simply—about how Pyotr Semyonovich got married to Mariya Ivanovna, that's all'. This formula
does not seem to have very exciting possibilities until one
reads some of the many stories by Chekhov to which it can
be applied.

The Teacher of Literature is one of these. It describes the
courtship and early married life of a young schoolmaster, Nikitin.
All that happens is that Nikitin falls in love with a girl called
Masha, proposes, gets married and gradually falls out of love.
The entire action of the story is seen through the young man's
eyes, and Chekhov conveys with his usual complete authenticity
the texture and flavour of the portion of life experienced by his
hero.

A complicated series of thoughts and sensations passes through
Nikitin's brain. Some of them are important—his marriage
plans and love for Masha; the majority are trivial and concern

certain smells, sights and sounds of everyday life which un-
accountably detach themselves as significant and vaguely disturbing. They succeed each other in apparently haphazard order
—just as such sensations always do in real life. It would perhaps have been difficult for Chekhov himself to say just why
he selected for mention at one moment the silhouette of a
brewery, at another the purring of a cat, or the sound of a
band in the park. Many of these themes recur several times,
an aspect of Chekhov's stories which has led some critics to
compare their construction with that of a piece of music—it
has even been said that they have *leit-motivs* like a Wagnerian
opera.

Chekhov's method was selective. He did not attempt a comprehensive catalogue of all his hero's sensations, such as has
been known to fill novels of several hundred pages with the
events of a single day, but merely picked out a few individual
items. These might not all have any immediately obvious logical
relevance, but they had a peculiar quality of evoking the atmosphere of the whole. His selection was evidently made with
great insight, for his stories have to a unique degree the power
of transporting their readers into another human mind. The skill
with which this remarkable form of mental transference is effec-
ted has often been claimed as one of Chekhov's chief gifts as
a writer. He was able to achieve it in almost all his later stories,
which is why W. Gerhardi is able to congratulate readers of
Chekhov on being able to live a hundred lives, while having paid
only for one.

D. S. Mirsky's phrase 'biographies of a mood' remains one of
the few successful attempts to find a portmanteau description
of these stories. Chekhov had, of course, been producing such
'biographies' long before he wrote *The Teacher of Literature*,
and the mood, or *nastroenie*, evoked in some of his early serious
stories was seen to have a special quality. This quality was developed to perfection in Chekhov's later fiction, and will always
be recognized as one of his greatest and most distinctive charms
as a writer. Though no attempt to analyse it is ever likely to go
very far, some of its more obvious elements have already been
indicated. One of these in particular, nature-description, continued to do Chekhov excellent service in the production of
atmosphere.

His method of describing nature had not altered in essentials
since he wrote *The Steppe*, and he still relied on flashes of

vivid detail to bring a whole scene before the reader's eyes. More than ever nature-descriptions were now relevant to the mood of one or other of the characters, and Chekhov still found it useful to stress this link by attributing human reactions to natural phenomena. Thus, in *The Teacher of Literature*, it is quite characteristic that the flowers in Masha's garden should participate emotionally in the proposal scene which they witness: 'in the dark grass, dimly lit by the moon, were sleepy tulips and irises, which seemed themselves to be awaiting a confession of love from somebody.'

Nature is also called into play in this story to help Chekhov to execute a neat and thorough Chekhovian figure, to which Mirsky first drew attention. During the first half of the story Chekhov sets a course in a straight line towards an apparently predictable goal. The straight line is Nikitin's courtship of Masha, which develops so delightfully that the reader begins to anticipate a conventional magazine-story ending. At a certain point, however, Chekhov's course begins, imperceptibly at first, to curve away from the line, and before very long it is proceeding in an entirely different direction. The curve is traced with such subtlety that it is hard to determine the exact point at which it begins. Nevertheless this point can be found if one looks for it, and it is typical that it should coincide with a description of nature.

One interesting feature in the production of atmosphere is the way in which Chekhov regularly provides hints calculated to link his scenes with the past and the future. He believed that a writer should make his readers feel, in addition to the personalities described, 'the human mass out of which they have come, the air they breathe and the background perspective—in a word everything.' It is not difficult to observe some of the ways in which he put this thesis into practice. Returning home on a foul night his Student, in the story of the same name, reflects that just such a wind had blown in the days of Ivan the Terrible and Peter the Great, and that under them there was just the same savage poverty and famine.

'There were the same tattered straw roofs, the same ignorance, misery, the same wilderness on all sides, the same darkness and feeling of oppression. All these horrors have been, are now, and will be, and life will become no better for the passing of another thousand years.'

In such passages Chekhov seems to be suggesting to his reader that this or that particular scene is merely a fragment chosen from the complex totality of human experience. The episodes which so absorb the passions of his heroes are to be thought of as something transient thrown up from a vast current stretching away indefinitely into the past and the future. The more sensitive of his characters consciously relate personal experience to its general historical context in this way, usually in brief hints which impart to their thoughts a characteristic melancholy beauty. Their reflections are not always as depressing as the one just quoted. Another typical passage, rich in Chekhovian atmosphere, is to be found in *The Lady with the Dog*, where Gurov and his mistress sit outside during the coming of dawn in a place called Oreanda, not far from Yalta.

'Yalta could hardly be seen through the morning mist, and white clouds stood motionless on the tops of the hills. The leaves on the trees did not move, cicadas chirped, and the monotonous, dull noise of the sea, borne up from below, spoke of peace and of the eternal sleep which awaits us. It used to make the same noise down there before Yalta and Oreanda existed, it makes it now, and will make it, just as indifferently and dully, when we are no longer here.'

Closely allied with this feature of Chekhov's atmosphere-building is his characters' habit of evoking memories and aspirations in their personal lives. Again and again they refer to the sensations of childhood, a period of life which tends above all to be surrounded with an aura of suggestive and intangible beauty, as Chekhov says of his Bishop:

'How wonderful, dear and unforgettable was his childhood. Why is it that this irrecoverable time, which has departed for ever—why is it that it seems brighter, gayer and richer than it actually was?'

The use of memory is especially noticeable in *An Artist's Story*, the events of which are recalled by the artist six or seven years after they occurred. He remembers his first glimpse of the house which was the scene of his ill-fated love, and it is typical that it should have made him feel for a moment 'the enchanting breath of something dear and very familiar, as though

o

I had once seen the same view in my childhood'. As he finishes his story the artist finds that his recollections of the house and of the girl he loves are becoming indistinct. They have already acquired the elusive and poignant quality which attaches itself to some deeply-felt emotion, half-buried in memory.

'I am already beginning to forget the house,' he concludes, 'and it is only occasionally, when reading or writing, that I suddenly and quite unexpectedly remember the green light of the window and the sound of my footsteps echoing in the fields at night as I returned home, full of my love, and rubbed my hands because of the cold. Even more rarely, at times when I am sad and weary with loneliness, I have indistinct memories, and gradually begin to feel that I too am remembered, that I am expected and that we shall meet. ... My darling, where are you?'

These are the last words in one of Chekhov's most celebrated stories, and they illustrate the fact that he rarely brings anything to a definite and final conclusion. He is concerned rather to stress the fact that life goes on, and that there is every reason to believe in the continuance of all its various complicated and disturbing qualities.

Chekhov recognized the great importance of love interest in fiction when he said of his own *Ward No. 6*: 'I am finishing a story which is very boring, because women and the element of love are quite lacking in it. I don't like that sort of story.' He certainly made up for the deficiency elsewhere. Few of his other stories are devoted quite so exclusively to the study of a love affair as *The Lady with the Dog*, but love occupies a very important place in nearly all of them, including most of those which were selected in an earlier chapter as evidence of Chekhov's social and philosophical views. Quite often the relationships described were made to do service as illustrations of these views—for instance in *My Life*, where Misail's marriage helped to discredit his philosophy of life, and in *Betrothed* where Nadya had to break off relations with Andrew before she could free herself from her vulgar and limited surroundings. Nadya made the right decision from Chekhov's point of view, whereas the heroine of another story, *At Home*, did not. Placed in a similar situation she submitted and married the dreary doctor and factory-owner Neshchapov.

The most obvious feature of love as portrayed by Chekhov is that it almost never works out to the satisfaction of either party, and *The Darling* would seem to contain the only exceptions to this rule in the whole of his later fiction. If Chekhov believed in the possibility of happy married life he certainly left little trace of this belief in his work. He seems to have regarded young love as an illusion, but an illusion so beautiful that he repeatedly used it for the evocation of atmosphere. His young men in love are liable to meet with one of three different fates, none of them enviable. Either their love is not returned, or they are separated from their beloved by circumstances, or, finally, they get married and the illusion ends in inevitable disillusion. All these experiences involve emotions and memories which, however frustrating to the participants, make ideal material for the construction of atmosphere.

It is not possible to do more than indicate the importance of this theme in Chekhov's stories. Love, it would seem, was the subject which fascinated him above all others, and he was concerned to present it, like all his themes, exactly as he saw it. There was certainly no problem to which he was less likely to pretend to have found a solution, and he said as much himself through the mouth of one of his characters in *About Love*.

'Hitherto only one uncontrovertible truth has been stated about love, to wit; "The thing is a great secret," and everything else which has been written and spoken about love has been, not a solution, but only a statement of questions which have simply remained unsolved. The explanation which seems as though it might fit one instance is no use in a dozen others, and the best thing in my opinion is to explain each instance in isolation, without trying to generalize. It is necessary, as doctors say, to individualize each separate case.'

VI

CHARACTERS AND HUMOUR

THE temptation to generalize about Chekhov's characters is not an easy one to resist. It will be remembered that Merezhkovsky called some of them unsuccessful men, and that Chekhov complained to Suvorin as early as 1888 that this was 'plugging the old routine'. He went on to say that: 'dividing people into successful and unsuccessful means looking at human nature from a narrow and prejudiced point of view. Are you successful or aren't you? What about me? What about Napoleon? One would need to be a god to distinguish successful from unsuccessful people without making mistakes. I'm going to a dance.'

In spite of Chekhov's irritation critics have continued to make similar classification. Mirsky in his *Modern Russian Literature* says that all Chekhov's characters 'may really be reduced to two types: the gentle and ineffective dreamer, and the vulgar and efficient man of action. There are infinite gradations in these; but the ineffective people, if sometimes funny, are invariably lovable, and the efficient people are vulgar.' Although this is a most helpful suggestion, Chekhov would no doubt have been delighted to see the way in which it promptly breaks down in the one instance where Mirsky applies it to an actual example. 'Nowhere,' he continues, 'is the contrast more marked than in *The Cherry Orchard*, between the old proprietors and the *nouveau riche* Lopakhin, who has all the virtues, but is successful, and for that reason alone detestable.' Lopakhin is certainly successful, at any rate financially, but is he really detestable? It is hard to see how anyone could take away such an impression from the play, and Chekhov's own remarks show that he regarded Lopakhin as neither detestable nor vulgar. He explained to Stanislavsky, whom he wanted to take the part, that Lopakhin 'is a decent man in every sense of the word. He must behave with decorum and intelligence. ... You mustn't lose sight of the fact that Lopakhin is loved by Varya, a serious and religious girl'.

Chekhov's characters do not fall into ready-made patterns, and are almost entirely free from the tendency to repetition of which he accused Turgenev's heroines. The production of this amazingly wide and diverse range of living figures can be claimed as one of his main achievements, and it was natural that he should have thought that any attempt to theorize about them robbed them of life and colour. However, there are some general points which it is interesting to bear in mind when reading the stories. Among these is a tendency for each character to enjoy the author's sympathy in so far as he possesses the quality of sensitivity. This is especially fascinating in stories like *Ionych*, where the hero starts off with a high degree of this quality and can be observed progressively shedding it with the passage of years. This process can be seen in reverse in *Betrothed* and *The Teacher of Literature* in which Chekhov describes its awakening where it has hitherto been dormant. In the latter story the birth-pangs of sensitivity in Nikitin were attended with a growing feeling of unhappiness, and this is in accordance with Chekhov's normal practice, for there is among his characters a high degree of correlation between sensitivity and unhappiness. These qualities often (though by no means always) go together with a lack of will power and a tendency to drift, which Chekhov describes with sympathy and a pleasing undercurrent of humour.

Conversely, the people who are reasonably satisfied and know what they want are very often submerged in dreary routine and vulgarity. They are clearly more futile in Chekhov's eyes than the sensitive types, and it is their very lack of sensitivity which enables them to preserve a greater degree of contentment. Chekhov often makes it clear that he approves of his sensitive characters, in spite of their unhappiness and flabbiness of will. He lets fall many hints that the more promising specimens among them hold out the best hope for the future of humanity, and often goes out of his way to suggest that their frustrations and indecisions will disappear when life begins to be organized in a more satisfactory way.

Chekhov's method of introducing his characters and bringing them to life for his readers has something in common with his technique of nature-description, for it exhibits a similar concentration on brevity and compactness. Again it is possible to contrast the method of Turgenev, who often settles down to a set-piece character study of important characters, expounding in detail their habits, temperaments and biographical background. Chekhov succeeded in dispensing with this, and usually managed with a few brief indications, often enlivened by an emphasis on some eccentricity typical of the person described. In the sphere of character-drawing he again revealed his unerring instinct for suggestive detail. Just as he believed that he could make his reader visualize a moonlit night by mentioning the glitter of light on a broken bottle, so he often found it possible to conjure up the personality of a man by insisting on some detail, such as his way of mispronouncing the letter R or his method of wrinkling his eyes when he smiled.

Chekhov often reverted in his later stories to the type of humorous caricature which he had perfected as *Antosha Chek-*

honte. His humour was never very far from the surface, and
continually imparted a lightness of touch, even to his most
sombre studies. Even *Ward No. 6* contains funny scenes—for
example, the occasion when Doctor Ragin appears before a
group of local officials who make a series of rudimentary tests
of his sanity. One character in the story, the preposterous
Mikhail Averyanych, is almost wholly comic, especially in the
ridiculous scene in Warsaw where he borrows Ragin's last
savings to pay his gambling debts, with a cry of 'Honour before
everything!' Similarly, the absurd Grandmother in *The Peasants*
and her indignation with the offending geese are conveyed in a
manner reminiscent of *Antosha Chekhonte*.

Quite often a reader unfamiliar with Russian literature may
wonder whether he is expected to laugh or cry when reading certain scenes of Chekhov. How, for example, is one expected to
react to the pathetic figure of the heroine's father in '*Anna on
the Neck*'? He is a poverty-stricken old schoolmaster who is
steadily going to the bad, and who is continually threatened with
dismissal because of his 'weakness'—a fondness for the bottle.
His two small sons have to follow him everywhere in order to
stop him from misbehaving himself, and their pathetic cries of
'Don't, Daddy, don't!' recur in the story as a repeated motif.
The Russian reader, who knew his Gogol and Dostoevsky, was
used to scenes of this type, where one might be expected to
smile and weep at the same time, and to which the critical
formula 'laughter through tears'—popularized by Gogol—was
often applied. Again and again Chekhov evokes this mingled
reaction, which is one of the most subtle effects at his disposal.

Even among the later stories there are a few in which the
comic element predominates, and which have features of plot
recalling the type of Little Story which Chekhov had long ago
written for the magazine *Fragments*. '*Anna on the Neck*' is one
of these. It describes the experiences of a young and beautiful
girl, Anna, who marries an elderly and insufferably pompous
official for his money. As the story develops he is seen to be a
dreary and obsequious nonentity with prototypes by the hundred
in Chekhov's early comic work. The story even has a snap ending such as was almost obligatory in the Little Story. This
comes when Anna, who has been very much afraid of her husband during her early married life, suddenly asserts herself and
turns the tables on him with a cry of 'Get out, you fool!' *The*

Man in a Case, which has already been discussed in some detail, is, of all Chekhov's later stories, the one which shows most resemblance to *Chekhonte,* especially in everything which concerns the central character, the schoolmaster Belikov. Belikov's habit of illustrating the sonority of the Greek language by screwing up his eyes, and pronouncing, with upraised finger, the word *anthropos,* is a typical piece of Chekhontian farce. So are nearly all Belikov's adventures in the story, especially when he receives an anonymous cartoon, bearing the inscription 'The Love-sick Anthropos', and showing him, complete with umbrella and goloshes, arm-in-arm with his prospective fiancée.

VII

LANGUAGE

BEFORE leaving the short stories it is worth looking briefly at Chekhov's prose style and use of language, matters in which his attitude accords closely with his general approach to literature. It is perhaps a commonplace to say that the qualities of simplicity and straightforwardness, which appear at their best in Chekhov's prose, are often the most difficult of attainment for a writer, and the most satisfying to his readers when attained. Chekhov seemed to find that his language acquired elegance and grace in so far as it became absolutely appropriate to his meaning; he described the quality he was looking for—which he knew could only be attained by a laborious process of re-writing and correcting—as 'musical'. Jarring notes must be avoided, as he once explained to Gorky. He said that in Gorky's early stories words like 'voluptuousness', 'velvetiness' and 'whisper' offended by over-repetition; a further blemish on Gorky's prose in his view was an excessive use of various foreign words— 'disc', 'accompaniment' and 'harmony'—which in their transliterated form had found a place in the Russian language.

It would be doing less than justice to Chekhov's own style to describe it as one which merely avoided such obvious errors as undue repetition and the use of ugly-sounding words. His descriptive passages are models of harmoniously-constructed Russian, beautiful and subtly evocative in spite of its simplicity. Gorky himself recognized Chekhov's pre-eminence as a writer of Russian prose, not only by requesting his comments on his own work, but also in critical articles. In one of these, an essay on Chekhov's *In the Ravine,* Gorky says: 'Chekhov is unapproachable as a stylist. When speaking of the growth of the Russian language, the literary historian of the future will say that this language was created by Pushkin, Turgenev and Chekhov.'

As Chekhov himself would have been the first to agree, style is an element in literature for the assessment of which there exists no exact criterion. In its absence critics have to be content to give their own personal impressions, and Chekhov's style is apparently a difficult one to estimate—at any rate it has given rise to differences of opinion between qualified judges. These differences are especially evident in the two fullest criticisms of Chekhov available in English: *Anton Chekhov* by William Gerhardi and *Contemporary Russian Literature* by D. S. Mirsky together with a shorter passage on Chekhov in *Modern Russian Literature* by the same author. To Gerhardi Chekhov's sentences 'have a very distinctive melodic strain', whereas Mirsky expressly states that his prose is not melodious. Mirsky actually refers to Chekhov's Russian style as a 'serious shortcoming': 'It is colourless and lacks individuality. He had no feeling for words. No Russian writer of anything like his significance used a language so devoid of all raciness and nerve.' Mirsky goes on to make the point that Chekhov, not being much of a stylist, has less to lose by translation than any other Russian writer.

So far as the translation question is concerned, Gerhardi again seems to disagree. At any rate he says that Chekhov's work loses a great deal in this process, and regards the versions of Constance Garnett as making 'the best of what needs must remain a bad job'. Gerhardi repeatedly praises the beauty and subtlety of Chekhov's language, and makes it clear that he is closer to Gorky than to Mirsky in his general estimate of Chekhov's style. The dialogue passages in Chekhov's stories have given rise to a similar divergence of opinion. Mirsky complains that the language of Chekhov's characters has no individual flavour: 'His characters all speak (within class limits and apart from little tricks of catchwords he lends them from time to time) the same language, which is Chekhov's own. They cannot be recognized, as Tolstoy's and Dostoevsky's can by the mere *sound of their voices*.' Here again it is doubtful whether Mirsky's opinion is representative, and an exactly opposite view is expressed in the excellent study of Chekhov by the Soviet critic Sobolev. Sobolev claims as one of Chekhov's outstanding characteristics the fact that every personage in his stories and plays 'talks in his own special language, individual to him; every character has his own voice and his own particular intonations'.

These are not the only points on which qualified judges would quarrel with Mirsky's survey, though many of them might agree that it is on balance one of the most valuable short criticisms of Chekhov available in any language. An element in it, which Mirsky himself stresses, is an irritation aroused in him by Chekhov's English enthusiasts, whom he regards as shallow and uninformed. His wish to deflate them may possibly have biased his critical judgment in places, though it has enabled him to perform the useful task of indicating certain other important Russian writers—such as Leskov—who have received less than their share of attention outside Russia.

Mirsky contrasts Chekhov's reputation in England and Russia. 'In Russia,' he says, 'Chekhov has become a thing of the past, of a past remoter than even Turgenev, not to speak of Gogol or Leskov.' For reasons which are obvious the life described by Chekhov must indeed seem very remote to the modern Russian reader. However, it is no longer true to say, as Mirsky does, that in Russia Chekhov is 'a classic who has been temporarily shelved.' There have been changes in his literary reputation both in Russia and England in the twenty-two years since Mirsky's book was written. In Russia Chekhov has come rather more into his own. V. Manuylov, author of a recent Russian book about him, quotes statistics to show how the number of his readers has grown since the Revolution; he mentions that sixteen million copies of his works have appeared since then, including translations into fifty-four languages of the Soviet Union. The growing interest of the ordinary reader has been accompanied by much serious and scholarly research by Soviet students of literature. Besides innumerable selections of stories, two complete critical editions of Chekhov have appeared. Much important documentary material, previously available only in manuscript, has now been published, and has been made the basis of numerous valuable biographical and critical surveys. As the result of all this Russia now has a considerable body of scholarship devoted to Chekhov.

In England the first rush of enthusiasm for Chekhov, which may have been naive and mistaken at times, has perhaps subsided in favour of comparative neglect, but also one may hope, of a truer and more sober appreciation. Chekhov's influence on English and American writers is unquestioned, and amongst those mentioned by Manuylov are such well-known names as Bernard Shaw, J. B. Priestley, Sherwood Anderson, Katherine Mansfield and Ernest Hemingway.

CHAPTER ELEVEN

Chekhov's Last Years: His Approach to Drama

I

GORKY, TOLSTOY AND BUNIN

IN the minds of most Russian readers Chekhov and Tolstoy (his senior by thirty-two years) were bracketed together as the two most important writers of the 'nineties. Towards the end of the decade a third writer, Maxim Gorky, had begun to emerge, and was already attracting a comparable degree of attention. These three dominated the Russian literary scene, and it was natural that they should be keenly interested in each other's work and personality. Opportunities for meeting occurred, usually in the Yalta area, and very friendly relations were established.

It will be remembered that Chekhov had made Tolstoy's acquaintance in 1895; it was towards the end of 1898 that he first came into contact with Gorky. Gorky, who was nine years his junior, took the first step. A newly-published volume of his stories had just been sent to Chekhov, and he followed it with a letter in which he asked for an opinion on his work, thus beginning an interesting correspondence. Gorky was a much more demonstrative character than Chekhov, upon whom he looked as his literary master. His attitude was one of mingled affection and admiration, and he expressed this in his letters, which were at first chiefly devoted to a discussion of literary matters. In his replies to Gorky and in other parts of his correspondence Chekhov made criticisms of Gorky's work, some of which have already been quoted because of the light they shed on his own attitude to writing. Chekhov had a great admiration for Gorky, though he had many reservations to make. 'Gorky in my opinion is a real talent,' he told another of his literary friends. 'His brush and colours are genuine, but he is somehow uncontrolled and flamboyant.' He admired the violence and sincerity with which Gorky wrote, but sometimes felt that they produced an unduly rhetorical effect.

Meetings between Chekhov and Gorky began in 1899 and strengthened the regard which they already felt for each other. Outwardly more conventional than Gorky, Chekhov was slightly put out by his friend's habit of wearing ostentatiously proletarian clothes. 'He's a tramp on the outside,' said Chekhov, 'but inside he's a fine enough man.' He had a great liking for Gorky, whom he arranged to meet in various parts of Russia. In 1900 the two friends travelled together in the Caucasus, and even planned to make a joint visit to China; in November of the same year they were together at a rehearsal of *Uncle Vanya* in Moscow, and in the following year Chekhov visited Gorky in Nizhny Novgorod. Most of their meetings, however, took place in the Yalta area, where Gorky lived from time to time during the last years of Chekhov's life, and where he and Chekhov often had the opportunity to visit Tolstoy together.

Correspondence between Chekhov and Gorky was kept up until Chekhov's death, and Gorky found frequent opportunities to pay tributes to his friend including the dedication to him of the novel *Foma Gordeev*. 'I think,' he wrote to Chekhov, 'that you are the first man I have met who is free and bows down before nothing,' and anyone familiar with Gorky's ideas will recognize this as the highest compliment he could pay. Some years after Chekhov's death Gorky wrote the memoirs to which reference has already been made, and which contain one of the most vivid and sympathetic accounts of Chekhov during the last years of his life. There can be no doubt that Chekhov's example and advice had considerable influence on Gorky, in particular by turning his attention to the stage. Gorky willingly fell in with this suggestion and his *Philistines* and *Lower Depths* were very soon rivalling Chekhov's own plays among the most successful items on the repertoire of the Moscow Art Theatre.

In 1902 both Chekhov and Gorky were involved in an incident which created considerable stir in Russia. To celebrate the centenary of Pushkin's birth the Russian Academy of Science had set up a 'Department of Belles Lettres', providing for the election of Honorary Academicians among outstanding living Russian writers. Chekhov, Tolstoy and Korolenko had been among those chosen at the first election in 1900. Chekhov received the news in the spirit of irony with which he always treated official honours, but it delighted his old cook, who announced with pride but not quite accurately that 'our Anton Pavlovich' had become a general. In 1902 a further election took place, and Chekhov was pleased to hear that Gorky too had now been made an Honorary Academician. This was rather a daring act by the Academy, because Gorky was viewed with extreme suspicion by the Government, and during the period of his friendship with Chekhov was often under police supervision for political reasons. When a copy of the election notice was forwarded to Nicholas II the trouble began. The Tsar was horrified, and wrote the words 'More than original!' in the margin, a sign of displeasure which made it necessary to withdraw the honour bestowed on Gorky. An announcement to this effect was made in the name of the Academy, though in fact the Academy had not been consulted at all. Owing to the censorship it was impossible for anyone to protest or explain the incident in public. Chekhov and Korolenko, who were disgusted at this piece of governmental sharp practice, retorted by sending in their resignations as Academicians. An attempt was made to induce Tolstoy to join them in this gesture but he merely replied that he had never considered himself an Academician, and thrust his nose in a book.

In the autumn of 1901 Tolstoy was forced by illness to move south, and took up residence at Gaspra, which was only a few miles away from Yalta. He was very seriously ill, and for a long time his death was thought to be imminent. The prospect weighed heavily on Chekhov. 'I fear Tolstoy's death,' he wrote. 'If he were to die it would leave a great empty place in my life.' When the danger-point was passed Tolstoy's admirers began to flock to Gaspra from all parts of Russia and Europe. Among them were Chekhov and Gorky, with whom Tolstoy was able to arrive at terms of intimacy and understanding impossible with the majority of his many visitors. Chekhov for his part was absolutely devoted to Tolstoy, claimed to understand 'every movement of his brows', and said that he had never loved any man so much as him. Personal contact even softened his determined hostility to Tolstoy's teaching, and in one letter of 1900 he actually went so far as to say: 'I am not a believer, but of all faiths I think Tolstoy's is the nearest to me, and the most suitable for me.'

According to Gorky, Tolstoy's attitude to Chekhov was one of fatherly love: 'Tolstoy loved Chekhov and when he looked at him always seemed to be caressing his face with his eyes, which were almost tender at such moments.' Tolstoy found Chekhov modest and unassuming, and on one occasion even compared him with a young lady. Chekhov's modesty seems to have caused him some embarrassment during Tolstoy's more outspoken moments. The old man once sprang the question: 'Did you go whoring much in your youth?' Whereupon Chekhov smiled confusedly, and, plucking his beard, said something inaudible. Tolstoy looked out to sea and said, using a 'salty peasant word', 'I was an indefatigable —— myself.' Chekhov became a favourite with Tolstoy's family, and even Tolstoy's wife, who disapproved of many of her husband's visitors, had a good word to say for him in her diary of October 12, 1901: 'A. P. Chekhov paid us a visit. We all liked him very much for his simplicity and ... talent, and found him a man near to us in spirit.'

It was the quality of simplicity which Tolstoy prized in Chekhov's stories, of which he had a very high opinion. He once called Chekhov a 'Prose Pushkin' and said: 'Chekhov is a real artist. You can read him several times.' In fact Chekhov's stories frequently were read aloud in Tolstoy's family circle, and one of them, *The Darling*, especially delighted the old man. Though he liked the stories Tolstoy thought that plays were 'not Chekhov's business'. He told Chekhov that he could not stand Shakespeare, but that Chekhov's plays were even worse than his.

In Yalta, Chekhov met other important Russian writers including Ivan Bunin. Bunin is especially worth mentioning because he has written two essays which are outstanding even among the rich memoir material about Chekhov. The first of these was written in 1904. Bunin explains that he first met Chekhov in 1895, and remembers him as a tall man with a deep baritone voice, neatly and pleasantly dressed. Bunin was young enough at the time to mistake Chekhov's extreme simplicity of manner for off-handedness, but this impression was corrected when they next met, four years later in Yalta. He found that Chekhov had much changed for the worse in appearance, but that he continued to produce an impression of elegance which had struck Bunin during their first meeting. In Yalta, Bunin was a regular visitor to Chekhov's house and the two became friendly though never really intimate. Bunin recalls the humour, which had been a feature of Chekhov's conversation ever since his early schooldays. So long as his health was not too bad he was continually thinking up absurd jokes, and in order to set the company laughing helplessly it was often enough for him to throw in a couple of words, accompanied by an artful gleam from above his pince-nez.

Like everyone else who met Chekhov, Bunin was especially struck by his sincerity and lack of affectation. He stresses Chekhov's reserve, and claims it as characteristic of his conversation that he should rarely mention his own sympathies and antipathies. 'I like this,' or 'I can't stand that', were not the sort of expressions he was heard to use. Bunin says that even the people most intimate with Chekhov 'never knew what was going on in the depths of his soul'—indeed, he suggests that Chekhov never was genuinely intimate with anybody.

The second essay, written in 1914, is a valuable commentary on Chekhov's reputation ten years after his death. Bunin notes that this reputation depended at this time more on the plays than on the stories, and states his own view that the plays are not Chekhov's most important work. His comments on Chekhov's other interpreters are especially welcome because he shares Chekhov's intellectual fastidiousness, and notes the amazing perversity with which critics have regularly chosen precisely the type of language which Chekhov himself most detested.

'For a long time,' says Bunin, 'nobody could call Chekhov anything but a "gloomy" writer, a "bard of the twilight", an "ailing talent", a man who looked at everything with hopelessness and indifference ... Now they've gone to the opposite extreme and keep plugging the sentence about the "diamond-studded heavens".' (A phrase from the end of *Uncle Vanya* where Chekhov allows one of his characters to speak with prophetic confidence about the future.) 'For the last ten years,' Bunin continues, 'they've been going on about "Chekhov's tenderness and warmth", "Chekhov's love of humanity", "the bard of *The Cherry Orchard*" ... All this makes intolerable reading. What would he have felt if he had read about his "tenderness"? This is a word which one must use very rarely and very carefully about Chekhov.'

Bunin goes on to specify further descriptions of Chekhov which he regards as lapses of taste. He takes Kuprin to task for giving an over-theatrical flavour to Chekhov's confident remarks about the future, especially at the point where Kuprin writes: ' "Do you know," Chekhov added suddenly with a serious face and in a tone of deep faith. "Do you know, in three or four hundred years the whole earth will turn into a blossoming garden." ' Other memoir-writers singled out by Bunin as offenders

include Korolenko, who spoke of Chekhov's 'grief about phantoms' and Elpatyevsky, who said: 'Chekhov was always drawn
by quiet valleys with their mists, hazy dreams and quiet tears.'
Anyone who cared to take the trouble could add an indefinite
number of even more absurd specimens to Bunin's list, especially
from Russians writing about Chekhov during the first decade
after his death.

Bunin drives the lesson home by saying that Chekhov was
'simple, sparing and to the point in his language, even in everyday life. He set enormous store by words. A pompous, false,
vulgar or bookish word produced a painful effect on him. He
had a fine way of speaking himself—always individual, clear
and accurate.'

II

CHEKHOV'S MARRIAGE

ALTHOUGH Chekhov always enjoyed feminine society, and met
many intelligent and attractive women, he did not fall in love
easily, and had to wait until nearly the fortieth year of his life
before forming his only profound and passionate attachment.
The numerous studies of marriage in his fiction are not the
work of one who would lightly embark on the role of husband,
and when he did so it was only after discovering a woman with
very exceptional qualities. He first met the actress Olga Knipper
(whom he married in 1901) during rehearsals of the Art Theatre
in the autumn of 1898. When he left for Yalta he had already
seen enough of her in two short meetings to carry with him the
pleasant impression that he would have fallen in love if he had
stayed behind.

They met again in Moscow in the spring of 1899 by which
time Olga had already made friends with Mariya Chekhov.
During this same spring Olga was a guest for three days at
Melikhovo, just before the estate was sold, and later in the year
there were further meetings in south Russia. It was not, apparently, until the following year that she and Chekhov realized the
full depth of their attachment to each other, and signalized it
by abandoning the formal 'you' for the intimate 'thou' in addressing each other. It was during this year that they decided to get
married, and they were careful to keep the engagement secret,
even from their own families. Secrecy was preserved until the
last moment.

On April 19, 1901, just before leaving for Moscow, Chekhov

wrote to Olga from Yalta: 'If you give your word that not a soul in Moscow will know about our wedding until it takes place, then I'll marry you—if you like, the day after my arrival. For some reason I am terribly scared of the ceremony and the congratulations and the champagne which one must hold in one's hand, while giving a vague smile.' The wedding took place on May 25th. So well was the secret kept that Ivan Chekhov actually met Anton an hour before the ceremony without learning what was afoot.

A doctor's examination which had been made a few days before the wedding had shown an aggravation of Chekhov's tuberculosis, and he was unfortunately compelled to combine his honeymoon with a *kumys* cure. *Kumys* was fermented mare's milk, which was believed to possess certain healing properties, and in order to drink it Chekhov took his bride to Aksenovo in the province of Ufa. Although circumstances were not as propitious as they might have been, Olga retained very happy memories of her honeymoon, and afterwards she often referred with pleasure to the stay at Aksenovo. Chekhov drank four bottles of *kumys* a day and had soon gained ten pounds in weight, though he said that he was uncertain whether to ascribe this improvement to marriage or to *kumys*. He appears to have been less enthusiastic than Olga about Aksenovo, referring in one letter to the 'horrible boredom, old newspapers, an uninteresting public and Bashkirs all around.' He continues the letter in terms which might be regarded as ungenerous to his bride: 'If it wasn't for the scenery, fishing and letters I would probably run away from here.' It was no part of Chekhov's character to overwhelm his friends with the ecstasies of a newly-married man when mentioning his change of status. 'Well, I've suddenly gone and got married,' he wrote to one friend shortly after the ceremony. 'To my new situation, i.e. the loss of certain rights and advantages, I have already grown accustomed, or nearly so, and I feel good. My wife is a very decent and intelligent person and a good soul.' Later on, writing to Potapenko after a long break in their correspondence, he concluded the letter: 'There aren't any special changes. However, I have got married. But at my age that is somehow hardly noticeable, like a bald patch on the head.'

These off-hand references are characteristic of Chekhov, and would give a misleading impression to anyone who took them seriously. He and Olga were very much in love, and were pro-

P

foundly happy together. Their married life was, however, beset
by troubles which did not originate in their relations to each
other. A recurring factor was the misery and frustration caused
by frequent enforced separations, due, as Chekhov told Olga,
'to the devil who planted germs in me and in you a love of art'.
At the time of their first meeting Olga was establishing herself as one of the foremost actresses in Moscow. She was completely devoted to the Art Theatre and in spite of her love for
Chekhov it was no part of her plan to leave the stage. Though
this suggestion was often discussed between them, Chekhov himself always insisted that she should not abandon her career.
Naturally enough, however, the conflict between husband and
career was a source of strain to Olga during these years. Apart
from rare and stolen visits she and Chekhov were able to spend
only the summer months together. During the rest of the year
they did what they could to console each other by writing
letters. These letters, most of which have since been published,
are extremely numerous, since they both wrote almost every day.
When letters failed to arrive frantic telegrams were often sent
to inquire the reason.

It was natural that Olga's letters should be fuller and longer
than Chekhov's. There was often very little doing in Yalta
during the winter months; frequently illness confined him to the
house, and he could often find little news to send except about
his health or the weather. Sometimes this failed to satisfy Olga,
who wanted to know all the thoughts that passed through her
husband's head. The whirl of life in Moscow naturally provided
her with a much richer fund of news, particularly as she had
to satisfy Chekhov's keen interest in the theatre, for he wanted
to know every detail of what was going on. During every theatrical season of their married life Olga was playing in one or more
of Chekhov's own plays and the roles she took were always
among the most important (Arkadina in *The Seagull,* Elena in
Uncle Vanya, Masha in *The Three Sisters* and Ranevskaya in
The Cherry Orchard). Naturally enough she often wanted to
ask Chekhov's advice, or to pass on the queries of other members
of the cast. Olga was a highly intelligent and sensitive woman
who had a keen appreciation of what her husband was trying to
do in these plays. She sometimes differed from Stanislavsky himself on points of interpretation, and it was often she who was
right. When Stanislavsky insisted on playing in the grand manner
the love scene between Astrov and Elena in *Uncle Vanya,* Olga

wrote to Chekhov expressing her misgivings. His reply showed that she was right in assessing the general tone of the scene as quiet and relaxed.

He was almost equally interested in the production of plays by other writers (especially Gorky), and to these many long passages in Olga's letters are devoted. The social life of the theatre also occupied a big part in her letters, and she so often reported her attendance at all-night parties that Chekhov expressed anxiety that her health might suffer. Some of these parties must have been magnificent affairs. One of which she speaks was given a new lease of life at seven o'clock in the morning, when Chaliapin, who had so far been in a gloomy mood, suddenly called for beer, and sang gypsy songs for the next three hours. Some of Olga's descriptions made Chekhov think with regret of the days when he had been able to give a respectable account of himself with the wine-bottle, and he could not help feeling very much out of things as winter life in Yalta pursued its monotonous course. It helped him to know that, despite the excitement of Moscow, Olga's thoughts were constantly with him. Her emotions were much more on the surface than his, and she was liable to much more violent changes of mood. Being an extremely highly-strung person she often found herself overwhelmed by intolerable grief at separation from her husband. In one of her letters she tells how she had almost broken down during the last act of *Three Sisters*:

'While I was standing by the pillar and listening to the music, irrepressible tears were flowing from me. I kept seeing you and I do not remember how I spoke the last words. When the curtain fell I burst out sobbing; they picked me up and took me to my dressing-room so that I did not appear for the curtain-calls.'

In another letter Olga gives an interesting study of her husband's character, in which she lays emphasis on his greater stability:

'You are lucky. You are always so even and untroubled; it sometimes seems to me that you are unaffected by any separations, feelings and changes. This is not because of any frigidity in your nature, or from indifference, but there is something in you which does not allow you to attach importance to the things of everyday life. You smile? I can see your face as you read my letter. I can see your smile and all your wrinkles, which I love so much, and the soft lines of your mouth, my dear one.'

Chekhov's mental make-up was a never-failing source of fascination to Olga. She felt that his thought processes were excitingly different from those of other men, but all she could say when she tried to express their special quality was that they were 'genuine and not invented'. Many of Olga's letters betray her wifely concern that Chekhov should be well fed and properly clothed. Had they cleaned his shoes and brushed his coat? Had he taken his medicine? Was his study in its usual state of 'literary disarray'? In his replies he often teased her by calling her a 'little German girl', for Olga's parents were Germans, who had emigrated from Alsace. On one occasion he quoted himself as a model German husband, and stated that he was wearing his long woollen pants to prove it.

In the second year of their marriage a further misfortune added to the worries occasioned by long separation. During a tour in Petersburg made by the Art Theatre in early 1902 Olga was taken ill and underwent an operation. It turned out that she had been pregnant without realizing it, and that her illness was due to a miscarriage. She was kept in hospital for some weeks, which delayed her journey to Yalta and the meeting to which they had both been looking forward so ardently. As soon as she felt well enough to travel she set off, but suffered a relapse on the steamer from Sevastopol to Yalta. She had to be removed from the boat on a stretcher. By the end of May she had recovered sufficiently to travel with Chekhov to Moscow, only to fall ill once more—on this occasion so seriously that her life was thought to be in danger. Chekhov's concern at her illness and constant vigils at her bedside were beginning to make dangerous inroads on his own failing health, but fortunately the crisis was over by mid-June.

Olga's miscarriage was a tragic disappointment to her and Chekhov, for they both longed to have a child. Unfortunately this never proved possible. It is not surprising that the troubles of this year left her in a state of unreasonableness. In the autumn Chekhov left to join his mother and sister in Yalta. Olga stayed behind in Moscow, having perversely and groundlessly convinced herself that his family did not want her to accompany him. She even entrusted to Chekhov a letter addressed to Mariya, the contents of which were offensive enough to cause general distress, one of the symptoms of her state of mind being a feeling of irritation against her sister-in-law. Some of her letters were sufficiently perverse even to arouse mild protests from Chekhov. Sometimes she accused him of regarding her 'merely as a woman' and not as a 'person', and at other times gave way to vague and undirected complaints such as 'I don't understand anything'. The misunderstandings of this year were symptomatic of the strain under which she was living, and did not seriously affect her devotion to Chekhov. She was a delightful and lovable woman, and made it possible for her husband to enjoy married happiness such as (to judge from his fiction) he must have believed to be a very uncommon thing.

III

The Cherry Orchard

CHEKHOV found the writing of plays an increasingly protracted process, and his last one, *The Cherry Orchard*, was the slowest of all to take shape. A number of references made in 1901 show that he already had a new play in mind. 'The next play I write for the Art Theatre,' he told Olga in March 1901, 'will definitely be funny, very funny—at least in intention.' Elsewhere he expressed a desire to present the Art Theatre with 'a four-act vaudeville or comedy', but it is impossible to say how far these intentions can be related to *The Cherry Orchard*. In January 1902 Chekhov again mentioned a new play to Olga, but it was still only a 'faint glimmering in the brain'. By the end of the year the subject was sufficiently thought out for him to be able to mention the title *The Cherry Orchard*, and he had a rough conception of what the characters would be. One of them was to be a 'stupid woman', a comic part which he designed for his wife. There was to be a further comic role for Stanislavsky. These were probably the mental prototypes of Varya and Lopakhin respectively. The central character of the play was to be an old woman. Would the Art Theatre have a suitable actress? 'If not, there won't be any play,' said Chekhov. The writing of *The Cherry Orchard* was spread over the months March to October 1903, and the commentary on its progress furnished by Chekhov's correspondence is especially full. The play was repeatedly altered and re-copied, but on one point Chekhov continued to insist—it was 'not a drama, but a comedy; in places even a farce'.

The Cherry Orchard was awaited with great impatience in Moscow, where it finally arrived in mid-October. Chekhov followed it with some advice from Yalta, stressing especially the point that there was not to be 'too much weeping' when it was acted. In December he arrived in Moscow himself for a stay of two months. This modification of his usual winter programme was made at the suggestion of the specialist Ostroumov, who maintained that the Moscow area would be less harmful to him than Yalta during the frosty season. It was an unexpected piece of advice, since hitherto Chekhov's doctors had united in sending him south for the winter. 'Try and make sense of this!' exclaimed Chekhov, disconcerted to learn that his uncongenial yearly exile had apparently been unnecessary. However, there was some disagreement on the point. In Yalta Doctor Altschüler expressed horror at the idea of Chekhov wintering in Moscow and even declared that Ostroumov must have been drunk when he made the suggestion. Caught between these conflicting opinions Chekhov decided that he might as well consult his own inclinations, and was thus able to attend rehearsals of *The Cherry Orchard* in December and January. This time he had more difficulty than usual in arriving at an understanding with Nemirovich-Danchenko and Stanislavsky. They were unable to agree that *The Cherry Orchard* was nothing more than a gay comedy, and irritated Chekhov by treating it as a 'drama of Russian life'.

Whether by accident or design the first performance of *The Cherry Orchard* had been fixed for January 17, 1904, which was Chekhov's nameday and birthday. That this might well be the last birthday of Chekhov's life was a thought which nobody liked to put into words, but which could not help occurring to all who saw him in his present utterly exhausted and emaciated condition. His friends in the Art Theatre decided to take what might be their last opportunity to express their love and admiration by making the première of *The Cherry Orchard* the occasion for a public celebration in his honour. The pretext was the twenty-fifth anniversary of his début as a writer, although this particular date was at least a year premature.

An impressive programme of speeches and presentations was arranged to take place in the interval between the third and fourth acts of the play, and a large number of prominent people, representing literary, theatrical and learned associations, arrived with gifts in their hands and the manuscripts of speeches in their pockets. *The Cherry Orchard* was well under way when a startling discovery was made. Chekhov was not in the theatre! The reason for his absence was not only ill-health. He had always been embarrassed to the point of genuine suffering by official honours, even when the recipients were other people. 'They spend twenty years running a man down,' he once told Bunin when discussing jubilee celebrations, 'and then present him with an aluminium goose-quill pen, and spend a whole day churning out solemn clap-trap to the accompaniment of kisses and tears.' Now that his own turn had come he simply could not face it, and his friends almost had to use force to make him leave his lodgings.

The third act was finishing when he reached the theatre. Pale and weak he took up his position on the stage, and the applause which broke out was such as to leave him in no doubt of the place he held in the affections of the audience. It is difficult for anyone except a Russian to appreciate the warm personal feeling with which he was greeted that night by people who, although many of them had never seen him before, knew and loved him for his writings, and who, moreover, still had the words of *The Cherry Orchard* ringing in their ears.

He had hardly taken his place on the stage when he was seized by a fit of uncontrollable coughing. People in the audience began to shout 'Sit down, Anton Pavlovich,' 'A chair for Anton Pavlovich,' but he insisted on remaining on his feet. The speeches and presentations began. There was an address on behalf of the Lovers of Russian Literature by Professor A. N. Veselovsky, and another on behalf of the Moscow Little Theatre by the actress Fedotova. There were many other speeches, including some by representatives of the liberal press, in which Chekhov had published so much of his best work. Finally Nemirovich-Danchenko rounded things off with an eloquent tribute in which he expressed what all his colleagues in the Art Theatre felt: 'Our theatre is so much indebted to your talent, to your tender heart and pure soul, that you have every right to say "This is my theatre".'

Knowing that his friends and admirers were sincerely trying to please him, Chekhov listened with great attention and seriousness. All the same there were times when those who knew him best caught a glint of ironical humour in his expression. One of these points occurred when a new speaker began his oration with the words 'Dear and much respected Anton Pavlovich'. Stanislavsky, who, as Gaev in *The Cherry Orchard*, had to deliver a speech to an old book-case beginning 'Dear and much respected book-case', caught Chekhov's eye at this moment. The exchange of glances showed him that Chekhov was as much amused by the coincidence as he was.

Nobody felt really happy when the ceremony was over. Although it had been a tremendous personal triumph, even the least sensitive member of the audience could see that it had caused Chekhov great mental and physical suffering. A few days later, exhausted and depressed, he took the train for Yalta, and there were few of his friends who did not realize that he was already a dying man.

IV

A 'REVOLUTIONARY' DRAMATIST

CHEKHOV was admirably fitted to become the leading dramatist of the Moscow Art Theatre because he thoroughly agreed with Nemirovich-Danchenko and Stanislavsky in wanting to get away from the conventions and atmosphere of the existing Russian stage. His four major plays—*The Seagull, Uncle Vanya, Three Sisters* and *The Cherry Orchard*—mark a break with tradition so startling that many critics call him a 'revolutionary' dramatist. In defining the revolution which he accomplished it is impossible to avoid paradoxical language—he is frequently said to have 'purged the theatre of theatricality', to have written 'undramatic drama' and 'tragedies, the essence of which consists in the absence of tragedy'.

Like the directors of the Art Theatre he objected to an over-concentration on a small number of characters, and seems to have been feeling his way towards this position as early as 1887 when he wrote *Ivanov*, in which he claimed that there was not a single hero or villain. Though *Ivanov* certainly lacked heroes and villains in the ordinary stage sense, it did contain, in the title role, a big part calculated to overshadow all the others, and suitable for performance by one of the old-style star actors. No such character appears in any of the four major plays. Naturally some of the parts are bulkier than others, but there is a much more even distribution of emphasis than had been customary in earlier drama.

Together with this tendency went a relative lack of action.

The average pre-Chekhov play seemed to move from one emotional crest to another, treating the audience to an exciting succession of fights, quarrels, confessions of love, adulteries, suicides, murders and the like. There are many passages in Chekhov's letters showing that he deliberately rejected this conception of the drama:

'After all, in real life,' he observed, 'people don't spend every minute shooting at each other, hanging themselves and making confessions of love. They don't spend all the time saying clever things. They're more occupied with eating, drinking, flirting and talking stupidities—and these are the things which ought to be shown on the stage. A play should be written in which people arrive, go away, have dinner, talk about the weather and play cards. Life must be exactly as it is, and people as they are—not on stilts. ... Let everything on the stage be just as complicated, and at the same time just as simple as it is in life. People eat their dinner, just eat their dinner, and all the time their happiness is being established or their lives are being broken up.'

This passage, similar to various statements by Chekhov on his approach to the short story, forms an excellent introduction to his method in the four major plays, although even in them he did not entirely dispense with such examples of stage action as shootings and confessions of love. His earlier dramatic work shows that an avoidance of such action had not always been part of his policy. This is particularly true of his earliest surviving play, which is sometimes referred to as *Platonov*, and which has considerably more than its share of startling effects. It includes, among many other examples of dramatic action, two unsuccessful attempts at murder, averted at the last minute, the murder of the hero, the attempt of one heroine to throw herself under a train, and a whole succession of hysterical love scenes. *Ivanov*, the next long play, also had a fair allotment of lurid incident such as is not usually encountered in ordinary life. Chekhov said of this play that he conducted it quietly and peacefully on the whole, but that at the end of each act he gave the audience a 'sock in the jaw'. It will be remembered that the most violent of these dramatic punches had been packed in the last act, which concludes with Ivanov's suicide on his wedding morning. It was a long way from this to the methods of the later plays. In *The Wood Demon*, which succeeded *Ivanov*, and was later transformed into *Uncle Vanya*, Chekhov was feeling his way towards his new approach. Unfortunately the harsh reception of *The Wood Demon* deterred him for a time from further experiment. The quieter manner adopted in this play led to its condemnation by critics on the ground that the treatment was more appropriate to a story or novel than to the stage. It is generally agreed to be unsuccessful, and even such a sympathetic member of the audience as Nemirovich-Danchenko pronounced it unfit for production.

Returning to the assault on the new drama, Chekhov produced in *The Seagull* the first representative specimen of his mature manner. In this play, as in its successors, he tends to avoid any concentration on exciting dramatic incidents. The characters are for the most part apparently absorbed in trivialities; they usually allow the audience to learn only in passing of important changes in their relationships and lives, such as might have been made the subject of vivid scenes by earlier dramatists. For example, the eventful career of Nina Zarechnaya (including her relations with Trigorin and his desertion of her) is hardly presented on the stage. The same applies to Treplev's two attempts at suicide, though on the second occasion the audience is allowed to hear the revolver shot. Revolver shots were for a long time Chekhov's last link with the more violent methods of the traditional theatre, and he said that he was very pleased when he managed to dispense with them for the first time in *The Cherry Orchard*.

The Cherry Orchard provides an especially interesting illustration of Chekhov's use of incident in his later plays. Though he talked about writing a play in which people do nothing more than 'arrive, go away, talk about the weather and play cards', he never managed to carry out this policy with complete ruthlessness. Something had to happen, even in a Chehkov play, and the main incident of *The Cherry Orchard* is one which seems to be very important to all the characters—the loss of the house and estate belonging to Gaev and his sister. There was a lot of fuss and worry about this, but it is typical that after the sale had taken place the whole affair should somehow seem very much less momentous. In fact Gaev himself gaily proclaims that 'now everything is all right. Before the sale of the cherry orchard we all suffered and got excited, but afterwards, when the question was finally and irrevocably decided, we all grew calm and even cheered up.'

Another way in which Chekhov wished to break with the old

theatre was by avoiding stock theatrical types. He shows what some of these were in another passage from his correspondence:

'Retired captains with red noses, bibulous reporters, starving writers, consumptive hard-working wives, honourable young men without a single blemish, exalted maidens, kind-hearted nurses—all these have been described already and must be avoided like the pit.'

Though he kept his plays free from these old favourites Chekhov feared that some of the characters might be misinterpreted along traditional stage lines, and it will be remembered that he did not even trust the Art Theatre to give the right interpretation in certain instances. Lopakhin in *The Cherry Orchard* must on no account be turned into a conventional stage merchant, nor Uncle Vanya into a stage landowner; the officers in *Three Sisters* must not strut about like stage soldiers—on all these points Chekhov gave explicit instructions. The characters were ordinary, simple people who must be played plainly and sincerely so as to create exactly the effect they would make in ordinary life. It was natural that Chekhov should also seek to avoid stock situations. 'Remember,' he wrote, 'that confessions of love, the deception of wives and husbands, tears, whether widows', orphans', or anyone else's, have long ago been described.' He goes on to say that 'the subject must be new and you can do without a plot.'

Plot occupies just as small a place in the plays as it does in the stories. To Chekhov the exchange of small-talk was often a sufficient vehicle for the presentation of complex and subtle emotions. Again and again his characters speak of trivialities at a time when their thoughts are quite clearly engaged on something quite different. A conversation illustrating this takes place at the end of *The Cherry Orchard* between Lopakhin and Varya, both of whom know that this is a likely moment for Lopakhin to propose, and that if he misses the opportunity his marriage with Varya is never likely to take place. All that comes out in the dialogue, however, is a few banalities about the weather, the fact that the thermometer is broken, and that Varya has lost something while packing. Though the dialogue turns on such neutral themes the real situation makes a greater impact on the audience than might have been possible if Chekhov had handled it directly.

Chekhov's indirect method often enabled him to obtain extremely subtle effects, but he was always ready to be simple and straightforward when the occasion demanded it. This is often noticeable in the way he introduces information to the audience. He has not always been to any particular pains to dovetail his exposition into natural dialogue in the way usually considered necessary by playwrights. His characters often give information which must clearly be known already to the people with whom they are conversing, and which is really intended for the audience. Olga's first speeches in *Three Sisters* are a case in point, for they include many items which would not be news to her sister Irina with whom she is speaking.

'Father died exactly a year ago, this very day, May 5th—your nameday, Irina. ... He was a General in command of a brigade. ... Father received his brigade and left Moscow with us eleven years ago.'

A similar straightforwardness of approach is to be found in numerous passages where various personages give character-sketches of themselves, again for the benefit of the audience.

Whether he was being direct or indirect, Chekhov's words were equally packed with meaning. Stanislavsky had a very keen appreciation of this, for as actor and producer he naturally made an especially thorough study of Chekhov's text. His general conclusion was that behind each of Chekhov's words 'there stretched a whole range of many-sided moods and thoughts, of which he said nothing, but which arose of their own accord in one's mind'. Stanislavsky found that a play like *Three Sisters* was so saturated with meaning that, although he acted in it hundreds of times, every single performance revealed something new to him about it.

v

ATMOSPHERE IN CHEKHOV'S PLAYS

THE quality of Chekhov's plays, so charged with emotional significance in spite of their surface innocence, has stimulated Russian critics to look for a suitable name to describe his technique. His drama has been called 'lyrical'; it has been called 'internal', as opposed to the earlier, 'external' variety, and it has also been called the 'drama of the under-water current', since the operative dramatic stresses are so often submerged. The most common description is 'the drama of *nastroenie*', a concept already discussed in relation to the stories, where it was shown that 'mood' or 'atmosphere' are the best English equivalents.

An examination of the plays shows that Chekhov's methods of presenting *nastroenie* are similar to those employed in the stories. The same use is made of memories of the past, hopes for the future, and the state of mind associated with unsuccessful love. Chekhov often chose to present situations particularly calculated to throw such sensations into relief. Leave-takings were very suitable for the purpose—for example, those involved in the departure of the regiment at the end of *Three Sisters*. It had been stationed for some years in the provincial town where the action takes place, so that, when it came to leave, intimate associations had to be broken off, with little prospect of them ever being renewed. The emotions attendant on such an occasion blended harmoniously into the Chekhov mood. Similar emotionally-charged partings are to be found in *Uncle Vanya* and *The Cherry Orchard*. Madame Ranevskaya's arrival at the beginning of the latter play shows that the reverse process is equally capable of evoking atmosphere. She arrives back in her home early one morning after an absence of several years and cannot restrain her tears at the sight of the old nursery where she slept as a little girl. She ranges from laughter to tears as she revives her memories of such varied things as her brother's habit of interspersing his conversation with imaginary billiard strokes, and the wonderful sight of the orchard in bloom.

In the plays, as in the stories, Chekhov also makes use of the beauties of nature in building up atmosphere. For example, the audience is not long allowed to forget the lake which figures so prominently in *The Seagull* that it has even been suggested that Chekhov regarded it as one of the *dramatis personae*. The cherry orchard plays an even more important part in conditioning the mood of the play to which it gives its name. 'White, white all over,' Madame Ranevskaya addresses her orchard on her return. 'Oh, my orchard! After a dark, foul autumn and a cold winter you are young again and full of happiness; the angels of heaven have not forsaken you.' Again and again the characters refer to the orchard. In the minds of Ranevskaya and her brother it is bound up with countless childhood memories. The old servant Firs remembers how forty or fifty years ago they used to send cherries by the wagon-load to Moscow and Kharkov, after

subjecting them to a special preserving process—now nobody
can remember the recipe. To Trofimov the orchard typifies
an obsolete social structure, but serves as a reminder of the
beautiful life which he believes is possible on earth. He develops this theme to Anya, the young daughter of the house.

'All Russia is our orchard. The earth is large and beautiful
and there are many wonderful places in it. Think, Anya, your
grandfather, your great-grandfather and all your ancestors were
serf-owners, possessors of living souls. Do you not feel that
human creatures are looking at you from every cherry in the
orchard, from every leaf and trunk? Don't you hear their
voices?'

Whereas all these characters relate the orchard to the past in
their various ways, the businessman Lopakhin is more concerned with its future. Nobody listens to him when he points
out that the cherry trees must be cut down so that summer
bungalows can be built. Finally the orchard has to be sold, and
it makes its last contribution to the atmosphere of the play at the
very end when the curtain goes down to the sound of axes as
the work of felling begins.

As anyone who has seen the play will remember, this is a particularly brilliant use of sound in the theatre. The same play
provides many other examples, including the dance music which
serves as a background to the third act—an eloquent commentary on the household crisis with which it coincides. An examination of the stage directions in the plays provides innumerable
more illustrations of Chekhov's feeling for sound. Stanislavsky
says that Chekhov himself sometimes used to confer with the
sound-effects man to make sure that the noises produced were
in exact accord with what he had in mind. At the beginning of
the third act of *Three Sisters* an alarm is sounded in warning
of a fire, and, according to Stanislavsky, Chekhov went to a
lot of trouble experimenting with various apparatus in the hope
of reproducing the typical and unmistakable 'soul-searing' note
of a church bell in a Russian provincial town. One remarkable
sound effect has caused some embarrassment to producers, and
illustrates the production of *nastroenie* on a more surrealist
level. This is the 'distant, dying and mournful sound of a break-
ing string', which is heard twice in *The Cherry Orchard*. The
play does not make it entirely clear how this noise is supposed

to have originated, but Chekhov certainly regarded it as important in evoking the right sort of mood in his audience. Stanislavsky was a more than eager co-operator in producing sound effects, and often seems to have overdone it in Chekhov's opinion. His introduction of bird calls and croaking frogs were not always appropriate to the season in which the scene was supposed to be taking place, and his fondness for choruses of chirping crickets was a standing joke. There was plenty of scope for his ingenuity in correctly reproducing the sounds which actually appeared in the stage directions. It should not be thought, however, that the plays were swamped with sound effects, for Chekhov retained his usual sense of balance in this matter. The point is not so much that he used such effects—they appear to a greater or lesser extent in any play—but that he used them with unusual subtlety. They were a particularly useful method of creating atmosphere, and one which is interesting because it was not available to Chekhov in the short stories.

VI

CHEKHOV'S PLAYS AND THE 'CHEKHOV LEGEND'

CHEKHOV'S plays raise once again the complicated question of his pessimism and of the 'Chekhov legend' in which it is embodied. This legend could not have arisen without some basis in fact, and the most superficial examination of the four last plays does something to show how it originated. The first of them, *The Seagull*, begins with this exchange of remarks:

'*Medvedenko*: Why do you always wear black?'
'*Masha*: I am in mourning for my life. I am unhappy.'

Andrew's soliloquy in *Three Sisters* is in the same style:
'Oh, where is my past, where has it disappeared to—the time when I was young, happy, intelligent, when my thoughts were fine, when my present and future were lit up with hopes? Why is it that, almost before we have begun to live, we become boring, grey, uninteresting, lazy, indifferent, useless, unhappy?

Only a small minority of Chekhov's personages are satisfied with their fate, and even these are usually people whose futility is patent to almost everybody else but themselves—the smug charlatan Serebryakov in *Uncle Vanya*, the absurd schoolmaster

Kulygin in *Three Sisters* and the conceited man-servant Yasha in *The Cherry Orchard*. These figures are clearly antipathetic to Chekhov. Decidedly exceptional is Doctor Dorn in *The Seagull*, who can look back with satisfaction to a reasonably happy and contented life, and who yet enjoys the respect of his fellows and the apparent approval of Chekhov. Another exception is the hard-working Doctor Astrov in *Uncle Vanya*, with his interest in forestry schemes. However, even Astrov describes himself as a man lost in the dark without a light to guide him, and this is pre-eminently true of the rest of Chekhov's heroes, who mostly drift along without knowing where they are going. They are not usually men of action, and such action as they take is generally ineffectual. Even when they fire revolvers, a form of violence which, as has been seen, Chekhov occasionally permits them, they are more likely than not to miss.

The characters lose few opportunities for airing their frustrations. The younger people usually want something in the future, and nearly always it is something which they do not look like getting. His three sisters have attached their mental fantasies to life in Moscow, where, they imagine, all their worries and cares would disappear at once. They never go there, of course, and even if they had gone it seems unlikely that it would have made much difference. With the older characters frustration often takes the form of laments over a wasted life and lost opportunities. Sorin in *The Seagull* suggests himself as a subject for a story on the theme *L'homme qui a voulu*.

'In my youth I wanted to become a writer—and didn't become one; I wanted to speak eloquently—and spoke revoltingly. ... I wanted to get married—and I didn't; I wanted to live in the town, and here I am ending my days in the country.'

When it is pointed out to Sorin that he has at any rate attained the distinction of becoming a senior civil servant, he replies that that was one of the things he hadn't wanted. Uncle Vanya regrets almost every feature of his past life, including the fact that he had not proposed to Elena before she became the wife of Serebryakov.

'Ten years ago I met her at my sister's house. She was seventeen at the time and I was thirty-seven. Why didn't I fall in love with her then and make a proposal? Why, it would have

been so easily possible! And now she would be my wife. ...
Yes ... Now we should both have been woken up by the
storms; she would have been afraid of the thunder, and I
would have held her in my arms and whispered, "Don't be
afraid." '

Among the sources of frustration in Chekhov's plays love
occupies pride of place. Broadly speaking no one is allowed to
be in love with anyone who is in love with them, and on the
rare occasions when this rule is broken some external circumstances can be relied upon to create an effective obstacle. In
The Seagull the love-pattern presents a remarkably complicated
picture, as follows:

> Medvedenko loves Masha
> Masha loves Treplev
> Treplev loves Nina
> Nina and Arkadina love Trigorin

This chain-formation was not repeated in any of the later plays,
but in them love is frustrated with equal consistency.

It is obvious that anyone prepared to identify Chekhov with
his own characters could find abundant evidence in the plays
to support the 'Chekhov legend'. During his lifetime the idea
sometimes did arise in Russia that Chekhov himself was a sort
of Uncle Vanya, but this impression dissolved as his work and
biography became better known. It was seen that Chekhov, far
from identifying himself with his gloomier heroes, was often
laughing at them, and it even began to be thought that he conceived his plays as scathing satires directed against the futility
and morbid self-pity of intellectuals belonging to his generation.
This view was almost equally mistaken. Perhaps Chekhov's attitude was puzzling because it was so simple. He was merely
following his usual policy of putting on the stage ordinary people
in an everyday environment. He might ridicule them or sym-
pathize with them (very often he seems to have been doing
both simultaneously) but his general attitude was not one of
wholesale condemnation or approval.

It is inevitable that the 'ordinary' people in Chekhov's plays
should produce an effect in some ways the reverse of ordinary in
England, since the characters and life described are so peculiar
by our standards. However, this very properly lends them an
extra element of interest on the English stage, provided that
they are acted (as they very often are) simply and sincerely, in

the way Chekhov intended. Chekhov's world must seem equally unfamiliar to all except the oldest generation of present-day Russians. It is worth remembering, however, that the plays were regarded by his contemporaries as true and representative pictures of their society. The fact that three of them are set in country houses belonging to the land-owning upper class does much to explain the accent on frustration. Members of this class could look back to a period earlier in the century when they had played a much more important part in Russian life. At the time when Chekhov was writing they had long forfeited their position of cultural leadership, and were fast losing their wealth. Any mention of a Russian landowner in literature of the second half of the nineteenth century is almost certain to be followed by the information that his estates are mortgaged and that he is heavily in debt. The more sensitive members of the class realized that their way of life was dying out, but they were so conditioned by education and environment as to be unable to do anything about it, and submitted to the social trend which brought about their complete extinction thirteen years after Chekhov's death. It was natural, therefore, that the country houses in which Chekhov sets his plays should distil an atmosphere of regret and aimlessness.

If Chekhov managed to present this situation without undue melancholy, it was due principally to the sympathetic humour with which he regarded it. This emerges in many ways, including the extraordinary manner in which he handles his dialogue —frequently used to emphasize the isolation of the characters one from another. Disconnected remarks are placed in juxtaposition to show how the various personages, absorbed in their own interests, ignore, or do not hear, what other people have to say. As an example of many-sided disjointed dialogue, Nemirovich-Danchenko singled out the second act of *Three Sisters*. This contains in a very short space of time a succession of remarks, often entirely disconnected, on a bewildering variety of themes, including the fact that Tusenbach has a triple-barrelled name, that Irina was rude to a woman in the post-office, that her new hair-style makes her look a boy, that Andrew has lost two hundred roubles at cards, that the doctor hasn't paid his rent for eight months, that life will be wonderful in two or three hundred years, and that Balzac was married at Berdichev. Among exchanges which emphasize the estrangement of the characters one from another, is included:

'*Natasha*: Babies understand very well. I said, "Hallo, Bobik. Hallo, darling," and he gave me a special sort of look. You think it's just a mother's partiality, but it isn't, I assure you. He's a remarkable child.

'*Solyony*: If that child was mine I'd cook him in a frying-pan and eat him.'

Mutual misunderstanding does not always operate on such a crude level, and a rather gentler example of this form of humour is to be found in a passage from *The Cherry Orchard*:

'*Dunyasha*: The clerk Epikhodov made me a proposal after Easter.

'*Anya*: You're always on about the same thing. .... I've lost all my hair-pins.

'*Dunyasha*: I just don't know what to think. He loves me. He loves me so much.

'*Anya*: (*tenderly, looking at the door of her room*) My room, my windows! Just as if I'd never gone away. I'm home! To-morrow morning I'll get up and run into the orchard.'

The element of humour became more noticeable with each play that Chekhov wrote, and it is most prominent in *The Cherry Orchard*. It will be remembered that Chekhov in his letters widely advertised the fact that he regarded this play as a farce, and it is quite true that many of the characters might have stepped straight out of one of his own vaudevilles—for example, Simeonov-Pishchik, whose name alone is ridiculous enough. This gentleman, with his inveterate borrowing, and claim to be descended from the horse which Caligula made a member of his Senate, is very much a figure of fun. When a servant offers his hostess a bottle of pills, he intervenes:

'You shouldn't take medicine, dear lady. ... It does you neither good nor harm. ... Give them to me, most respected lady. (*Takes the pills, pours them on his palm, blows on them, puts them in his mouth and drinks them down with kvas.*)'

This is not the only excursion into farce in the play. People fall downstairs, break billiard-cues and lose their goloshes. At least half of the characters are presented in comic terms. These include, apart from Simeonov-Pishchik, the absurd governess

Charlotta Ivanovna, most of the servants, and Gaev with his general ineptitude, mock billiards strokes and eloquent speeches which are liable to be addressed to the furniture. Similar comic touches appear in the other plays, though they figure most prominently in *The Cherry Orchard.*

Chekhov himself was seriously convinced that *The Cherry Orchard* and—what is more surprising—*The Three Sisters* were 'gay comedies, almost vaudevilles'. Stanislavsky has recorded his insistence on this point in the face of much opposition. 'Right up to his death Chekhov could not reconcile himself with the idea that *The Three Sisters* and *The Cherry Orchard* were sorrowful tragedies of Russian life.' Neither Chekhov himself nor the 'sorrowful tragedy' school of thought seem to have expressed the true position on the subject. The plays are not comedies or tragedies in the accepted sense of either word, nor are they exclusively gay or sorrowful. They contain rather an extremely subtle blend of both elements. That the evocative atmosphere peculiar to Chekhov should combine harmoniously with broad farce is perhaps a surprising fact, but *The Cherry Orchard* is there to prove the possibility of such a combination.

CHAPTER TWELVE

Chekhov's Last Months

RETURNING to Yalta in February 1904, Chekhov began to recover a little from the exhaustion caused by his jubilee, and started to plan the future; although he had written very little since the turn of the century, many new and attractive literary subjects were passing through his mind, and among his various projects was another four-act play. He was not only taken up with what he was going to write, but also announced his intention of travelling. He was going now to Sweden, now to Switzerland; he was going on a world tour. The outbreak of the Russo-Japanese War gave him another idea—he decided to have himself sent to the front as a medical officer.

Chekhov's doctors must have shaken their heads when they heard that he was talking in this way, and it is difficult to know how far he can have been serious in making such plans. Was he the victim of an illusion of well-being said to be common in advanced tuberculosis cases, or was it that he was trying with his usual kindness to shield his wife and family from thoughts about his death? It is difficult to know, but there were times when he allowed himself to take a more realistic view, and told Olga 'we have not long to live together'. The truth of this was more obvious than ever when he returned to Moscow for the last time in May 1904.

He arrived in a state of utter collapse. People who had known him a few years previously were profoundly shocked by what they saw when they visited his sick-room. Though something of his humorous and kindly expression remained in his eyes, Chekhov was so ill as to be otherwise unrecognizable. Clearly the end could not be far away; he admitted as much to some of his visitors, although in front of Olga he tried to pretend that there was still hope.

After a few weeks a slight improvement enabled him to go, on his doctors' advice, to the German spa Badenweiler in the Black Forest. He left with Olga on June 3rd. A halt was made in Berlin, where the celebrated German specialist, Professor

Ewald, examined him. From Badenweiler he was soon writing to say that his health was returning, 'not in drams, but in hundredweights,' and he showed that he was at any rate well enough to maintain his usual interest in the little details of life, the spelling of his own name as 'Tschechow', and the tasteless way in which German women dressed. He had soon recovered enough energy to express indignation at the 'desperate boredom' distilled by Badenweiler, and started planning an extension of the trip. Pathetically enough his last letter, written on June 28th, is largely concerned with the details of sailings from Marseilles, whence he hoped to return to Russia by sea. Two days previously he had written to his sister to announce the onset of a genuine recovery in his health.

The end came quickly and unexpectedly on the night of July 1st-2nd. About supper-time he was feeling fairly lively and began to sketch out to Olga a subject for a story. It was to describe the scene in a hotel at supper-time. The characters, consisting of all sorts of 'fat bankers and red-cheeked Englishmen', arrive back in their hotel to find no meal prepared because the cook has run away. The story was to describe the effect of this 'blow in the stomach' on 'all these spoilt people'.

After sketching out this story Chekhov fell asleep, but as night approached he woke up, and, for the first time in his life called for a doctor. When the doctor arrived Chekhov said that he was dying. Attempts to revive him were of no avail. When an ice-pack was placed on his heart Chekhov said, 'You don't put ice on an empty heart'. The doctor then ordered that he should drink champagne, and with the words 'It's a long time since I drank champagne' Chekhov emptied the glass, turned over on his side and died.

The body was removed to Petersburg in a railway wagon which, owing to some oversight, bore the inscription 'Fresh Oysters'—an incident which would certainly have amused Chekhov with his keen appreciation of the incongruities attendant upon solemn occasions. From Petersburg the body was conveyed to Moscow, where matters began to be ordered in a more appropriate spirit by a committee set up to supervise his funeral. The news of Chekhov's death had called forth national mourning on a scale which surprised even his warmest admirers, and as the procession passed through the city vast crowds of people turned out to do him honour. The traffic of Moscow had to be diverted, and the police authorities, in the nervous atmosphere of the time, feared that the crowds might begin to demonstrate against the Government. However, on this occasion the citizens of Moscow were thinking more of the dead man than of their political wrongs. Chekhov was buried amid scenes which left no doubt of the affection and admiration accorded to him by his fellow-countrymen—affection and admiration which, in the years which followed, were destined to increase and to reach other countries, in a way his natural modesty would never have allowed him to imagine as remotely possible.

SELECT BIBLIOGRAPHY

I. BIBLIOGRAPHIES IN ENGLISH

Two most useful bibliographies, published by the New York Public Library and containing in all nearly five hundred items, give a comprehensive picture of the literature relating to Chekhov published in English —translations of his writings, biographical and critical studies, memoirs, essays, articles etc. They are:

Chekhov in English: A List of Works by and about him. Compiled by Anna Heifetz. Ed. and with a Foreword by Avrahm Yarmolinsky (New York, 1949) and

The Chekhov Centennial Chekhov in English: A Selective List of Works by and about him, 1949-60. Compiled by Rissa Yachnin (New York, 1960).

Bibliographies in English will also be found in the books by David Magarshack (*Chekhov: a Life*) and Ernest J. Simmons mentioned in Section II, below. Magarshack provides a bibliographical index of Chekhov's writings in alphabetical order of their English titles and Simmons includes a list of bibliographies in Russian.

II. BIOGRAPHICAL AND CRITICAL STUDIES

Leon Shestov, *Anton Tchekhov and Other Essays* (Dublin and London, 1916).

William Gerhardi, *Anton Chekhov: a Critical Study* (London, 1923).

Oliver Elton, *Chekhov* (The Taylorian Lecture, 1929; Oxford, 1929).

Nina Andronikova Toumanova, *Anton Chekhov: the Voice of Twilight Russia* (London, 1937).

W. H. Bruford, *Chekhov and his Russia: a Sociological Study* (London, 1948).

Irene Nemirovsky, *A Life of Chekhov*. Tr. from the French by Erik de Mauny (London, 1950).

David Magarshack, *Chekhov: a Life* (London, 1952).

David Magarshack, *Chekhov the Dramatist* (London, 1952).

Vladimir Yermilov (Ermilov), *Anton Pavlovich Chekhov, 1860-1904*. Tr. Ivy Litvinov (Moscow, 1956: London, 1957).

W. H. Bruford, *Anton Chekhov* (London, 1957).

T. Eekman, ed., *Anton Chekhov, 1860-1960* (Leiden, 1960).

Beatrice Saunders, *Tchehov the Man* (London, 1960).

Ernest J. Simmons, *Chekhov: a Biography* (Boston, Toronto, 1962; London, 1963).

Kornei Chukovsky. *Chekhov the Man*. Tr. Pauline Rose (London, n.d.)

III. LETTERS AND MEMOIR MATERIAL ETC.

Letters of Anton Chehov to his Family and Friends. Tr. Constance Garnett (London, 1920).

The Note-books of Anton Tchekhov together with Reminiscences of Tchekhov by Maxim Gorky. Tr. S. S. Koteliansky and Leonard Woolf (Richmond, 1921).

Letters on the Short Story, the Drama and Other Literary Topics. By Anton Chekhov. Selected and ed. Louis S. Friedland (New York, 1924).

Konstantin Stanislavsky, *My Life in Art*. Tr. J. J. Robbins (London, 1924; New York, 1956).

The Life and Letters of Anton Tchekhov. Tr. and ed. S. S. Koteliansky and Philip Tomlinson (London, 1925).

The Letters of Anton Pavlovitch Tchehov to Olga Leonardovna Knipper. Tr. Constance Garnett (London, 1926).

Anton Tchekhov. Literary and Theatrical Reminiscences. Tr. and ed. S. S. Koteliansky (London, 1927).

Vladimir Nemirovitch-Dantchenko, *My Life in the Russian Theatre*. Tr. John Cournos (London, 1937).

The Personal Papers of Anton Chekhov. Introduction by Matthew Josephson (New York, 1948).

Lydia Avilov, *Chekhov in my Life: a Love Story*. Tr. with an Introduction by David Magarshack (London, 1950).

Konstantin Stanislavsky, *Stanislavsky on the Art of the Stage*. Tr. with an introductory essay on Stanislavsky's 'System' by David Magarshack (London, 1950).

The Selected Letters of Anton Chekhov. Ed. Lillian Hellman, tr. Sidonie Lederer (New York, 1955).

IV. SOME OTHER CRITICAL AND BIOGRAPHICAL WORKS

Amfiteatrov, A. V., *Slavnye Mertvetsy*, Works, Vol. XIV (Petersburg, 1910-14).

Balukhaty, S., *Problemy dramaticheskogo Analiza* (Leningrad, 1927). *Chekhov Dramaturg* (Leningrad, 1936).

Batyushkov, F. D., *Na Pamyatnik A. P. Chekhovu* (Petersburg, 1906).

Bunin, I. A., *Works*, Vol. VI (Petrograd, 1915).

Chekhov, Michael P., *Anton Chekhov i ego Syuzhety* (Moscow, 1923). *Vokrug Chekhova* (Moscow-Leningrad, 1933).

Derman, A., *Tvorchesky Portret Chekhova* (Moscow, 1929). *Anton Pavlovich Chekhov. Kritiko-biografichesky Ocherk* (Moscow, 1939). *Moskva v Zhizni i Tvorchestve A. P. Chekhova* (Moscow, 1948).

Ermilov, V., *Dramaturgiya Chekhova* (Moscow, 1948).

Feyder, V., *A. P. Chekhov. Literaturny Byt i Tvorchestvo po memuarnym Materialam* (Leningrad, 1928).

Gorky, M., *Izbrannye literaturno-kriticheskie Statyi* (Moscow, 1941).

Grigoryev, M., *Stsenicheskaya Kompozitsiya chekhovskikh Pyes* (Moscow, 1924).

Ivanov-Razumnik, R. V., *Istoriya russkoy obshchestvennoy Mysli* (Petersburg, 1911).

Izmaylov, A., *Chekhov. Biografichesky Nabrosok* (Moscow, 1916).

Kireev, D., *Chekhov. Zhizn i Tvorchestvo* (Moscow, 1929).

Kogan, P. S., *A. P. Chekhov. Biografichesky Ocherk* (Moscow, 1929).

Manuylov, V., *A. P. Chekhov* (Leningrad, 1945).

Maude, Aylmer, *The Life of Tolstoy.* 2 volumes (London, 1930).

Mirsky, D. S., *Modern Russian Literature* (London, 1925). *Contemporary Russian Literature* (London, 1926).

Morozov, M., *Chekhov v otsenke angliyskoy i amerikanskoy pechati* (*Oktyabr* 7-8 (1944) pp. 162-8).

Myshkovskaya, L., *Chekhov i yumoristicheskie Zhurnaly 80-kh godov* (Moscow, 1929).

Ovsyaniko-Kulikovsky, D. N., *Istoriya russkoy Intelligentsii.* 5th edition (Petrograd, 1914).

Roskin, A., *Antosha Chekhonte* (Moscow, 1940).

Simmons, Ernest J., *Leo Tolstoy* (London, 1949).

Shestov, L., *Tvorchestvo iz Nichego*, Works, Vol. V (Petersburg, 1908); the section about Chekhov is translated by S. S. Koteliansky and J. Middleton Murry in *Anton Chekhov and other essays* (London, 1916).

Sobolev, Y., *Chekhov. Statyi, Materialy, Bibliografiya* (Moscow, 1931). *Chekhov* (Moscow, 1934).

Teodorovich, I. A., *O Gorkom i Chekhove* (Moscow, 1930).

INDEX

Works of Chekhov, Russian periodicals and certain technical expressions are followed by the Russian transliterated form in brackets. Date of writing, first publication or performance is given for Chekhov's plays and stories.